W9-BYZ-101

SECOND EDITION

Programmer's Guide to Drupal

Jennifer Hodgdon

Beijing · Boston · Farnham · Sebastopol · Tokyo

Programmer's Guide to Drupal

by Jennifer Hodgdon

Copyright © 2016 Poplar ProductivityWare, LLC. All rights reserved.

Printed in the United States of America.

Published by O'Reilly Media, Inc., 1005 Gravenstein Highway North, Sebastopol, CA 95472.

O'Reilly books may be purchased for educational, business, or sales promotional use. Online editions are also available for most titles (*http://safaribooksonline.com*). For more information, contact our corporate/institutional sales department: 800-998-9938 or *corporate@oreilly.com*.

Editor: Allyson MacDonald	**Indexer:** WordCo Indexing Services, Inc.
Production Editor: Matthew Hacker	**Interior Designer:** David Futato
Copyeditor: Eileen Cohen	**Cover Designer:** Ellie Volckhausen
Proofreader: Jasmine Kwityn	

December 2012:   First Edition
October 2015:   Second Edition

Revision History for the Second Edition
2015-10-08:   First Release

See *http://oreilly.com/catalog/errata.csp?isbn=9781491911464* for release details.

The O'Reilly logo is a registered trademark of O'Reilly Media, Inc. *Programmer's Guide to Drupal,* the cover image of a French angelfish, and related trade dress are trademarks of O'Reilly Media, Inc.

While the publisher and the author have used good faith efforts to ensure that the information and instructions contained in this work are accurate, the publisher and the author disclaim all responsibility for errors or omissions, including without limitation responsibility for damages resulting from the use of or reliance on this work. Use of the information and instructions contained in this work is at your own risk. If any code samples or other technology this work contains or describes is subject to open source licenses or the intellectual property rights of others, it is your responsibility to ensure that your use thereof complies with such licenses and/or rights.

978-1-4919-1146-4

[LSI]

Table of Contents

Preface

Welcome! This book is meant to launch you into the world of programming with the open source web content management system known as *Drupal*. My hope is that with the aid of this book, you will pass smoothly through the stage of being a novice Drupal programmer, while avoiding the mistakes that many expert Drupal programmers made in their first Drupal programming endeavors. If you make an effort to learn the "Drupal way" of programming, you can look forward to many enjoyable and fruitful years of programming with Drupal.

 Probably every experienced Drupal programmer has a slightly different definition of the Drupal way of programming, although there are many commonalities. My interpretation of the Drupal way is set out in Chapters 2 and 3; I've tried to stick to the commonalities in the definition that most Drupal programmers would agree on.

Intended Audience

The first edition of this book was written primarily for people with a background in programming who are new to using and programming with Drupal. If you fit this profile, the main reason to read this book is that whatever your programming background, your experiences have taught you certain lessons—and only some of them apply well to Drupal. My main goal in the first edition was to make you aware of which lessons are which, and help you make a successful transition to being an expert Drupal programmer: someone who knows just how and where to apply your programming skills to have the greatest effect.

The second edition of this book retains this goal but is also aimed at experienced Drupal 7 programmers who want to make the transition to Drupal 8. Because both Drupal 7 and Drupal 8 are included in this book, programmers who fit this profile will be able to compare the Drupal 7 programming methods, APIs, and concepts that they are familiar with to their Drupal 8 equivalents.

In addition, this book should be useful for the following audiences:

- Anyone working with Drupal who wants to understand how it works "under the hood"
- Drupal site builders and themers who have realized they need to do some programming for customization and want to do it the Drupal way
- Drupal users who want to contribute to the Drupal open source project by programming

The backend of Drupal and most of its code is written in PHP, utilizing some variety of SQL for database queries. Accordingly, this book concentrates on PHP and database programming for Drupal, although there are definitely opportunities to program in Flash, JavaScript, and other frontend languages with Drupal.

Because this book was written for a programming audience, it assumes knowledge of the following:

- The basics of the Web and HTTP requests
- The basics of PHP programming and programming in general (standard programming terminology is not explained)
- Object-oriented programming in PHP, especially for the Drupal 8 sections
- How to use Drupal core and existing add-on modules to build web sites

See "Where to Find More Information" on page 199 to find resources about these topics, if you need additional background.

How to Use This Book

In order to get the most out of this book, I would suggest that you start by reading Chapter 1 and making sure you are familiar with all the material in it. If you have never installed Drupal at all or tried to use it, you should definitely do that too. There are installation instructions in the *INSTALL.txt* file that comes with Drupal (this file is in the *core* subdirectory in Drupal 8), or at *https://drupal.org/documentation/install*.

Then I'd suggest reading Chapters 2 and 3 carefully, to learn about the dos and don'ts of Drupal programming; there are also many programming examples in those chapters. If you've never before done any Drupal programming or looked at any Drupal code, there are suggestions at the beginning of Chapter 2 for finding some code to look at before or while you read those chapters. I would especially recommend downloading Examples for Developers (*https://drupal.org/project/examples*), which is a comprehensive set of programming examples covering *Drupal core* (the base Drupal system, not including add-on modules). The Examples project is maintained by many contributors within the Drupal community, and it is an excellent resource.

After reading about Drupal's principles and common mistakes, look through Chapter 4 so you know what's there, and then come back to individual topics and examples when you need them. Of course, this book would never be able to cover every possible topic in Drupal programming, so if you find you need an example that isn't covered here, try the Examples for Developers project. If it isn't covered there either, there are many Drupal programmers who blog, so a web search may be helpful.

Drupal 7 programmers transitioning to Drupal 8 may also find it useful to look up familiar functions and hooks in the index (or by searching an ebook version). In most cases, the Drupal 8 version of the programming task will be covered in the same section or the following one.

Finally, Chapter 5 offers a few closing tips and suggestions, and many sections of this book have suggestions for further reading. In particular, this book does not contain the complete documentation for every Drupal function and class that it mentions or uses; you can find this information on the official Drupal API reference site, *https://api.drupal.org*. See "Using api.drupal.org" on page 201 for more details.

 All of the code in this book is available for download from the book's website. The downloaded code contains additional documentation headers and test code beyond what is included in the book. See "How to Contact Us" on page xii.

Drupal Versions

Every few years, the Drupal project releases a new *major version* of Drupal (Drupal 6, Drupal 7, etc.). Each major version of Drupal brings large, incompatible changes to the architecture and API, and generally, programming that you do for one major version cannot be used without modification in other major versions. *Contributed modules* (additional modules downloaded from *drupal.org*) also make large, incompatible architectural and API changes with their releases (Views 6.x-2.x versus 6.x-3.x, for instance).

The code samples in this book are compatible with either Drupal 7 or Drupal 8 as noted, and with particular Drupal 7 or 8 versions of contributed modules as noted in their sections. The descriptive sections of this book are also written primarily with Drupal 7 and 8 in mind.

Conventions Used in This Book

The following terminology conventions are used in this book:

- Although on some operating systems directories are called folders, this book always refers to them as directories.
- Sample site URLs use *example.com* as the base site URL.
- Sample modules have machine name `mymodule`, and sample themes have machine name `mytheme`.

The following typographical conventions are used in this book:

Italic
> Indicates new terms, URLs, email addresses, filenames, and file extensions

`Constant width`
> Used for program listings, as well as within paragraphs to refer to machine names and program elements such as variable or function names, databases, data types, environment variables, statements, and keywords

`Constant width bold`
> Shows commands or other text that should be typed literally by the user

`Constant width italic`
> Shows text that should be replaced with user-supplied values or by values determined by context

This icon signifies a tip or suggestion.

This icon signifies a note.

This icon indicates a warning or caution.

Using Code Examples

Supplemental material (code examples, exercises, etc.) is available for download at *https://github.com/oreillymedia/programmers_guide_to_drupal*.

This book is here to help you get your job done. In general, if example code is offered with this book, you may use it in your programs and documentation. You do not need to contact us for permission unless you're reproducing a significant portion of the code. For example, writing a program that uses several chunks of code from this book does not require permission. Selling or distributing a CD-ROM of examples from O'Reilly books does require permission. Answering a question by citing this book and quoting example code does not require permission. Incorporating a significant amount of example code from this book into your product's documentation does require permission.

We appreciate, but do not require, attribution. An attribution usually includes the title, author, publisher, and ISBN. For example: "*Programmer's Guide to Drupal, Second Edition* by Jennifer Hodgdon (O'Reilly). Copyright 2016 Poplar Productivity-Ware, LLC, 978-1-4919-1146-4."

Drupal is an open source project, and its code is uses the GNU Public License (GPL). Some Drupal project code is reproduced in this book (clearly labeled); use of this code needs to comply with the GPL. See the *LICENSE.txt* file distributed with Drupal code downloads for more information.

If you feel your use of code examples falls outside fair use or the permission given above, feel free to contact us at *permissions@oreilly.com*.

Safari® Books Online

Safari Books Online is an on-demand digital library that delivers expert content in both book and video form from the world's leading authors in technology and business.

Technology professionals, software developers, web designers, and business and creative professionals use Safari Books Online as their primary resource for research, problem solving, learning, and certification training.

Safari Books Online offers a range of plans and pricing for enterprise, government, education, and individuals.

Members have access to thousands of books, training videos, and prepublication manuscripts in one fully searchable database from publishers like O'Reilly Media, Prentice Hall Professional, Addison-Wesley Professional, Microsoft Press, Sams, Que, Peachpit Press, Focal Press, Cisco Press, John Wiley & Sons, Syngress, Morgan pass:

[Kaufmann], IBM Redbooks, Packt, Adobe Press, FT Press, Apress, Manning, New Riders, McGraw-Hill, Jones & Bartlett, Course Technology, and hundreds more. For more information about Safari Books Online, please visit us online.

How to Contact Us

Please address comments and questions concerning this book to the publisher:

O'Reilly Media, Inc.
1005 Gravenstein Highway North
Sebastopol, CA 95472
800-998-9938 (in the United States or Canada)
707-829-0515 (international or local)
707-829-0104 (fax)

We have a web page for this book, where we list errata, examples, code downloads, and additional information. You can access this page at *http://bit.ly/ prog_guide_drupal2e.*

To comment or ask technical questions about this book, send email to *bookquestions@oreilly.com.*

For more information about our books, courses, conferences, and news, see our website at *http://www.oreilly.com.*

Find us on Facebook: *http://facebook.com/oreilly*

Follow us on Twitter: *http://twitter.com/oreillymedia*

Watch us on YouTube: *http://www.youtube.com/oreillymedia*

Acknowledgments

Writing this book would not have been possible without the worldwide Drupal open source project community. For the first edition, I would especially like to acknowledge the support of the women of Drupal and the members of the Seattle and Spokane Drupal Groups. Without their help and encouragement, I would never have even gotten in touch with O'Reilly (thanks, Angie!), much less decided to write this book. The daily cheerleading of my partner, Zach Carter, was also a great help in completing it.

The second edition would not have been possible for me to write if I had not first gained an understanding the new Drupal 8 API. This understanding came through discussions with the Drupal community in the *#drupal-contribute* IRC channel and the Drupal issue queues, especially while I was writing landing-page topics for *https:// api.drupal.org.* I would especially like to thank Károly Négyesi (chx), Tim Plunkett (tim.plunkett), and Sascha Grossenbacher (berdir) for their patient explanations and careful patch reviews during this process, and Angie Byron (webchick) for envisioning and organizing the API documentation topics effort.

I would also like to thank Will Hartmann (PapaGrande), Michelle Williamson (micnap), Melissa Anderson (eliza411), Katherine Senzee (ksenzee), and Michael J. Ross (mjross) for providing technical reviews of the first edition of this book, and Károly Négyesi (chx) and Michelle Cox (Michelle) for providing technical reviews of the second edition. Their careful reading and thoughtful comments spurred many improvements to the text and code in the book, and I am greatly indebted to them. The careful copyediting of the second edition by Eileen Cohen was also very much appreciated.

And finally, I would like to thank my editors at O'Reilly, Meghan Blanchette for the first edition and Allyson MacDonald for the second edition, for many valuable suggestions, and Meghan in particular for patiently guiding me through my first experience with the publishing process. I'd also like to thank Matthew Hacker in Production, without whom the second edition would not have come out.

## CHAPTER 1

Overview of Drupal

This chapter contains overviews of the Drupal software and open source project, how Drupal has evolved from its beginnings through the latest version (Drupal 8), how Drupal performs its core function (handling HTTP requests), the Drupal cache system, and Drupal's automatic class loading system. You will need to be familiar with this information in order to understand and use the rest of the book, so you'll probably want to at least skim through it, if not read it in depth.

What Is Drupal?

Depending on who you talk to, you'll hear Drupal called a *content management system (CMS)* or a *content management framework (CMF)*, a platform that you can use to build a custom CMS—and both are accurate. It can be called a CMS because after installing only the base Drupal software, you can create a basic website and manage the content online. On the other hand, it can be called a flexible CMF because most people choose to add additional modules to Drupal in order to build more complicated websites with more features, and Drupal also allows you to create fully custom modules.

Drupal is *free and open source software (FOSS)*, governed by the GNU General Public License (GPL) version 2 (or, at your option, any later version). The licensing means that Drupal is free for you, or anyone else in the world, to download, use, and modify, as long as you comply with the license terms.

If you have never read the GPL and plan to use Drupal, you would be well advised to do so (even more so if you plan to do any Drupal programming, for yourself or others). The GPL governs not only what you can do with Drupal software itself, but also what you can do with any add-ons you download from *drupal.org*, code you find on *drupal.org* documentation pages, and any *derivative work* (work that contains GPL-licensed work, verbatim or with modifications) that you or others create. It's also written in plain English and is quite a good read (for programmer types anyway); you can find it in the *LICENSE.txt* file distributed with Drupal core, or at *http://gnu.org*.

And finally, Drupal is also a project and a community. Unlike some FOSS software that is developed primarily by one company that later releases the source code to the public, Drupal is continually evolving due to the efforts of a worldwide community of individuals and companies who donate their time and money to create and test Drupal software, write the documentation, translate it into other languages, answer support questions, keep the *drupal.org* web servers running, and organize get-togethers on a local and worldwide scale.

Drupal Core

Drupal core is the name of the package you can download from *https://www.drupal.org/project/drupal*, consisting of a set of PHP scripts (some with embedded HTML markup), JavaScript, CSS, and other files. This software interacts with a web server (typically, Apache), a database (MySQL, PostgreSQL, and SQLite are supported by Drupal core versions 7 and 8, and others are supported by add-on modules), and a web browser to provide the basics of a CMS:

- A URL request dispatch system
- A user account management system with flexible *permissions* and *roles*
- Online content editing
- An API for Drupal programmers
- A *module* system, which lets you enable and disable functionality in a modular way and download additional code to expand functionality
- A *theme* (template) system, which lets you override how everything from a button to an entire page is displayed
- An *installation profile* system, which governs what modules and themes are installed when you first install Drupal and allows downloading of complete Drupal *distributions* for special-purpose sites

- An *internationalization* system, which allows you to translate your site into other languages
- A *block* system that allows you to place chunks of content in various regions of a site's pages
- A navigation *menu* builder
- A flexible *taxonomy* system that supports categories, tags, and user-defined taxonomy vocabularies
- Optional modules supporting commenting, content fields, RSS aggregation, search, lists of content and other site components, and site features such as forums and polls (depending on the Drupal version, some of these may require downloading add-on modules instead of being part of Drupal core)
- The ability to set up a site in different languages and translate content (depending on the Drupal version, some add-on modules may be required to make a multilingual or non-English site)
- Logging of system events and errors
- An automatic class loading system
- In Drupal 8, a file-based configuration management system
- In Drupal 8, a *plugin* API, which is used in many Drupal systems
- In Drupal 8, the *services* concept and the *dependency injection container*, which allow overrides of basic Drupal functionality

Drupal Add-Ons: Modules, Themes, Distributions, and Translations

Drupal is modular software, meaning that you can turn site features and functionality on and off by enabling and disabling modules. In Drupal 7 and earlier versions, you can disable a module to turn off its functionality while retaining its data so it can be enabled again. However, in Drupal 8, this is not allowed: to turn off a module you have to uninstall it completely, losing its data. Drupal core comes with a few required modules and several optional modules; you can download thousands of additional *contributed modules* from *https://www.drupal.org/project/modules*. Most modules have configuration options that you can modify from the Drupal administration interface, by logging in to the Drupal-based site using an account that has been given appropriate permissions. The permission system is flexible: you can define named roles, which are granted specific permissions (the permissions are defined by modules), and you can assign one or more roles to each user account.

Drupal's theme system separates the content from the specific HTML markup and styling. This means that if you want to redesign the site's layout or styling, you can do so by downloading a new theme from *https://www.drupal.org/project/themes*, purchasing a commercially available theme, or creating one yourself. Once a theme is installed and enabled, it takes effect immediately to change the look of your site without the necessity of editing your content pages. The theme system has a cascading system of inheritance and overrides, including the ability to define *sub-themes*, which allows you to use the default display or the display from a theme you have downloaded for some aspects of the output, and override the parts you want to change; the overrides can be at anything from the lowest level (e.g., the presentation of buttons) to the full page.

You can also download Drupal in a distribution, which consists of Drupal core, an installation profile, and a collection of contributed modules and themes that work together to provide a more functional site for a specific purpose. Distributions are available at *https://www.drupal.org/project/distributions* for ecommerce, government, nonprofits, and many other purposes.

And finally, you can download translations for Drupal and its contributed modules, themes, and distributions from *https://localize.drupal.org*. This allows you to build a non–English language site fairly easily with both Drupal 7 and Drupal 8. Multilingual sites can also be built using Drupal; in Drupal 7, this requires downloading several contributed modules and is fairly complex, but Drupal 8 core has much more multilingual functionality built in and is much more streamlined. See *https://www.drupal.org/documentation/multilingual* for more on building multilingual sites.

Finding Drupal add-ons

Here are the main ways to find Drupal add-ons (modules, themes, or distributions):

- To find a specific add-on that you know the name of, visit *https://www.drupal.org* and type the name into the search box.

- If the add-on that you're looking for is not in the first few results, try restricting the search to modules or themes, using the filters in the right sidebar (there is no way to restrict to distributions from a *drupal.org* search, as of summer 2015).

- Alternatively, start by navigating to *https://www.drupal.org/project/modules*, *https://www.drupal.org/project/themes*, or *https://www.drupal.org/project/distributions*, and searching from there. You can also search from these pages by keyword, Drupal version compatibility, or category (modules only).

- You can try guessing the URL, which is always *drupal.org/project/*, followed by the *machine name* of the project. The machine name is composed of lowercase letters, numbers, and underscores, but because the machine names are chosen by developers, some are hard to guess and they may take a couple of tries. For example, the Panels module is at *https://www.drupal.org/project/panels*; the Omega theme is at *https://www.drupal.org/project/omega*; the XML Sitemap module is at *https://www.drupal.org/project/xmlsitemap*.

- Of course, you can always try your favorite web search engine, with keywords "Drupal module" and the name of the module.

The Evolution of Drupal

Drupal started out as a message board, created by founder Dries Buytaert at the University of Antwerp in 1999. Once this message board was established, its members started exploring ideas for its improvement, and these were added to the software. Eventually, Dries named the software Drupal, and he released it on January 15, 2001, as an open source project so others could work on it. By June 2002, when version 4.0.0 was released, Drupal had expanded to a more flexible CMS, with new modules handling blogs, polls, taxonomy, and generic content, and a system for add-on modules and themes. The 4.x.y, 5.x, and 6.x versions continued the process of adding new CMS functionality and refining the API.

 Don't worry if you don't know what all of the terminology in this section means yet! It will be explained later in the book, where programming with each of the related subsystems of Drupal is explored.

January 2011 saw the first full release of Drupal version 7, which brought several major changes to the Drupal software and its API:

- There was a major usability push. A group formed to do usability testing, and its findings resulted in the redesign and reorganization of administrative pages.
- The accessibility of the administrative interface was also vastly improved, due to the efforts of a dedicated group of people interested in accessibility, and the recognition in the Drupal community as a whole of its importance.
- A completely new database API, based on the PHP Data Objects (PDO) library, was added. This took Drupal 6's concept of database portability, which was accomplished through a set of wrapper functions, and made it object-oriented, more robust, more secure, and more industry-standard.
- A class autoloader was created and added to Drupal core.
- The concept of *entities* was introduced, encompassing content items from the Node module, user accounts, taxonomy terms, and comments. The system also allowed add-on modules to define their own entity types.
- In conjunction with entities, a system for fields on entities was added to Drupal core (previously, this had been in the Content Construction Kit, or CCK, contributed module, and it only worked on node content items). Many field modules were also added to Drupal core, including modules to handle file and image

uploads, and output images in different sizes. Because nearly every Drupal site needs this functionality, getting it into Drupal core was a key Drupal 7 milestone.

- A new Render API was introduced, with the goal of delaying rendering until later in the page-generating process, so that the page can be altered before it is rendered. This was based on the Form API that existed in earlier versions.

- An automated testing system was introduced, which had previously been in a contributed module. Tests were added to Drupal core for much of the basic functionality, and these tests were run on every proposed Drupal core patch, to guard against regression. This greatly improved the quality of the Drupal core source code and of contributed modules that made use of it.

- The API for defining installation profiles was revised and streamlined.

Drupal 8 introduces even more changes:

- The usability and accessibility teams have continued to improve the usability and accessibility of the administrative UI.

- A mobile team was formed, which has made sure that both the administrative UI and the core themes work well on mobile devices (phones and tablets).

- Underneath the UI, the internals of Drupal have been radically transformed from a mostly ad-hoc, specific-to-Drupal, procedural-code-based system into a mostly object-oriented system that incorporates code from many outside open source projects. To do this, the Drupal 8 core development community has had to overcome the "not invented here" attitude seen in many open source projects; the idea is that the Drupal project should use code from other projects where possible, and improve that code if necessary (to the benefit of other open source projects), rather than trying to invent everything itself. In addition, some of the core systems of Drupal were rewritten as portable PHP classes without Drupal-specific dependencies, with the idea that they could be used by other open source projects.

The internal systems and APIs that are radically changed in Drupal 8 include:

- The system for handling URL requests, which was native to Drupal in previous versions, has been replaced by the URL request handler from the Symfony project. Symfony is an open source PHP web development framework.

- A system for swappable services has been added, and many aspects of Drupal core functionality have been converted to services (allowing contributed modules to replace them). The service framework also comes from the Symfony project.

- An object-oriented plugin system has been added, and many of the hooks from previous versions of Drupal have been converted to plugins. This means that modules have increasing amounts of object-oriented code and reduced amounts of procedural code. The plugin framework comes from the Symfony project and the Doctrine project.

- Some informational hooks from previous versions of Drupal have been converted to using YAML-formatted files to provide the information.

- The system for storing configuration information, which was interconnected with other data and somewhat ad hoc in Drupal 7 and previous versions, has been replaced by a new API. Configuration is now easy to export and import, making it fairly straightforward to share configuration among sites or store it in a revision control system.

- The theme system has been converted to use the templating system from the Twig project, instead of the Drupal-specific PHP-based templates and functions used in Drupal 7 and previous versions.

- The class loader from the open source Composer project replaces the Drupal-specific class loader from Drupal 7.

- Some functionality previously in contributed modules, such as the Views module, has been added to Drupal core. On the other hand, some of the less-used Drupal core modules, such as the Poll module, have been converted to contributed modules and removed from Drupal core.

How Drupal Handles HTTP Requests

When Drupal is installed properly and the web server receives an HTTP request that corresponds to the Drupal site, the main Drupal *index.php* file is loaded and executed by the server to handle the request. It is important for Drupal programmers to understand how Drupal handles such requests. This process changed significantly between Drupal 7 and Drupal 8, so it is discussed in two separate sections.

Further reading and reference:

- "The Drupal Cache" on page 10
- "Registering for URLs and Displaying Content" on page 88
- "Where to Find More Information" on page 199 (web technology section—to find resources for learning about how web servers process requests in general)
- Symfony framework: *http://symfony.com*
- Composer project: *https://getcomposer.org/*

HTTP Request Handling in Drupal 7

Here is an overview of the HTTP request processing sequence in Drupal 7:

1. Drupal determines which *settings.php* file to use for the HTTP request (you can set up Drupal to serve multiple sites, each with its own *settings.php* file), and this file is loaded and executed.

2. The database connection and configuration/variable system are initialized.

3. If a request is coming from an *anonymous user* (a site visitor who is not logged in), the *page cache* is checked to see if output has previously been cached for the same requested URL. If so, the cached output is returned to the web server, and Drupal is done. Drupal page caching does not apply to *authenticated* (logged-in) users.

4. PHP session variables are initialized.

5. The language system is initialized, and various files are loaded and executed (core include files and enabled modules' *.module* files).

6. Drupal determines whether the site is *offline* (also known as being in *maintenance mode*) or *online*.

7. If the site is offline, Drupal retrieves the offline message stored by an administrator as the page content. Other functions are called to generate some sections of the page content.

8. If the site is online, or if an authorized user is accessing a page while the site is offline, Drupal determines which functions need to be called to generate the content for the request, and it calls these functions. They ideally return *render arrays* that include the page data and other information necessary to render the page, but they could also return rendered or partially rendered content. During this process, if the page request includes a Drupal Form API form submission, the submitted data is processed and sent to form validation and/or submission handler functions.

9. Drupal determines what *delivery method* to use for the page and calls the appropriate delivery function.

10. For HTML page requests, the default page-delivery function prints HTTP headers, uses the theme to render the render array elements into HTML, prints the HTML output (which effectively sends it to the web server), saves user session information to the database, and exits. The Ajax request-delivery function is similar, but it renders into JavaScript Object Notation (JSON) output instead of using the theme system to render to HTML. Modules can also define custom page-delivery methods.

HTTP Request Handling in Drupal 8

The major change in Drupal 8's HTTP request handling from all previous versions of Drupal is that Drupal 8 uses the Symfony framework to handle HTTP requests. Here is an overview of the HTTP request processing sequence in Drupal 8:

1. The dynamic class loader and error handlers are started. At any time after this point, if an operation requires a connection to the database, it will be initialized.

2. Drupal determines which *settings.php* file to use for the HTTP request (you can set up Drupal to serve multiple sites, each with its own *settings.php* file), and this file is loaded and executed. Note that the setup for multiple sites in Drupal 8 requires a *sites.php* file; in Drupal 7, you could get by with special names for the site directories.

3. The Drupal *kernel* is initialized, which starts up the *dependency injection container* (which defines *services* provided by classes). At any time after this point, if an operation requires the configuration system, it will be initialized.

4. PHP session variables and cookies are initialized.

5. The *page cache* is checked to see if output has previously been cached for the same request conditions (known as *context*) and URL. If so, the cached output is returned to the web server, and Drupal is done.

6. Various files are loaded and executed (core include files and enabled modules' *.module* files).

7. Symfony's HTTP request system handles the request and returns the result to the browser. In this system:

   - Modules can register *routes*, which map URLs and context to *controller* classes. Controller classes come in several flavors, including those that produce generic page output, and those that present forms and process form submissions.

   - Symfony determines the best match to the context and chooses the controller method to execute.

   - The controller either returns a Symfony response object containing HTTP header and content information, or a Drupal *render array*. Symfony response objects are handled directly by the Symfony framework; render arrays are handled by a Drupal subsystem that converts the array into the main content for the page or request, optionally *decorates* it with blocks or other markup, and wraps the result in a Symfony response object.

   - Symfony returns the response information to the browser.

   - Modules can also register *event subscribers* to intercept and override various steps in the response process. Core modules use event subscribers for many purposes, including translating URL aliases to system URL paths, enabling *maintenance mode*, handling language selection, and providing dynamic URL routes.

The Drupal Cache

Drupal has a *cache* system, which allows modules to precalculate data or output and store it so that the next time it is needed it doesn't have to be calculated again. This can save a lot of time on page loads, at the expense of some added complexity: any module that uses caching needs to take care to clear its cached data whenever the data is invalidated due to changes in dependent data.

Both Drupal core and add-on modules cache information using this system. Here are a few examples (not all of them apply to all versions of Drupal):

- Page output (page caching can be turned off from the Performance configuration page)
- Block output (block caching can be turned off from the Performance page in Drupal 7 but is always on in Drupal 8 for cacheable blocks)
- Information collected from hooks; for example, Drupal 7 entity type and field definitions
- Lists of available plugins in Drupal 8 plugin managers
- Theme information, including the list of theme regions and theme-related information from modules and themes
- Form arrays

Programmers and site builders new to Drupal quickly learn that the first thing to try, if they are having trouble with a site or if programming changes they have recently made are not being recognized, is to clear the cache. You can clear the cache by visiting the Performance configuration page and clicking the cache clear button, or by using Drush. The Drush command to clear the cache in Drupal 7 is **drush cc all**; in Drupal 8, use **drush cr** (which clears the cache and also rebuilds the dependency injection container; more about that later in the book).

 The rest of this section provides details of the cache API, which you can skip for now and return to when you need them.

Further reading and reference:

- See *https://api.drupal.org* to find full documentation of the cache functions mentioned in the following sections (there is a "Cache API" topic for Drupal 8; in Drupal 7, look up the individual functions).
- See "Principle: Drupal Is Alterable" on page 17 to learn more about hooks and plugins in general, "Using the Drupal Form API" on page 109 to learn about forms, and "Drupal 8 Services and Dependency Injection" on page 35 to learn about services and the dependency injection container.
- For more information on Drush, see "Drupal Development Tools" on page 204.
- "Rebuilding the container" on page 38.

Examples—using the cache:

- The Cache example in Examples for Developers (*https://www.drupal.org/project/examples*) illustrates how to use the Cache API.

Drupal 7 Cache API

The Drupal 7 cache system has a fairly simple API, consisting of the cache_set() and cache_get() functions (with a few variations), as well as cache_clear_all() and drupal_flush_all_caches() to clear cache information. Modules can register to have their caches cleared by implementing a *hook* (hooks are module entry points to altering Drupal) called hook_flush_caches(). All cached data is stored in the database, usually in tables whose names start with cache_.

Drupal 8 Cache API

The Drupal 8 cache API uses *services*, so that different sets of cached data, or *bins*, can use different storage mechanisms. In Drupal 8, all cache functionality starts by calling \Drupal::cache($bin), passing in the name of the cache storage bin you want to use, to get an instance of the correct cache class; this class will implement \Drupal \Core\Cache\CacheBackendInterface. Many cache applications use the default bin. Alternatively, if you have a $container variable in a class method, you'll call:

```
// The name of the service for a particular cache bin is
// 'cache.' . $bin.
$cache_class = $container->get('cache.' . $bin);
```

Once you have a cache class, your module can call methods such as set(), get(), and invalidate() to store, retrieve, and invalidate your cached data. If your module uses a custom cache system, it should implement hook_cache_flush() to flush the data when a cache clear is requested via the drupal_flush_all_caches() function, and you may need to implement hook_rebuild() as well. However, if you store your data in cache bins that Drupal core defines, your cached data will automatically be flushed.

For efficiency, the Drupal 8 cache system also has a tagging mechanism, which is used to flush parts of the cache (rather than the whole cache) when data they're related to is changed or removed. For instance, if your module is caching data related to a particular node content item, you should tag it with the node ID when you add it to the cache, by calling:

```
// $cid is a unique cache ID key for your data, which is $data.
// $nid is the ID of the node whose data is cached.
$cache_class->set($cid, $data, CacheBackendInterface::CACHE_PERMANENT,
    array('node:' . $nid));
```

Tags are passed in as the fourth argument; here, the node tag is given a value equal to the node ID related to this cached data. Then, when calls to the core Node module modify this node content item, it will call cache methods to invalidate all cached data that was tagged with this node ID. There is also a node_list cache tag, which indicates your data is a list of node content items; this tag is invalidated whenever any node is changed, added, or deleted.

You can define custom tags for your module's caches and use them to invalidate groups of cached data when appropriate by calling:

```
\Drupal\Core\Cache\Cache::invalidateTags($tags);
```

There is one more concept in caching, which is used in the request-rendering pipeline. The idea is that the content of a page (or other request result) may depend on various variables, such as the user who is viewing the page, the user's roles, the page language, the time zone, or other factors; these factors are collectively known as the *cache context*. For details on how to add cache information to a render array, see the "Render API Overview" topic page on *https://api.drupal.org*.

Automatic Class Loading in Drupal

Drupal core versions 7 and 8 both include systems for automatic loading of files containing PHP class, interface, and trait declarations (in the rest of this section, class refers to either a class or an interface, or a trait in Drupal 8). The basic idea of both systems is the same:

- Integrate with PHP's native class-autoloading system, in which functions can be registered as class loaders.
- Reduce the load on the server by loading files containing class definitions only if those classes are being used in a particular page request.

- Reduce the burden on developers by automatically loading files containing class definitions, instead of making them load the classes explicitly in code.

Drupal 7's class-loading system is a homegrown (specific to Drupal) system called the *registry*. Here is how it works:

1. Drupal determines when the class registry needs to be updated; for example, when you enable or disable modules, update a module version, or clear the Drupal cache.

2. When the registry needs to be updated, Drupal makes a list of files it needs to scan. These include files explicitly listed in enabled modules' *.info* files, as well as *.inc* files in the Drupal core *includes* directory.

3. Each of these files is scanned for PHP class declarations.

4. The resulting list of which files contain which class declarations (the registry) is saved in the database.

5. During start-up, Drupal registers its `drupal_autoload_class()` and `drupal_autoload_interface()` functions as PHP autoload functions. When an undefined class is accessed in PHP code, the PHP engine calls these functions, which read the registry database to locate the file the class is defined in, and then include the file so that the class is defined.

 Drupal 7 class names have to be globally unique. Always name your classes with a prefix that makes them unique, such as your module name.

Early in the development cycle for Drupal version 8, a decision was made to stop using the homegrown registry system developed for Drupal 7, and instead incorporate the class loader from the Composer open source project, which is based on the *PSR-0* and *PSR-4* standards, and PHP namespaces. Here is how this system works:

1. Classes are declared to be in a PHP namespace with a PHP `namespace` declaration. Drupal uses namespaces beginning with the name `\Drupal`, and the namespace(s) for a particular module `mymodule` should begin with `\Drupal\mymodule`.

2. Files that depend on classes outside their own namespace have PHP `use` declarations for the outside classes.

3. Each class declaration is in its own file.

4. The directory that each class file goes in depends on its namespace. Examples:

- An add-on module's `\Drupal\mymodule\subnamespace\Foo` class would go in the *src/subnamespace/Foo.php* file under the main module directory.

- Classes that are for Drupal core broadly, and not part of a particular Drupal core module, are found under the *core/lib* directory; for example, the `\Drupal\Component\Datetime\DateTimePlus` class is located in the *core/lib/Drupal/Component/Datetime/DateTimePlus.php* file.

- Classes that have been adopted from outside projects are found under the *vendor* directory; for example, the `\Symfony\Component\DependencyInjection\Container` class is located in the *vendor/symfony/dependency-injection/Container.php* file.

5. Drupal provides information about its namespace and directory conventions to the Symfony class-loading system. For instance, it tells Symfony to look in enabled modules' *src* directories for class files, but not in disabled modules' directories.

In PHP, namespaces in `namespace` and `use` declarations do not start with a backslash, although the *fully qualified namespace*, used in other places in code, always starts with a backslash. In this book, Drupal 8 classes are always referred to with their fully qualified namespace, to avoid ambiguity.

6. When a class is needed, the Symfony class loader automatically locates and loads the include file so that the class is defined.

As a side effect of the Drupal 8 class-loading system, each module needs to be in its own directory or subdirectory in Drupal 8 (in Drupal 7, you could put several modules into the same directory). The name of the directory that directly contains the main module files needs to match the module's machine name exactly (in Drupal 7, this did not need to be the case).

Further reading and reference:

- Namespaces in PHP: *http://php.net/manual/language.namespaces.php*
- Composer project: *https://getcomposer.org/*
- PSR-0 standard: *http://bit.ly/psr-0_standard*
- PSR-4 standard: *http://bit.ly/psr-4_autoloader*

Examples—class loading:

- Code examples in this book involving classes include information on what to name the file, where to put it, and what needs to go into the module information file (in Drupal 7 only) so that the class-loading system can locate it.

## CHAPTER 2

Drupal Programming Principles

Experienced programmers learn, through training and experience, a set of principles and best practices to apply whenever they approach a problem they want to solve with programming. These include general practices such as "comment your code" and "choose clear variable names," which apply to all programming languages and situations, and some that are specific to a particular domain. Drupal has its own set of programming principles (covered in this chapter); learning them and following them should help you be a more effective Drupal programmer.

If you are completely new to Drupal programming, you might find it useful to look at some Drupal code before or while reading this chapter. One suggestion would be to download Examples for Developers (*https://www.drupal.org/project/examples/*). You could try out the Page and Block examples, and take a look at their source code. Or, you might consider browsing through one of the Drupal core modules in the Drupal 7 *modules* directory or Drupal 8 *core/ modules* directory, although they are not documented as tutorials. The Statistics module for Drupal 7 and 8 (which tracks view statistics and provides a block showing popular content) or the Email module for Drupal 8 (which provides a field for storing email addresses) would be good choices.

Principle: Drupal Is Alterable

Drupal is intended to be used as a platform for building web applications, so one of its fundamental principles is that nearly everything about it needs to be customizable, and it needs to be customizable without having to edit the Drupal core source code. Because you're not supposed to need to edit the base code to build any type of web application with Drupal, both Drupal core and contributed modules are (ideally) fully *alterable*, meaning that they provide mechanisms that you can use to customize and add to their behavior and output.

The basic idea is that instead of editing code you downloaded, you should instead create an add-on module or theme using the standard Drupal alteration mechanisms. In some cases, you will have a choice of using either a module or a theme, but a good rule of thumb is that if your aim is to change the presentation of data, such as the exact HTML markup and CSS, you should create a theme, and if your aim is to change the way Drupal behaves, add new features, or change what data is being output, you should create a module. If you need to do both, you probably will be best off separating out the presentation changes from the behavior and data changes, and creating both a theme and a module.

You'll also need to figure out what type of alteration you need to do. One type of alteration mechanism available in Drupal is a *hook*. A hook is a PHP file or function you can put into a module or theme, which will be *invoked* (called or included) at an appropriate time by a Drupal core or contributed module in order to let your module or theme alter (or add to) behavior and output. All versions of Drupal offer several different types of hooks:

- *Generic hooks*, which allow modules to define additions to Drupal behavior by defining a function.

- *Alter hooks*, which allow modules to make modifications to existing Drupal behavior by defining a function.

- *Theme hooks*, which allow themes to modify the output that is sent to the browser. Theme hooks come in two varieties: some use *theme functions* (the theme defines a function to modify the output), and some use *theme template files* (the theme has a file that modifies output); in Drupal 8, nearly all are template files. Drupal 7 template files are PHP files with extension *.tpl.php*, and Drupal 8 template files are Twig files with extension *.html.twig*.

  Theme hooks come with *theme preprocessing hooks* and *theme processing hooks*, which modules and themes can both use to alter the information that is sent to the theme function or template file for output.

Drupal 8 offers several additional mechanisms for altering and adding to Drupal behavior:

- A *plugin* system, which has replaced many of the generic hooks from Drupal 7 with an object-oriented system whereby modules can add classes that define additions to Drupal behavior.

- The *dependency injection* system, which allows modules to replace fundamental core systems of Drupal (or *services*), such as the mechanism for storing cached data.

- An *event* system, which allows modules and core components to define and dispatch events, and other modules to subscribe and respond to them.

- A new Symfony-based *routing* system, which allows modules to define URLs and their output by defining *routes* and *controllers*, and to alter what happens at various points during an HTTP request using the event system.

- A new YAML-based system for defining default menu links, contextual links, and other data for various Drupal core systems.

So, in Drupal 7 and earlier versions (at least, from the point of view of a PHP programmer), modules are mostly collections of hook *implementations* (PHP functions that define the hook's output or behavior), and themes are mostly collections of theme hook *overrides* (PHP functions or template files that define how output is presented); both themes and modules can also contain supporting code, CSS, JavaScript, images, and other files. In Drupal 8, most modules will contain fewer hook implementations, as many of these are replaced by classes and YAML-based files.

Why Not Just Hack (Edit) the Code?

Unlike in some other programming communities, the word "hack" in the Drupal community has definite negative connotations: hacking specifically means editing code that you downloaded from *drupal.org*, in order to make a change that you need for a site. Hacking is highly discouraged; "hacking core," or editing the Drupal core files, is considered to be the worst offense. There are several reasons:

- Hacking is usually unnecessary, as there should be a hook or other mechanism available that will let you accomplish your goal without hacking.

- If you have hacked Drupal core or other downloaded code, updates will be much more difficult, because you will need to reapply your hack after downloading a new version of the code. All downloaded code is at least occasionally updated with security fixes, bug fixes, and new features.

- If you program with hooks, plugins, and other alteration mechanisms instead of hacking, you can turn off your changes by disabling your module. If you hack code, you will need to "unhack" it to turn off your changes.

- You may find that there isn't a mechanism available for altering the behavior you want to alter, or you may be tempted to hack in order to fix a bug or add a new feature to a module. If you instead turn your hack into a patch, it becomes a benefit to you and the Drupal community if it is added to the module or to Drupal core, and when you next update, your fix will be included.

Further reading and reference:

- The following sections explain how to set up a module or theme so Drupal will recognize it, and the basics of programming with Drupal's generic altering mechanisms: hooks, plugins, events, and dependency injection.

- Routes and routing events for Drupal 8 are covered in "Registering for a URL in Drupal 8" on page 92 and "Altering Routes and Providing Dynamic Routes in Drupal 8" on page 98.

- Patches: "Reporting Issues and Contributing Code to the Drupal Community" on page 83.

Setting Up a Module or Theme

To set up a module or theme, follow these steps:

1. Pick a *machine name* or *short name* for the module or theme. This is usually a sequence of letters and underscores, sometimes with numbers, that must follow PHP's function-naming conventions, as it will be used as a function and/or namespace prefix (use the machine name as a prefix for all functions you define in your module or theme). Pick a name that is not already in use by a project on *drupal.org*, to avoid later conflicts. Throughout this book, the convention is that you are creating a module called mymodule or a theme called mytheme. The maximum length of a module or theme machine name is 50 characters.

2. Create a directory for your theme or module. See "Where to put modules and themes" on page 22 to figure out where to put this directory. In Drupal 7, you would normally name the directory the same as your module or theme's machine name; in Drupal 8, this is required.

3. For Drupal 7, create a file called *mymodule.info* or *mytheme.info* inside your directory, which is a plain text file that contains information about the module or theme. In Drupal 8, create a file called *mymodule.info.yml* or *mytheme.info.yml*. The exact syntax of this file tends to vary from version to version of Drupal and is slightly different for modules and themes, so check the online documentation, or copy a file from a module or theme provided in Drupal core or the Examples for Developers project to use as a starting point. Here are minimal examples for Drupal 7 and Drupal 8 modules (the syntax of this portion is the same for themes):

```
; Drupal 7 module .info file
; Comments start with ;
; The name displayed on the Modules or Themes list.
name = My Module
; The longer description displayed on the Modules or Themes list.
```

```
description = Longer description of this module.
; The Drupal core version this module or theme is compatible with.
core = 7.x

# Drupal 8 module .info.yml file
# Comments start with #
name: 'My Module'
description: 'Longer description of this module.'
# A required line telling Drupal this is a module.
type: module
core: 8.x
```

4. Create a PHP base file for your module or theme, inside the same directory. For Drupal 7, the base file is called *template.php* for a theme (which is where your theme function overrides will go) or *mymodule.module* for a module (which is where your hook implementations and other functions go), and the file can be completely empty. For Drupal 8, the base file can be omitted if you do not need to define any functions or implement hooks. If you do need it, the base file is called *mytheme.theme* for a theme or *mymodule.module* for a module.

You are now ready to put implementations and overrides of hooks, plugins, etc. into your module or theme.

Further reading and reference:

- Documentation of *.info* file syntax for Drupal 7 modules: *http://bit.ly/module_info*.

- Documentation of *.info.yml* file syntax for Drupal 8 modules: *http://bit.ly/info_yml*.

- Documentation of *.info* file syntax for Drupal 7 themes: *http://bit.ly/theme_info*.

- Documentation of *.info.yml* file syntax for Drupal 8 themes: *http://bit.ly/theme_info_yml*.

- Check if a proposed machine name for your module or theme is already in use by trying the URL *drupal.org/project/your_proposed_name*.

Examples:

- The code download for this book consists of a module and theme for Drupal 7 and 8. See "How to Contact Us" on page xii.

- There are theme info file examples in "Defining Theme Regions for Block Placement" on page 77.

Where to put modules and themes

In Drupal 7 and earlier versions, modules and themes that you download or create should generally go into the *sites/all/modules* and *sites/all/themes* directories. Each module or theme project should be in its own subdirectory, such as *sites/all/modules/views* for the Views project. You can also organize modules into subdirectories; for example, you could create *sites/all/modules/contrib* and *sites/all/modules/custom* directories for downloaded contributed modules and your own custom modules, respectively.

If you have a multisite installation and want a module or theme to be available for only one of the sites, you can put it in *sites/specific_site/modules* or *sites/specific_site/themes*. See *https://www.drupal.org/documentation/install/multi-site* for more information on this topic.

In Drupal 8, all of the Drupal core code (include files, modules, themes, etc.) has been moved to the *core* directory, and while you can still put your downloaded and custom modules into *sites/all*, there are also top-level *modules* and *themes* directories available. The use of these top-level directories is recommended, except for site-specific modules and themes in a multisite installation. Within these top-level directories, you are still free to organize your modules into subdirectories.

Creating a sub-theme

Drupal allows you to define a theme that inherits or derives from another theme. The terminology is that the *sub-theme* derives from a *base theme*; the base theme can be part of Drupal core or can be a contributed or custom theme, and there can be an arbitrarily long chain of inheritance in sub-themes. To indicate that a theme you are creating is a sub-theme of another theme, add this line to your *mytheme.info* (Drupal 7) or *mytheme.info.yml* (Drupal 8) file:

```
# Drupal 7 mytheme.info file:
base theme = machine_name_of_base

# Drupal 8 mytheme.info.yml file:
base theme: machine_name_of_base
```

The main thing that a sub-theme inherits from its base theme is the template files. Drupal 8 core provides a special base theme called Classy (machine name: `classy`) that contains templates whose HTML markup is peppered with many class attributes, allowing for very specific CSS styling in your sub-theme. Also, by design, the Classy theme has only a minimal amount of CSS, so you won't have to counteract or override its choices much in your own theme. The core themes Seven (the administration theme) and Bartik (the user-facing theme) both derive from Classy, which allows them to define a very small set of templates and do most of their styling work with CSS. If you are defining a Drupal 8 theme, you may find it useful to use Classy as a base theme, and you can use these two core themes as a model. In Drupal 7, you'd need to sub-theme Bartik to get similar behavior, but there is much more CSS to override in Bartik than in the Drupal 8 Classy theme.

If you are not fond of the class attributes that Classy and Bartik have in their markup, you might prefer to use the Stark theme (machine name: stark, available in both Drupal 7 and 8) as your base theme. The Stark theme is a more basic starting point than Classy or Bartik, as it does not have any templates of its own—it just uses the base templates provided by modules. In Drupal 7, you will find that there are still class attributes in the markup, but in Drupal 8, nearly all of them have been removed from the base templates, in order to give themers better control over what classes appear in their HTML markup.

There are also many contributed base themes available. Many theme developers choose to use a base theme that provides responsive behavior (the core themes in Drupal 7 are not responsive to mobile device sizes, since they were developed before responsive design was common) or integrates with a JavaScript and/or CSS web framework they are familiar with.

The Basics of Module and Theme Hook Programming

To implement a hook or override a theme hook, follow these steps:

1. Set up a module or a theme, following the instructions in "Setting Up a Module or Theme" on page 20.

2. Figure out which file your hook override or implementation needs to go in. Most hook implementations and theme function overrides go in the base module or theme file. However, theme templates are their own files, and there are also a few hook implementations that belong in other files. For instance, implementations of install-related hooks such as hook_schema() and hook_update_N() go into the *mymodule.install* file, and the contributed Views module for Drupal 7 uses two separate files for its hooks. Always read the reference documentation for the hook you are implementing to find out where its implementation belongs.

3. Within your base module or theme file, or the alternative file where your particular hook implementation belongs, define a function to implement the hook or override the theme function (skip this step for theme templates). For a generic module hook called hook_foo(), the function must be named mymodule_foo(). For a theme hook function called theme_foo(), the function must be called mytheme_foo(). For the function body, often there is a good starting point in the hook documentation or the theme hook function you are overriding.

4. To override a theme hook template file, copy the template file you are overriding to your theme directory, or preferably to a *templates* subdirectory (this is required in Drupal 8), keeping the same filename.

5. Edit the function or file to make the desired changes.

6. Enable your module or theme.

7. As you are programming and testing, if you add a new hook implementation or theme override to an enabled module or theme, you will need to clear the Drupal cache so that Drupal will recognize your change. For some informational hooks, you will also need to clear the cache when you make a change to the function body, to force Drupal to call your hook implementation function again and read the new information. In general, it's always a good idea while you are developing for Drupal to clear the cache after any change, or if Drupal is not behaving the way you expect.

Further reading and reference:

- "The Drupal Cache" on page 10.
- If you know the name of a hook, documentation can be found by searching for the hook function or template filename on the Drupal API site (*https://api.drupal.org*), such as `hook_block_info`, `theme_table`, *block.tpl.php*, or *block.html.twig*. When searching, do not put `()` after function names.
- If you do not know the name, there are lists of hooks on the API site: the "Hooks" topic lists all Drupal core generic and alter hooks, and the "Default theme implementations" (Drupal 7) or "Theme system overview" (Drupal 8) topic lists all Drupal core theme hooks.
- To learn about universal and specific theme preprocess and process hooks that you can define, check the documentation of the `theme()` function in Drupal 7, and the "Theme system overview" topic in Drupal 8.
- Hook documentation pages on the API site give you documentation about the purpose of the hook, parameters, return value, which file the hook should be located in, a list of places where the hook is invoked (that is, which Drupal system will call your hook implementation function), and a list of other implementations in Drupal core. The function body for a hook function is a sample implementation.
- Theme hook and template documentation pages on the API site tell you where the theme hook is used and document the variables you can use in your output. The theme function body or file content is the default implementation, which you can copy as a starting point for your override. There should also be links to the default preprocessing and processing functions, which you can add to by implementing hooks.

Examples—implementing hooks:

Making Your Module Output Themeable

Drupal's theme system is designed to separate the data and content from the styling and presentation: the module has control over the data and content, and the theme that is in use should have full control over styling and presentation, including HTML markup. The basic principle that makes this work is that all data that is rendered into HTML should be passed through the Drupal theme system.

In Drupal 7, data can be rendered by calling the theme() function directly, or by passing a *render array* (an array containing the data to be output and formatting parameters) into the drupal_render() function (which calls theme() internally). Render arrays that are returned from page- or block-generating functions are also rendered internally by a call to drupal_render().

In Drupal 8, as much as possible, render arrays should be returned from all functions that return output, and these will be rendered by calls to internal functions; the `theme()` function does not exist in Drupal 8 for modules to call directly, and calling `drupal_render()` directly is also discouraged (and probably will not work).

As an example, whenever a block from the core Block module is rendered in Drupal 7, a call is made to `theme('block', $block_data)`, rather than having the Block module simply output an HTML `<div>` containing the data. This allows your theme to override the default *block.tpl.php* theme template file, replacing the default `<div>` with different HTML if desired. In Drupal 8, the process is slightly different and the default template file is *block.html.twig*, but eventually, the same theme call is made internally, and your theme can override the Twig template file.

Theme Functions and Templates Versus Render Arrays

There is often confusion around the relationship between theme functions or templates and render arrays. The basic idea is that each element in a render array is *rendered* (converted into an HTML string) by a theme function or theme template.

Modules that you write should follow the same principle: they should generally return render arrays from functions that provide block and page output, and define custom theme functions or templates as needed (as described in this section), to render the data into HTML, rather than defining the HTML markup directly. This way, the theme system can override your module's theme functions or templates and retain control of the markup. Here is an outline of the steps:

1. See if there is already a theme hook or *render element* for the type of output you are generating. For instance, if you are generating an HTML table, you should use the Drupal core `'table'` theme hook instead of defining your own hook. If a theme hook or render element already exists, skip the rest of this section; a good way to discover this is to find a function that generates similar output in Drupal core and see how it's being done.

2. If there is not already an appropriate theme hook or render element, define a custom theme hook by implementing `hook_theme()` in your *mymodule.module* file. For example (for either Drupal 7 or 8):

```
function mymodule_theme($existing, $type, $theme, $path) {
  return array(
    // The array keys are names of the theme hooks you are defining.
    'mymodule_hookname' => array(
      // Input variables.
      'variables' => array(
        // These are passed as an array to theme(), which passes them on
        // to your theme function or template. Here, provide default values.
        'input1' => '',
      ),
```

```
    // If you want to use a template, include this line; for a theme
    // function in Drupal 7, leave it out.
    'template' => 'mymodule-hookname',
  ),
);
}
```

3. Define a default implementation of your theme hook in your module. If your theme hook is named 'mymodule_hookname', this is either a theme function called theme_mymymodule_hookname() or a theme template file called *mymodule-hookname.tpl.php* in Drupal 7, with templates being preferred. In Drupal 8, it should be a Twig template file *mymodule-hookname.html.twig*, which needs to go in the *templates* subdirectory of your module. Template files should print the data in appropriate HTML markup; theme functions should compose a string containing the data and HTML markup and return that. For example:

```
// Sample theme function (avoid theme functions in Drupal 8):
function theme_mymodule_hookname($variables) {
  return '<div>' . $variables['input1'] . '</div>';
}

// Same output as a PHP template file for Drupal 7:
<div><?php print $input1; ?></div>

// Same output as a Twig template file for Drupal 8:
<div>{{ input1 }}</div>
```

4. If you are using a PHP theme template in Drupal 7, declare it in your *mymodule.info* file with a files[] = mymodule-hookname.tpl.php line. This is not necessary in Drupal 8.

5. Try to keep the programming in your theme function or template file to a minimum—it should just be printing the output inside some HTML markup. Any programming logic should ideally be done before the theme function is called, or if it is only related to formatting, it should be put into a function called template_preprocess_mymodule_hookname(), defined in your *mymodule.module* file. This function will automatically be called to preprocess the input data into the variables that can be printed by the template file.

6. Call theme('mymodule_hookname', $data) directly in your module (Drupal 7 only), or set up a render array (preferable) to render the data. If you are calling directly, $data is an associative array of the variable inputs defined in your hook_theme() implementation; if calling indirectly, you can set the #theme element in the render array to 'mymodule_hookname':

```
// Direct call of theme() -- Drupal 7 only.
$data = array('input1' => t('Hello World!'));
$output = theme('mymodule_hookname', $data);
```

```
// Indirect call of theme.
$build['hello'] = array(
  '#input1' => t('Hello World!'),
  '#theme' => 'mymodule_hookname',
);
$output = drupal_render($build); // Better to return $build instead.
```

Further reading and reference:

- Overriding theme hooks and implementing generic hooks: "The Basics of Module and Theme Hook Programming" on page 23.
- The "Default theme implementations" (Drupal 7) or "Theme system overview" (Drupal 8) topic on *https://api.drupal.org* lists all Drupal core theme functions and template files.
- "Creating Render Arrays for Page and Block Output" on page 102.
- For more advanced theming, you can also define your own render element type, which would include a theme hook. In Drupal 7, this is done with `hook_element_info()`. Drupal 8 uses render element plugins; see the `\Drupal\Core\Render\Element\ElementInterface` documentation for details.

Examples—setting up theme hooks:

- "Defining a Content Entity Type in Drupal 8" on page 139
- The Theming example in Examples for Developers (*https://www.drupal.org/project/examples*)

The Basics of Drupal 8 Plugin Programming

The *plugins* concept was introduced to Drupal in Drupal 8. Plugins allow modules to define things like entity types, fields, blocks, text filters, etc.; in Drupal 7 and earlier versions, the hook system was used for these purposes. Here is an overview of how the plugin system works:

- A Drupal core or contributed module can define a *plugin type*. The plugin type consists of (usually) a PHP interface, a *discovery* mechanism, and (usually) a PHP base class. In most cases, the discovery mechanism is based on *annotation* that is added to the documentation header of plugin classes.
- The module defining the plugin type uses a *plugin manager* class to collect plugin implementations from other modules and instantiate their classes.
- Other modules can define implementations of the plugin type by creating a PHP class that implements the plugin interface, is annotated using the annotation scheme, and (optionally) extends the base plugin class. The class needs to have a

namespace and be properly placed for autoloading. If the discovery mechanism uses a hook or other mechanism, the plugin module will also need to implement a hook or perform other steps, and class annotation will not be necessary.

The remainder of this section describes in more detail these three parts of the plugin system. Even if you only intend to implement plugin types defined by other modules, read through the sections on defining plugin types and plugin managers, because there are concepts and data defined there that you will need when you implement your plugin.

Further reading and reference:

- "Automatic Class Loading in Drupal" on page 12.
- "Setting Up a Module or Theme" on page 20.
- This section concentrates on the annotation-based plugin system, which is the system that most Drupal plugins use. You can read about other discovery mechanisms in more depth in the Plugin API documentation section at *http://bit.ly/ plugin_api*.
- Find documentation for classes and interfaces mentioned in this section on *https://api.drupal.org*. Also, the "Annotations" topic for Drupal 8 lists all of the Drupal core plugin types that use annotations and describes how to annotate them.

Defining a plugin type

To define a plugin type, assuming you want to use the annotation-based discovery mechanism, your module will need to define a PHP interface and an annotation class. As an aid to modules that are implementing your plugin type, it is also desirable to define a base PHP class (which is often abstract) that provides helper methods and implements the plugin interface's methods in the manner that most implementing plugins would want to use.

The purpose of the interface is to define how your plugin-defining module will interact with the implemented plugin classes. As an example, the Drupal core Block system defines a plugin type that other modules can use to define blocks that an administrator can display on the site. An implementing block plugin needs to define who can see the block, what the block should display, and optionally, a configuration form. Accordingly, the Block system defines the following interface for block plugins (slightly simplified):

```
namespace Drupal\Core\Block;

interface BlockPluginInterface {
  // Define who can see the block.
```

```
    public function access();

    // Output the block.
    public function build();

    // There are also methods related to configuring the block,
    // returning the block title, and suggesting a machine name.
}
```

The \Drupal\Core\Block\BlockBase abstract class defines a default constructor, a default access() method that checks the visibility settings on the block, and a few more helper methods, but leaves the build() method undefined (there is no point to defining a default block output, because each block plugin presumably would have different output). Plugins are not required to extend the base abstract class, but they are required to implement the interface.

The annotation for a plugin is a set of static data that the plugin-defining module delineates in an annotation class, and that implementing plugins provide in a documentation header. This data must include a unique machine name or ID for the plugin implementation. If that is the only data a plugin type needs, the annotation class can just be a one-line extension of the simple \Drupal\Component\Annotation \PluginId class. If you need more data in your annotation, extend \Drupal \Component\Annotation\Plugin and include member variables for the other data. In the case of Block plugins, the annotation class is \Drupal\Core\Block\Annotation \Block, and it looks like this:

```
/**
 * Defines a Block annotation object.
 *
 * @Annotation
 */
class Block extends Plugin {
  /**
   * The plugin ID.
   *
   * @var string
   */
  public $id;

  /**
   * The administrative label of the block.
   *
   * @var \Drupal\Core\Annotation\Translation
   */
  public $admin_label;

  // There are a couple of additional member variables.
}
```

Note that if you are defining your own plugin type, you will need to be sure to include the documentation block before the class, with a line saying @Annotation. This tells Drupal that your class is an annotation class.

It is also a good idea to document each member variable in your annotation class, in a manner similar to the example shown here, so that modules implementing your plugin will know what data type is expected, and whether it is translatable data or not. Any string information that will be presented to site administrators or other users should be translatable; machine names should not be translatable.

Creating a plugin manager

Once your module has defined a plugin type, you need to define a plugin manager class to discover and list the plugin implementations from other modules. Here are some examples of how Drupal core uses plugin managers:

- The Block system uses a plugin manager that lists available blocks defined by modules, so that administrators can configure which blocks to display where on the site.
- The Field UI module uses a plugin manager that lists available field types defined by other modules, so that administrators can attach these fields to content types and other entities, and configure their data, forms, and display.
- The Image module uses a plugin manager that lists available image effects, so that administrators can define image styles that apply effects to images.

The steps to define and use a plugin manager are as follows, assuming an annotation-based plugin discovery method.

First, in your *mymodule.services.yml* file, define a *service* for managing your type of plugin. Defining a service means that you are declaring a class that you would like to use for managing this type of plugin and declaring the arguments that will be used to instantiate this class (which are usually other services).

For example, the core Block system has this in *core/core.services.yml*:

```
services:
  plugin.manager.block:
    class: Drupal\Core\Block\BlockManager
    parent: default_plugin_manager
  default_plugin_manager:
    abstract: true
    arguments: ['@container.namespaces', '@cache.discovery', '@module_handler']
```

Note that arguments starting with @ are names of other services that are defined by the Drupal core or modules.

The second step is to define the manager class that you declared in your services file, usually extending \Drupal\Core\Plugin\DefaultPluginManager. Most plugin manager classes have only a constructor method and leave the rest to the base class; some plugin manager classes have other methods that they need for their particular application. The Block plugin's manager class looks like this (slightly simplified):

```
class BlockManager extends DefaultPluginManager {
  public function __construct(\Traversable $namespaces,
    CacheBackendInterface $cache_backend,
    ModuleHandlerInterface $module_handler) {

    // Call the parent constructor to set up plugin discovery.
    parent::__construct('Plugin/Block', $namespaces, $module_handler,
      'Drupal\Core\Block\Annotation\Block');

    // Invoke hook_block_alter() to let modules alter the list of
    // discovered plugins.
    $this->alterInfo('block');

    $this->setCacheBackend($cache_backend, 'block_plugins');
  }

  // There are several other methods and member variables.
}
```

Plugin Data Needed by Plugin Implementers

If you are implementing a plugin, you will need to figure out the annotation class, plugin interface, plugin base class, and plugin namespace. The Drupal core plugin types all have this information in the documentation header of the annotation class, so start there; if you are defining your own plugin type, find a Drupal core example and put similar documentation in your annotation class for developers to use.

If you can't locate the information you need in the annotation class's documentation header, the next starting point is to find the plugin manager class, whose constructor method contains most of this information. The first code line of the plugin manager constructor method is particularly rich in information:

```
parent::__construct('Plugin/Block', $namespaces,
  $module_handler, 'Drupal\Core\Block\Annotation\Block');
```

The first argument to the parent constructor gives the plugin subdirectory where you will need to put your plugin, and by implication, the namespace. In this example, the subdirectory is *Plugin/Block*, meaning that block plugins need to be in the *src/Plugin/Block* subdirectory under the main implementing module directory, and correspondingly, their namespace needs to be \Drupal\mymodule\Plugin\Block.

The last argument gives the name of the annotation class for this type of plugin.

Also, some modules may want to alter other modules' plugin definitions. They can do that by implementing an alter hook, which you'll also find in the constructor:

```
$this->alterInfo('block');
```

This says that the hook is called hook_block_alter(), and it will be passed an array of discovered block plugin definitions, whose keys will be the block plugin IDs and whose values will be the annotation information from each defined plugin.

Once you have defined your plugin manager class, the last steps are to instantiate and use the class. To instantiate a plugin manager class, call the get() method on the Drupal container object, passing in the name of the service that you defined. For example, in \Drupal\block\BlockListBuilder::createInstance(), the container object is in local variable $container, and there is a call to $container->get('plugin.manager.block') to instantiate a block manager class, which is then stored in the $blockManager class property in the constructor.

Then you can call methods on the plugin manager. For instance, on the same class, the buildForm() method calls:

```
$plugins = $this->blockManager->getSortedDefinitions();
foreach ($plugins as $plugin_id => $plugin_definition) {
  // ...
}
```

And several other places in Drupal core, you can find calls to:

```
$this->blockManager->clearCachedDefinitions();
```

This tells the block plugin manager to clear its cache of plugin definitions, because something has happened that affects the plugin definition data (such as when the \Drupal\block_content\Plugin\Block\BlockContentBlock plugin is used by an administrator to add or update a custom block).

Further reading and reference:

- "Drupal 8 Services and Dependency Injection" on page 35

Implementing a plugin in a module

A module that implements a plugin type needs to define a class that implements the defined plugin interface, with the defined plugin annotation added as a documentation block immediately before the class declaration. Here are the steps to follow:

1. You'll need some information before you start—see "Plugin Data Needed by Plugin Implementers" on page 32. You'll want to start by finding the annotation class or the plugin manager class. You can discover available annotation classes by

looking at the "Annotations" topic on *https://api.drupal.org*, or searching the code base for classes with @Annotation in their documentation header. Plugin managers generally extend \Drupal\Core\Plugin\DefaultPluginManager, which should help you find them if necessary.

2. In the example of a Block plugin, the interface is \Drupal\Core\Block\Block PluginInterface, the base class is \Drupal\Core\Block\BlockBase, the annotation class is \Drupal\Core\Block\Annotation\Block, and the namespace subdirectory is Plugin\Block. For most plugins, the namespace is something like Plugin\(type), but different plugins use different conventions for (type), and some use subdirectories.

3. Define a class in your module's namespace that implements the interface (the easiest way is usually to extend the base class) and is annotated using the defined annotation scheme, in the correct namespace. The annotation goes into a documentation block directly before the start of your class, and looks like this:

```
/**
 * Provides a block for (whatever your block does).
 *
 * @Block(
 *   id = "mymodule_myblockname",
 *   admin_label = @Translation("Admin label for my block"),
 * )
 */
class MyModuleMyBlockName extends BlockBase {
    ...
```

Notes:

- Keys in the annotation array that match the member variable names in the annotation class are providing overrides of default values.

- Annotation syntax is similar to PHP array syntax, but it has a few differences:

  — In place of => for a PHP array key/value mapping, use =.

  — The keys are not quoted. However, if an annotation value is itself an array, the keys of that array are quoted, and the array is enclosed in curly brackets.

  — Only use double-quotes in values. Single quotes will not work.

- If you are providing a translatable string in annotation, wrap it in @Translation().

Examples—implementing plugins:

- "Registering a Block in Drupal 8" on page 101.
- "Defining a Content Entity Type in Drupal 8" on page 139 (has example of arrays in annotation).

- "Defining a Configuration Entity Type in Drupal 8" on page 149 (has example of arrays in annotation).
- "Defining a field widget in Drupal 8" on page 165.
- "Defining a field formatter in Drupal 8" on page 169.
- In Drupal core, class files under *core/modules/*/src/Plugin/** are either plugin implementations or plugin type definitions.

Drupal 8 Services and Dependency Injection

Basic concepts: Services, Containers, and Dependency Injection

Drupal version 8 adopted the concept of *services* from the Symfony project. The basic idea is that the functionality of Drupal should be separated into separate classes, each providing a self-contained chunk of functionality known as a *service*. For instance, Drupal core has a service for translating user interface text, several services for caching different types of information, and a service for providing aliases for internal URL paths. Each service has a machine name, such as `string_translation`, `cache.default`, or `path.alias_manager`.

Closely allied with the services concept is the *dependency injection container*, or *container*. Again, this comes from the Symfony framework, which defines the `\Symfony\Component\DependencyInjection\ContainerInterface` interface. The container is the central place for retrieving the classes that provide services, via its `get()` method. The top-level `\Drupal` class has a `getContainer()` method to retrieve the container class, a `service()` method to retrieve a single service, plus several helper methods for retrieving commonly used Drupal services.

If you write code that uses functionality provided by a service, you should always make sure to get the service via either *service location* (calling `ContainerInterface::get()` or methods on the `\Drupal` class), or *dependency injection*. Dependency injection can be done in two ways:

- If your code is itself defining a service, you can inject dependencies on other services via the `arguments` component of the service definition in the **.services.yml* file. The next section shows how to do this.
- Many base classes and interfaces in Drupal have either `create()` or `createInstance()` methods that are called by default manager and factory classes to create instances of these classes. The methods have a `$container` argument passed in; you can call `$container->get()` in your override of this method to obtain a service class and store it in a member variable on your class.

Examples—using services and dependency injection:

- "The Drupal Cache" on page 10
- "Simple configuration API in Drupal 8" on page 45
- "State API in Drupal 8" on page 47
- "Internationalizing User Interface Text" on page 49
- "Drupal core's main permission system" on page 64
- "Registering for a URL in Drupal 8" on page 92
- "Generating Paged Output" on page 107
- "Basic Form Generation and Processing in Drupal 8" on page 114
- `MyEntityTypeDeleteForm` from "Defining a Configuration Entity Type in Drupal 8" on page 149
- "Querying and Loading Entities in Drupal 8" on page 160

Defining a service

In your modules, you can define services by putting them in a *mymodule.services.yml* file in your module's main directory. Each service definition starts with the machine name, and subsequent lines contain data about the service, such as the default class that provides the service, and arguments (usually other services) for the class constructor. For example (from *core/core.services.yml*, with some arguments omitted):

```
services:
  path.alias_manager:
    class: Drupal\Core\Path\AliasManager
    arguments: ['@path.alias_storage', '@path.alias_whitelist']
```

The other part of providing a service is to define the default class, and normally also an interface that defines the methods that overriding classes need to implement.

Examples—service defining:

- "Creating a plugin manager" on page 31
- "Altering Routes and Providing Dynamic Routes in Drupal 8" on page 98
- The classes listed in the central *core/core.services.yml* file or various Drupal core modules' **.services.yml* files

Service tags

Some services are tagged with *service tags* in their service definition. For instance, all of the cache bin services are tagged with `cache.bin`:

```
# From the core/core.services.yml file:
cache.default:
  class: Drupal\Core\Cache\CacheBackendInterface
  tags:
  - { name: cache.bin }
```

In this case, the tag allows Drupal's cache mechanism to locate available cache bins
and use them appropriately; if your module adds a new cache bin, it will need to tag
its service definition. See "Drupal 8 Cache API" on page 11 for more on the cache
system.

Overriding services

The final concept around services is that they are alterable: the *services.yml* file
defines the *default* class for a service, but a module can override this choice by providing a different class to be used instead. If you want to do this, here are the steps.

First, you will need to define a class to use as your alternative service provider. You
will probably want to extend the default service provider class and override methods
whose functionality you want to change, so that you can be sure that all needed methods are present. Put this class into your module's namespace.

Next, define a class that implements the \Drupal\Core\DependencyInjec
tion\ServiceModifierInterface interface. This class must have a specific name to
be automatically recognized by Drupal as a service modifier: the name must start
with a CamelCase version of your module's machine name, followed by ServicePro
vider. For instance, if your module's machine name is foo_bar, then your service
modifier class must be called FooBarServiceProvider. Also, it must be in the top-
level namespace for your module (in this case, \Drupal\foo_bar), and therefore it
must be located in the *src/FooBarServiceProvider.php* file under your main module
directory. (In contrast to the other examples in this book, I used foo_bar instead of
mymodule for the machine name of the module, to illustrate what happens in the common case of a module with an underscore in its machine name.)

There is only one method in this interface: alter(). Here is a simple example:

```
public function alter(ContainerBuilder $container) {
  $definition = $container->getDefinition('name.of.service');
  $definition->setClass('Drupal\mymodule\MyNewServiceClass');
}
```

Further reading and reference:

- "Automatic Class Loading in Drupal" on page 12.
- If you're interested, here are some additional details on the internals of this process. First, \Drupal\Core\DrupalKernel::discoverServiceProviders() is
  what actually makes a list of classes with the right names and namespaces,

as well as the list of *services.yml* files. Then `\Drupal\Core\DependencyInjection` `\Compiler\ModifyServiceDefinitionsPass::process()` is what checks to see if the classes implement `ServiceModifierInterface`, and if so, calls their `alter()` methods.

Rebuilding the container

As you are developing code for Drupal 8, if you make changes to plugin annotations, routing definitions, administrative links, and other similar aspects of your PHP code and YAML files, you'll need to do an operation known as "rebuilding the container" in order to get Drupal to recognize your changes. The reason is that Drupal parses this information and caches it in PHP files or the database; this information isn't cleared during a normal cache clear.

There are two ways to trigger a container rebuild:

- At the command line, use the **drush cr** command, if you have the Drush development tool installed.
- From the browser, navigate to *example.com/core/rebuild.php*.

Further reading and reference:

- "The Drupal Cache" on page 10
- "Drupal Development Tools" on page 204

Interacting with the Drupal 8 Event System

The Symfony framework defines the concept of *events*. Each event is identified with a unique name; events are *dispatched* by the Symfony framework during the HTTP response process, as well as by other Drupal components and modules. Drupal modules can set up *event subscribers*, which are classes that register to take action when particular events are dispatched.

To define and dispatch an event:

1. Choose a name for your event, which must be unique.
2. Define a class constant whose value is the name of your event.
3. Define a class to contain the data relevant to the event, which must extend `\Symfony\Component\EventDispatcher\Event`.
4. In your event-dispatching class or code, call the `dispatch()` method on the `event_dispatcher` service. The first argument is your event name, and the sec-

ond is an event data object, which you'll need to instantiate with the necessary data.

To respond to an event:

1. Create an event subscriber class, which implements `\Symfony\Component\Event Dispatcher\EventSubscriberInterface`.

2. Define the `getSubscribedEvents()` method in your class, which specifies which events you are subscribing to, and which methods on your class to call for each one. Alternatively, there are base classes available for some specific types of event subscribers, which may implement this method for you but require you to implement other methods.

3. Write the individual methods that will respond to the events. Their single parameter will be the data object from the event dispatch.

4. Define a service in your *mymodule.services.yml* file, tagged with `event_subscriber` and referencing your class. For example:

```
services:
  mymodule.subscriber:
    class: Drupal\mymodule\My\Class\Name
    tags:
    - { name: event_subscriber }
```

Further reading and reference:

- "Drupal 8 Services and Dependency Injection" on page 35
- The "Events" topic on *https://api.drupal.org*, which includes a list of defined events
- Symfony's documentation on events: *http://bit.ly/eventdispatcher*

Examples—event responding:

- "Altering Routes and Providing Dynamic Routes in Drupal 8" on page 98

Principle: Drupal Separates Content, Configuration, and State Data

Any website built with a content management system has data that can (at least, in principle) be separated into three types of information:

Content

The text, images, files, and other information that is being presented to the site visitor. Content information can be further separated into types (e.g., the text of sidebar blocks, the text and images in the main body area of site pages, and the comments on a blog), each of which has its own set of properties (or fields). On many sites, some content information is open to editing and creating by nonexpert or even anonymous site users. Content tends to change often and grow over time.

Configuration

Information about the site structure and settings; defines how to collect the content information and present it to the site visitor. In Drupal, this includes your content type settings, field settings, views, and so on. Configuration information tends to be fairly stable over time and only change when new features or functionality are being added to the site; it is usually managed by a site administrator. Some configuration data can be separated into types with properties in the same way as content (e.g., content type settings are one type, and views are another); other configuration data is more atomic (e.g., the name of your site).

State

Information about the current state of the site. A good example of this type of information in Drupal is the time of the last cron job run. State information changes often.

Separating the storage of configuration, state, and content information on a site is very useful, because it allows you to set up strategies for deployment, staging, and sharing of data among sites—generally, the information flows for content and configuration are not the same, and state information is not desirable to share at all. So, in your programming with Drupal, it is a good idea to figure out whether the information you will be storing should be classified as content, configuration, or state before you start. The distinction is open to opinion in many cases, but you should make a determination and then use the appropriate mechanism to store your data.

Information Storage in Drupal 7

Drupal 7, unfortunately, does not have a perfect system for separating configuration, state, and content information. It is mixed together in the database, so the system does not lend itself easily to deployment strategies:

- Simple configuration information and most state information is serialized and stored in the `variable` table in the database, using the `variable_set()` and `variable_get()` functions.

- The simple configuration information in the `variable` table can be overridden by $conf entries in the *settings.php* file.

- Complex configuration information is stored by individual modules in the database in a custom manner of their choosing.

- Content is ideally stored using *entities* and fields; however, many modules instead use a custom database schema to store content information. Content does not generally have a universal ID that would facilitate synchronizing and sharing content among sites.

- A site builder can export most configuration information to PHP code by using the contributed Features module. The Strongarm module also allows you to export simple configuration variable values using Features, if you prefer not to put them in your *settings.php* file. In principle, this allows site configuration to be shared among sites or deployed from staging to the live site. In practice, however, not all configuration information can be managed using this method, and this solution is not perfect.

- Content information can be synchronized and shared among sites using the contributed Migrate module, or a combination of Views and Feeds modules; both methods require a significant investment in time and/or coding to set up.

Further reading and reference:

- See *https://api.drupal.org* for documentation of `variable_*` functions.
- "Principle: Drupal Is Database-Independent" on page 54.
- "Programming with Entities and Fields" on page 129.
- Features module: *https://www.drupal.org/project/features*.
- Strongarm module: *https://www.drupal.org/project/strongarm*.
- Migrate module: *https://www.drupal.org/project/migrate*.
- Feeds module: *https://www.drupal.org/project/feeds*.
- Views module: *https://www.drupal.org/project/views*.

Information Separation in Drupal 8

Although Drupal 8 still stores most of its information in the database, the configuration, state, and content information has a much cleaner separation than in previous versions of Drupal. At least, that is true if you use the Drupal APIs to access information, instead of attempting direct database queries. Here is an outline of the Drupal 8 information separation system:

- The current configuration information for a site is stored in the site's active configuration storage, either in the filesystem or in the database (database by default).

- Configuration information can be exported and imported via files, so you can share it with other sites. Configuration you are importing goes in the site's staging configuration directory; the location of this directory is defined in your *settings.php* file.

- If file storage is being used for configuration information, it will be read from the active configuration directory (as configured in *settings.php*) and cached for efficiency (see "The Drupal Cache" on page 10).

- There is a Configuration API in Drupal for modules to use to define, create, update, and read configuration data. This is described in "Configuration API in Drupal 8" on page 42.

- State information is stored in the database, and there is a State API that modules can use to create, update, and read state data. This is described in "State API in Drupal 8" on page 47.

- Content information is stored using *entities* and *fields*. See "Programming with Entities and Fields" on page 129 for more information.

- Each content entity item has a *universally unique identifier (UUID)* which is unique across sites. Storing content in entities keeps it separate from configuration and state information, and this fact and the presence of UUIDs facilitate import, export, staging, and deployment strategies.

Configuration API in Drupal 8

Drupal 8's Configuration API consists of the following parts:

- The native format for configuration data is YAML files, with defined schema.

- Simple global configuration information, such as the name of the website, is stored and retrieved using `Config` objects.

- Configuration information that has multiple copies, such as views, content types, and other definitions, is stored and retrieved using *configuration entities*.

The following sections describe each of these parts of the configuration system.

Configuration file format and schema in Drupal 8

Drupal 8's configuration files are written in YAML format. Your extension (module, theme, or installation profile) can provide default configuration data in files in its *config/install* directory under the main extension directory. Some extensions put all their settings in a single *myextension.settings.yml* file; if it makes more sense to separate the settings into separate files, you can also use multiple subsystem files named *myextension.subsystem_name.yml*. Configuration files for configuration entities (views, content types, etc.) have specific naming conventions, which must be followed. The configuration files in *config/install* will be imported when your extension is first enabled; changes to these files have no effect after this point.

Some configuration has outside dependencies. For instance, configuration for a node content type depends on the Node module, and configuration for a view depends on the Views module. If your module provides configuration that depends on other modules, you have two choices:

- You can make your module depend on the other module. In this case, put the dependent configuration in the *config/install* directory along with the rest of your configuration.

- You can provide the configuration in the *config/optional* directory and avoid having a module dependency. When your module is installed, if the modules this configuration depend on are already installed, your configuration will be imported into the site. Or, if those modules are installed later, your module's *config/optional* directory will be scanned again for configuration whose dependencies have now been met, and the configuration will be imported then.

Within each YAML file, the configuration data is essentially an associative array, with keys and values, which can be flat or nested. For instance, your *mymodule.settings.yml* file might look like this:

```
submit_button_label: 'Submit'
name_field_settings:
  field_label: 'Your name'
  field_size: 50
```

You also need to provide a YAML-formatted configuration schema file, *config/schema/mymodule.schema.yml* under your main module directory, which describes the data types of the configuration data items, as well as the labels they should have when configuration is being translated. In this example, the schema file would contain:

```
# Schema for My Module configuration.
mymodule.settings:
  type: config_object
  label: 'My module settings'
  mapping:
    submit_button_label:
      type: label
      label: 'Label for submit button'
    name_field_settings:
      type: mapping
      label: 'Settings for name field'
      mapping:
        field_label:
          type: label
          label: 'Label for name field'
```

```
field_size:
  type: integer
  label: 'Size of name field'
```

Notes:

- The top-level data type needs to be `config_object` for simple configuration like this. For configuration entities, it would be `config_entity`.

- There are many other data type options, such as the `boolean` and `float` scalar types, and the `path` (a Drupal path) and `text` (a translatable string) complex types.

- The `label` type holds a single-line plain-text translatable string.

- The `text` type can contain multiple lines and HTML, and is also translatable.

- The `string` type is also available, for nontranslatable single-line text. You can use this type for machine names.

- The labels in the YAML schema file are used as an aid to translation. While it is not technically necessary to provide labels for nontranslatable configuration data, it is still a good idea for consistency and documentation.

- Although the native format for configuration is YAML files, configuration is normally stored in the Drupal database.

- You can import and export YAML configuration information using the core Configuration Manager module UI. If you use the UI to export a single configuration, it will tell you the correct filename to use. This is useful in developing the configuration files to put in your module's *config/install* or *config/optional* directory.

- There is a hard limit on the length of a configuration filename: without the extension, it cannot exceed 250 characters.

Further reading and reference:

- Drupal configuration YAML files: *http://bit.ly/drupal8_config_file*
- Drupal configuration YAML schema: *http://bit.ly/config_schema*
- YAML: *http://yaml.org*
- Another way to manage configuration during development: *https://www.drupal.org/project/config_devel*

Examples—configuration schema files:

- "Defining a Configuration Entity Type in Drupal 8" on page 149

Simple configuration API in Drupal 8

Once you have a configuration file defined for your module, as described in "Config-uration file format and schema in Drupal 8" on page 42, you can use the simple con-figuration API to store and retrieve configuration information in code. When your module is installed, the values will be the defaults defined in your module's *config/ install* and/or *config/optional* YML file or files; these can be overridden by an admin-istrator, presumably using a settings form supplied by your module.

To use the configuration API, you start by getting a \Drupal\Core\Config\Config object from the config.factory service, and then you can use its methods to get, set, and save data. You'll need to distinguish between getting an editable configuration object without *overrides* (the raw version), or an object with overrides suitable for display in the UI (read more about overrides later in this chapter). For example, assuming that *mymodule.settings.yml* is the name of your module's configuration file, and it contains the data shown in the example in "Configuration file format and schema in Drupal 8" on page 42:

```
// Code without dependency injection or $container variable:
// - Get a non-editable version (with overrides):
$config = \Drupal::configFactory()->get('mymodule.settings');
// - Get an editable version (without overrides):
$config = \Drupal::configFactory()->getEditable('mymodule.settings');
// With dependency injection, or if you have a $container variable:
$config = $container->get('config.factory')->get('mymodule.settings');
$config = $container->get('config.factory')->getEditable('mymodule.settings');

// Get the whole config array, and then extract one component:
$all = $config->get();
$button_label = $all['submit_button_label'];
// Or, if you only need this one component, one step:
$button_label = $config->get('submit_button_label');

// Get another component:
$name_field_info = $all['name_field_settings'];
// Or, in one step:
$name_field_info = $config->get('name_field_settings');

// Drill down:
$name_label = $name_field_info['field_label'];
// Or, in one step:
$name_label = $config->get('name_field_settings.field_label');
```

Each of the preceding get() operations has a corresponding set() operation, such as:

```
// Store changes locally in your editable config object:
$config->set('submit_button_label', $new_label);
```

If you are changing settings, you also need to call the save() method at the end of the operation, in order to make your changes permanent:

```
// Make the changes permanent:
$config->save();
```

Further reading and reference:

- Services background: "Drupal 8 Services and Dependency Injection" on page 35

Configuration entities in Drupal 8

As discussed in "Principle: Drupal Separates Content, Configuration, and State Data" on page 39, some configuration data can be separated into types. For example:

- Content types, managed by the Drupal core Node module, which are a special case of content entity bundle configuration entities
- Views, managed by the Drupal core Views module
- Date formats, managed by the Drupal core System module

This type of configuration data is managed by defining a *configuration entity*, rather than using the simple configuration API discussed in the previous section. The process of defining a configuration entity is described fully in "Defining a Configuration Entity Type in Drupal 8" on page 149.

Configuration overrides in Drupal 8

The configuration system in Drupal 8 also has an override system, which allows configuration values to be overridden and translated. There are three types of overrides: global, language, and dynamic. When you are retrieving configuration values, if you use the get() method on a configuration object, you will get the value with overrides, and if you use the getEditable() method, you will get the value without overrides. The general principle is that when editing configuration, you should use the nonoverridden value, and when using or displaying configuration, you should use the overridden value.

Global overrides can be provided for a site by adding entries to the global $config variable in your *settings.php* file. For example, to override the submit button label in your main module settings from the example earlier in this section:

```
$config['mymodule.settings']['submit_button_label'] = 'New label text';
```

Language overrides are provided by the Language module, and the Configuration Translation module allows users to translate their configuration. Dynamic overrides can be provided by modules by defining a service tagged with config.factory.override.

Further reading and reference:

- More details about configuration overrides: *http://bit.ly/config_override*
- Services background: "Drupal 8 Services and Dependency Injection" on page 35

State API in Drupal 8

To use the Drupal State API, start by getting the state object, which implements
\Drupal\Core\State\StateInterface, from the state service:

```
// Code without dependency injection or $container variable:
$state = \Drupal::state();
// Dependency injection, or $container variable:
$state = $container->get('state');
```

Next, if you have some module-specific state information to save, you need to choose
a unique machine name for it; the convention is to prefix it with your module's
machine name. Then, you can save your state information by calling:

```
$state->set('mymodule.my_state_variable_name', $value);
```

To retrieve the value:

```
$value = $state->get('mymodule.my_state_variable_name');
```

And if for some reason you want to completely remove the state information for that
variable, perhaps because it is not relevant anymore due to a configuration change:

```
$state->delete('mymodule.my_state_variable_name');
```

You can also set and get other modules' state information, after locating the correct
machine name of the state variable. For instance:

- Setting node.node_access_needs_rebuild to TRUE indicates that the node permissions tables need to be rebuilt.
- A TRUE value for system.maintenance_mode indicates that the site is currently in maintenance mode.
- The system.cron_last variable stores the time of the most recent cron run.

Further reading and reference:

- Services background: "Drupal 8 Services and Dependency Injection" on page 35

Principle: Drupal Is International

Drupal core and Drupal contributed modules and themes are, ideally, constructed so that their user interface elements use English by default but can be translated into other languages. Less universally (but still ideally), modules and themes are also constructed so that any user-entered text for configuration or content can be translated. If both of these principles are followed:

- You can build an English-language site.
- You can build a site whose language is not English.
- You can build a multilingual site.
- You can use the translation mechanism to change the default English user interface text supplied by a module (for instance, changing the text on a button or link), without altering the module code.

When you program for Drupal, even if you don't think you will ever need to translate your site, it is still a good idea to follow this principle, because:

- Markets and the reach of websites expand, and you might eventually need to translate your site.
- You might decide to contribute the module on *drupal.org* so that others can use it, and some users will speak other languages.
- It's a good Drupal coding habit to get into, in case you ever want to contribute code to the Drupal project.
- At least for built-in user interface text, it's not very difficult anyway.

Unicode Strings

When programming with an international audience in mind, it is important to remember that not all text is ASCII—character sets for much of the world are instead multibyte Unicode characters. Some of the standard PHP string functions, such as `strlen()`, `strtolower()`, etc., do not take this into consideration and are not safe to use for multibyte characters. Instead, you can use Drupal's multibyte-safe equivalent functions: `drupal_strlen()`, and so on in Drupal 7; these functions are wrappers to static methods on the core `\Drupal\Component\Utility\Unicode` class in Drupal 8.

Internationalizing User Interface Text

The basic tool for internationalizing user interface text in the modules and themes you create is Drupal's t() function. Any text that will be shown to an administrative user or a site visitor should be enclosed in t(); before the text is printed, Drupal will translate it to the appropriate language. For instance:

```
// Bad:
$button_text = 'Save';
// Good:
$button_text = t('Save');
```

For translation to work properly, the first argument of t() must always be a literal string—it cannot contain variables. (This is because the first arguments to t() are extracted from code to build the database of strings that need translation.) If you need to substitute variable information into your string, t() has a mechanism:

```
// Bad:
$message_string = t("Hello $user_name");
// Good:
$message_string = t('Hello @user_name', array('@user_name' => $user_name));
```

As you can see, it doesn't really take much effort to make basic module-defined or theme-defined user interface text translatable.

Notes on internationalizing user interface text:

- There are additional Drupal functions you can use to internationalize numbers, dates, and JavaScript text; these are collectively known as the Drupal Localization API. There is an "Internationalization" topic on *https://api.drupal.org* for Drupal 8 that gives examples of these functions, plus some other strings that are automatically internationalized.

- There is a Drupal.t() function that is the equivalent to t() for use in JavaScript code, in both Drupal 7 and Drupal 8.

- In Drupal 7, there is an st() function for use in contexts where the full Drupal localization system is not available (such as during installation).

- In Drupal 8, string translation is technically provided by the string_translation service; many classes have a t() method, which supports dependency injection. If a base class you are using has a t() method, use it rather than calling the t() function. There is no need in Drupal 8 for an st() function.

- If you are defining a class in Drupal 8 and the base class does not have a t() method, use \Drupal\Core\StringTranslation\StringTranslationTrait to add it.

- In Drupal 8, you will also need to use the `@Translation` annotation when defining a plugin, in order to make its text strings translatable.

Further reading and reference:

- Find Drupal localization functions on *https://api.drupal.org* listed in the "Formatting" and "Sanitization functions" topics. The "Internationalization" topic for Drupal 8 also has some useful information.
- Read more about the Localization API at *https://www.drupal.org/developing/api/localization*.
- Annotation: "The Basics of Drupal 8 Plugin Programming" on page 28.
- "Drupal 8 Services and Dependency Injection" on page 35.
- Traits are new to PHP 5.4. See *http://php.net/manual/language.oop5.traits.php*.

Internationalizing User-Entered Text in Drupal 7

If you are building a module that has user-entered settings or user-entered text that is then displayed to other users, and you want your module to be fully internationalized so that it can be used on a multilingual site, you need to provide a way for the user-entered text to be translated. The `t()` function only works for literal text strings, so it cannot be used for this purpose.

Unfortunately, in Drupal version 7 there is no Drupal core API for translating user-entered text in a uniform way. But there are several methods that can be used to make your user-entered text translatable:

- Store user-entered text in individual Drupal *variables*, using the `variable_get()` and `variable_set()` functions. If each string of user-entered text is stored in its own variable, and the variables are declared using the contributed Variable module's `hook_variable_info()`, site builders can use the contributed Internationalization module to translate this text. This is most appropriate if you just have a few administrator-entered text strings that need to be translated.
- For settings that form a list, use a Drupal core taxonomy vocabulary to manage the list instead of managing it in your own module. The taxonomy terms can then be translated using the contributed Internationalization module. To set up a vocabulary, you will need to add the following code to your module's `hook_enable()` implementation in the *mymodule.install* file (`mymodule_enable()` function):

```
// Create the vocabulary if it doesn't already exist.
$vocabulary = taxonomy_vocabulary_load(variable_get('mymodule_vocabulary', 0));
if (!$vocabulary) {
```

```
    $vocabulary = (object) array(
      'name' => t('Some appropriate name'),
      'machine_name' => 'mymodule_appropriate_name',
      'description' => t('Some appropriate description'),
      'module' => 'mymodule',
    );
    taxonomy_vocabulary_save($vocabulary);
    variable_set('mymodule_vocabulary', $vocabulary->vid);
  }
```

- For more complicated collections of settings, or content to be displayed on the site, use a node with fields to store the information, or define a custom Drupal *entity* with *fields* to store your settings. The collections of settings can then be translated using the Entity Translation module.

Further reading and reference:

- General information about programming with hooks: "The Basics of Module and Theme Hook Programming" on page 23
- Defining entity with fields: "Defining an Entity Type in Drupal 7" on page 132
- Internationalization module: *https://www.drupal.org/project/i18n*
- Variable module: *https://www.drupal.org/project/variable*
- Entity Translation module: *https://www.drupal.org/project/entity_translation*

Internationalizing User-Entered Text in Drupal 8

The situation for internationalizing user-entered text in Drupal 8 is much better than in Drupal 7. There are two methods, depending on the nature of the text: whether it is considered configuration or content information.

Content text in Drupal 8 should be stored in *fields* on *entities*; either use an entity type provided by Drupal core (node, taxonomy, etc.), use an entity type provided by a contributed module, or define your own custom entity type. Once you have stored your user-entered data in an entity, it can be translated using the Content Translation module, which is part of Drupal 8 core.

Configuration text in Drupal 8 can also be translated, as long as your module uses the core configuration system to store its configuration data. Configuration components of `label` and `text` types are translatable, and the core Configuration Translation module provides a user interface for translating this data.

Further reading and reference:

- "Principle: Drupal Separates Content, Configuration, and State Data" on page 39

- "Programming with Entities and Fields" on page 129
- "Configuration API in Drupal 8" on page 42

Principle: Drupal Is Accessible and Usable

The World Wide Web Consortium (W3C) defines *accessibility* as meaning that people with disabilities can perceive, understand, interact with, and contribute to a website, and its Web Accessibility Initiative (WAI) has many resources for learning about accessibility and testing websites for accessibility. The Drupal project has an active accessibility team, and one of Drupal's guiding principles is that its administrative backend and its visitor-facing output should both be as accessible as possible. The Drupal accessibility team has helped to improve the accessibility of Drupal by maintaining documentation on accessibility, testing Drupal for accessibility problems, and pushing the Drupal project to adopt industry-wide accessibility standards.

Another principle that ideally guides web design is *usability*: the idea that websites' user interfaces should be easy to use and learn. The Drupal project has an active usability team, and a commitment to high usability of the Drupal administrative interface is one of Drupal's guiding principles. The Drupal usability team has done usability studies and proposed changes that have greatly improved the usability of Drupal—there was a large usability push for Drupal version 7, and another for Drupal 8.

Related to usability is a focus on mobile platforms: increasingly, websites are accessed through mobile phones, tablets, and other small devices rather than through desktop browsers, so for a website to be truly usable, all of its content and functionality needs to be mobile-friendly. Accordingly, Drupal 8 adopted a "mobile first" design philosophy for both its administrative interfaces and its public-facing output, with the aim of making sure that an administrator or site visitor on a mobile device would have a rich and fully functional experience.

At times, usability and accessibility can be at odds; a mobile-first orientation can also be at odds with optimal desktop browser usability. However, there are usually designs that can be adopted that are reasonably good for all users. For instance, usability studies might show that a drag-and-drop interface for ordering menu items is much faster and more intuitive than an interface where you assign numerical weights to define the order, but blind users and users who have mobility limitations that preclude use of a mouse cannot use drag-and-drop interfaces, so the drag-and-drop interface has accessibility problems. To satisfy both usability and accessibility principles, you can supply the drag-and-drop interface along with a link that lets users switch to the numerical weight interface if needed. In the mobile versus desktop realm, an interface that provides more information when you hover your mouse over an area might be quite usable for someone using a mouse on a standard computer, but how do you "hover" on a mobile phone interface? In this case, the design philosophy would be to make sure this information is available in some other way for mobile device users.

So, instead of thinking that usability and accessibility are incompatible, the guiding principle of combining usability and accessibility should be to make the user interface for a task as easy to use and learn as possible for users without mobility, sight, or other limitations, while providing alternatives that allow users with these limitations to be able to accomplish the task. In addition, when thinking about and testing for usability, different types and sizes of devices and browsers should be considered. Drupal aims to follow these principles, and you should also try to adopt them in your own programming. Here are some things you can do to improve accessibility and usability in your programming:

- Familiarize yourself with the usability and accessibility guidelines of the Drupal project.
- When providing a user interface in your own module, use the same user interface patterns as Drupal core (they have already been tested for usability and accessibility, and uniformity also means easier learning).
- When adding an administrative page for your module, put it in an appropriate section of the existing administrative user interface hierarchy of Drupal core, so people can find it easily.
- Test your user interfaces and theme for accessibility.
- Make sure that all information you present is available in text format (not just in images or diagrams), so screen reader users can access it. Search engines also only index text information, so making your site accessible in this way will also help its visibility in search engines.
- Make your theme and user interface designs adaptable to different screen sizes and magnifications. This will help with both usability on mobile devices and accessibility for people who need to magnify their screens.

Further reading and reference:

- World Wide Web Consortium (W3C): *http://w3.org*
- Web Accessibility Initiative (WAI)—includes resources for accessibility testing and worldwide standards: *http://www.w3.org/WAI/*
- Drupal accessibility team: *https://groups.drupal.org/accessibility*
- Drupal accessibility guidelines and resources: *https://www.drupal.org/about/accessibility*
- Drupal usability team: *https://groups.drupal.org/usability*

- Drupal usability guidelines: *https://www.drupal.org/ui-standards*
- Drupal mobile development guide: *https://www.drupal.org/documentation/mobile*

Principle: Drupal Is Database-Independent

Although most Drupal sites use MySQL (or a compatible clone) as the database back-end, Drupal version 7 (and later versions) can be used with a variety of databases. Drupal core supports MySQL, PostgreSQL, and SQLite (or some subset, depending on the Drupal version), and contributed modules add support for other databases, including at least partial support for non-SQL databases, such as MongoDB. Drupal core also provides several database-related customizations, such as the ability to prefix database table names with a string, or different strings for different tables, and to fall back to a different database if the default database is not available.

In order to facilitate this portability, Drupal provides a Schema API and a Database API, which work together as a framework for defining and querying database tables. The Schema API has been fairly stable for several versions of Drupal. The Database API was completely overhauled for Drupal 7 and is based on the standard PHP PDO library; it is also sometimes referred to as *DBTNG* (Database, the Next Generation).

Because Drupal is written in PHP, it is possible in your own programming to avoid using the Drupal Schema and Database APIs and instead use the PHP database-specific query functions you may be familiar with to query the database directly. But this is not a good idea, because:

- Using the Database API helps make your queries more secure from SQL injection bugs.
- The Schema API is actually easier to use for creating and modifying tables than writing your own SQL queries, and the code is easier to read and maintain. The Database API takes an effort similar to writing your own SQL queries.
- You might sometime want to switch to a different database for performance reasons.
- You might sometime want to use different site set-up choices, such as setting up development and staging sites with different database options.
- You might want to contribute your module to the Drupal open source project so that others can use it, and contributed code should be database-independent.
- It's a good habit to get into, in case you ever want to contribute code to the Drupal project.

It should be noted that one of the best ways to make sure to stay independent of the database is to avoid direct use of the database entirely. For instance, instead of creating a module to store information in its own custom database table, consider whether you can use Drupal's taxonomy, node, or entity system instead. Or perhaps you can use a contributed module, along with a custom plugin.

Drupal 8

In Drupal 8, unless you are developing core systems, direct database queries are deprecated in most cases in favor of other APIs (entity system, configuration system, etc.), so if you find yourself wanting to use a database query, you should check to see if there is an API you should be using instead. For the most part, only these core API functions themselves should be making direct database queries.

Further reading and reference:

- The rest of this section has more details on the Database and Schema APIs.
- Avoiding database programming entirely: "Mistake: Programming Too Much" on page 71.
- Security concerns: "Principle: Drupal Is Secure; User Input Is Insecure" on page 61.
- Drupal Schema API: *https://www.drupal.org/developing/api/schema*.
- Drupal Database API: *https://www.drupal.org/developing/api/database*.
- Modules providing alternative database integration: MongoDB (*https://www.drupal.org/project/mongodb*), Microsoft SQL Server (*https://www.drupal.org/project/sqlsrv*), Oracle (*https://www.drupal.org/project/oracle*).
- Group for people interested in enterprise applications (including database integration): *https://groups.drupal.org/enterprise*.

Setting Up Database Tables: Schema API and hook_update_N()

If your module needs to set up its own database tables, create them by implementing hook_schema() in your *mymodule.install* file. Drupal will then take care of creating the tables when your module is enabled, as well as deleting them when your module is uninstalled. For example, to define a database table called 'mymodule_foo' with fields 'bar' and 'baz':

```
// This code works in Drupal 7 or 8.
function mymodule_schema() {
  $schema = array();
  $schema['mymodule_foo'] = array(
    'description' => 'Untranslated description of this table',
    'fields' => array(
```

```
      'bar' => array(
        'description' => 'Untranslated description of this field',
        'type' => 'varchar',
        'length' => 50,
        'default' => '',
      ),
      'baz' => array(
        'description' => 'Untranslated description of this field',
        'type' => 'int',
        'unsigned' => TRUE,
        'default' => 0,
      ),
    ),
    'primary key' => array('baz'),
  );
  return $schema;
}
```

 The Schema API is flexible enough to define all aspects of database tables, including fields of different types, indexes, and so on. See the Schema API documentation for details: *https://www.drupal.org/ developing/api/schema*.

Once you have enabled a module and its database tables are created, you may find that you need to make a change to the database schema, such as adding a field, deleting a field, adding a new database table, and so on, to correspond to a new feature you have added to your module. The Schema API provides a standard way to do this:

1. Add a hook_update_N() implementation (also known as an *update function*) to your *mymodule.install* file, which will update the database using functions such as db_add_field(), db_create_table(), and so on. Update functions are named sequentially, and each builds upon the previous schema and updates. The comment directly before the function is shown on the Pending Updates page when you run the *example.com/update.php* script, so make this comment coherent and descriptive. For example, this function would change the length of the 'bar' field to 150 characters, and also add a new 'bay' field:

```
/**
 * Make one field wider and add a new field in the mymodule_foo table.
 */
function mymodule_update_7001() {
  // This code works in Drupal 7 or 8. In Drupal 8, name the function
  // mymodule_update_8001, however!
  db_change_field('mymodule_foo', 'bar', 'bar', array(
    'description' => 'Untranslated description of this field',
    'type' => 'varchar',
    'length' => 150,
```

```
      'default' => '',
    ));
    db_add_field('mymodule_foo', 'bay', array(
      'description' => 'Untranslated description of this field',
      'type' => 'varchar',
      'length' => 50,
      'default' => '',
    ));
  }
```

2. Edit your original hook_schema() implementation function, making corresponding changes to the schema.

3. Make changes in your module code to use the new schema.

4. If this is for a site you manage, run the update script by visiting *example.com/update.php*. You will be presented with a list of pending updates, which should include the update function you just created and show the description from the function comment.

Do not attempt to call Drupal Database API functions such as Drupal 7's drupal_write_record() that rely on the schema from inside an update function, because the schema will be in an unknown state while the update function is running.

Correspondingly, never reference your hook_schema() implementation in an update function—always write out the full array values in your calls to db_change_field() and similar functions. The reason is that if you ever decide to share your module with someone else, you will not have control over when the updates are run, so you don't know at the moment of running a particular update function what the state of the schema in hook_schema() might be.

Further reading and reference:

- General information about programming with hooks: "The Basics of Module and Theme Hook Programming" on page 23.

- Drupal Schema API: *https://www.drupal.org/developing/api/schema.*

- Look up hook_schema and hook_update_N on *https://api.drupal.org* for full details of their return values.

- The functions that update database tables, such as db_change_field(), can be found in the *database.inc* include file (in Drupal 7, this is in the top-level *includes* directory; in Drupal 8, it's in *core/includes*). You can look this file up on *https://api.drupal.org* to find a list of all its functions.

Examples—setting up database schema:

- In defining a Drupal 7 entity: "Step 2: Implement hook_schema()" on page 134
- The DBTNG example in Examples for Developers (*https://www.drupal.org/ project/examples*)

Querying the Database with the Database API

If your module needs to query the Drupal database directly—whether querying its own tables or tables provided by Drupal core or another module—you will need to use the Drupal Database API to ensure that your queries are secure and portable. The Database API provides the db_query() function, which you can use to make simple queries, and a dynamic API that can be used for arbitrarily complex queries.

Very simple queries

For the simplest SELECT queries, you can use the Drupal db_query() function:

```
// This exact query works in Drupal 7 only, because the table schema has
// changed.
$result = db_query('SELECT * FROM {users} u WHERE u.status = :status',
  array(':status' => $desired_status));
foreach ($result as $record) {
  // $record will be a PHP object with fields corresponding to the table fields.
  $user_name = $record->name;
  // ...
}
```

Notes:

- The name of the database table being queried must be enclosed in {}. When Drupal runs the query, this table name will be prefixed as necessary.
- Variable inputs to the query use *placeholders*, which start with : and should contain only letters (numbers, underscores, etc. will not work in all cases). The second argument to db_query() is an array giving the values of the placeholders. Never put variable inputs directly into your query strings, especially if they originate in insecure user input.
- If a placeholder is a string, do not enclose it in quotes in the query—the variable substitution will take care of adding the quotes as necessary. For instance:

```
// Bad:
"WHERE u.name = ':name'"
// Good:
"WHERE u.name = :name"
```

- Only use db_query() for simple, static SELECT queries that you are certain will run on any database engine. If you have doubts about portability, or if the query string needs to be built up dynamically using programming logic, use the dynamic query API described in the next section.

- Some Drupal database tables have permission implications (for instance, the Node module has a rich permission system for restricting access to certain content by certain users or roles). When querying such tables, do not use db_query(), because the query will need to be modified by Drupal to enforce the correct permissions. Use the dynamic query API or the entity query API instead.

- Drupal also has a built-in pager system that greatly simplifies making multiple-page queries. You will need to use the dynamic query API to use this system.

Dynamic queries

For queries that involve paging, SQL functions such as LIKE, grouping, tables with access restrictions, or anything other than a SELECT, you will need to use Drupal's dynamic query functions instead of the simple db_query() function. These functions allow you to build up a query in a database-independent way and then execute it to get the same type of result set returned by db_query().

For example:

```
// Equivalent to:
//   SELECT title, nid, created FROM {node} n WHERE n.status = 1
// with node access enforced.
// Only for Drupal 7.
$result = db_select('node', 'n')
  ->addTag('node_access') // Enforce node access permissions.
  ->fields('n', array('title', 'nid', 'created')) // Fields to return.
  ->condition('n.status', 1) // WHERE condition.
  ->execute();
foreach ($result as $node) {
  // $node will be a PHP object with fields corresponding to the table fields.
  $title = $node->title;
  // ...
}
```

Notes:

- This specific query will only work in Drupal 7, due to database table changes; however, the function and method call syntax is the same in Drupal 8. But do remember that direct database queries in Drupal 8 are usually a mistake unless you are developing Drupal core systems.

- Unlike when using the simple db_query(), do not enclose table names in {}.

- The addTag() method is used when you are querying a table with permissions considerations. For instance, the Node module has a complex permissions system, which is enforced for you in database queries if you add the 'node_access' tag to your query.

Some query methods allow *chaining*, as illustrated in the previous example, because they alter the query in place and return the altered query object. Some do not: notably, addField() and the join methods. If you use a nonchaining method, use syntax like this:

```
// Equivalent to:
//   SELECT n.changed AS last_updated, n.title, n.nid, u.name FROM
//   {node} n INNER JOIN {users} u ON u.uid = n.nid WHERE
//   n.status = 1
// with a pager, 20 items per page, and node access enforced.
// Drupal 7 only.
$query = db_select('node', 'n');
$query->addField('n', 'changed', 'last_updated'); // Field with an alias.
$query->innerJoin('users', 'u', 'u.uid = n.uid'); // Join.
$query = $query->extend('PagerDefault'); // Paging.
$result = $query
  ->fields('n', array('title', 'nid'))
  ->fields('u', array('name'))
  ->addTag('node_access')
  ->condition('n.status', 1)
  ->limit(20) // Number of items per page.
  ->execute();
```

Notes:

- This query also only works for Drupal 7, because paging is different in Drupal 8 and database tables have changed. See the following text for the Drupal 8 version.

- When using a PagerDefault query, as in the previous example, add a standard pager to your output by calling theme('pager'). This will let Drupal handle all the details of getting the right items on each page.

In Drupal 8, when querying nodes and other *entities*, you should really use an entity query instead of the bare Database API. For purposes of illustrating the paging system, however, here is the Drupal 8 version of the previous query:

```
// Equivalent to:
//   SELECT nd.changed AS last_updated, nd.title, nd.nid, u.name FROM
//   {node} n
//   INNER JOIN {node_field_data} nd ON n.nid = nd.nid AND n.vid = nd.vid
//   INNER JOIN {users_field_data} u ON u.uid = nd.uid WHERE
//   n.status = 1
// with a pager, 20 items per page, and node access enforced.
//
// DO NOT REALLY RUN THIS IN DRUPAL 8 -- use an entity query instead!
```

```
//
$query = db_select('node', 'n'); // Base table; two joins below.
$query->innerJoin('node_field_data', 'nd', 'n.nid = nd.nid AND n.vid = nd.vid');
$query->innerJoin('users_field_data', 'u', 'u.uid = nd.uid');
$query->addField('nd', 'changed', 'last_updated'); // Field with an alias.
$query
  ->extend('Drupal\Core\Database\Query\PagerSelectExtender') // Add pager.
  ->limit(20) // 20 items per page.
  ->fields('nd', array('title', 'nid')) // More fields.
  ->fields('u', array('name'))
  ->addTag('node_access') // Enforce node access.
  ->condition('nd.status', 1);
$result = $query->execute();
foreach ($result as $node) {
  // $node will be a PHP object with fields corresponding to the table fields.
  $title = $node->title;
  // ...
}
```

Further reading and reference:

- Avoiding database programming entirely: "Mistake: Programming Too Much" on page 71.
- Security concerns: "Principle: Drupal Is Secure; User Input Is Insecure" on page 61.
- Drupal Database API: *https://www.drupal.org/developing/api/database*.
- Detailed documentation for the database functions and classes can be found on *https://api.drupal.org*.

Examples—dynamic queries:

- "Querying and Loading Entities in Drupal 8" on page 160
- Paged queries and output: "Generating Paged Output" on page 107
- The DBTNG example in Examples for Developers (*https://www.drupal.org/project/examples*)

Principle: Drupal Is Secure; User Input Is Insecure

When programming for the web, you always need to think about security. One basic principle to follow is to consider all user-provided input to be insecure, whether it is provided by a trusted user such as a site administrator (who could be the target of hacking), a semitrusted user such as someone with a generic user account on your site, or an anonymous site visitor. With that in mind, whatever you do in your Drupal programming that involves user-provided input, that input will need to be cleansed or checked in some way to make it more secure before you use it to generate any output. There are also other standard web security concerns, such as preventing various types of hacking attacks, that you'll need to keep in mind in your programming.

Besides these principles, which apply to all web programming, Drupal has an additional security concern: your programming needs to respect Drupal's permission system. For instance, although a module you write can include code to run arbitrary database queries, only information from the database that a particular user has permission to view should be shown to that user. And although a module you write can technically call any Drupal API function at any time, you should not call functions without checking that the user has permission to perform their actions.

Both Drupal core and Drupal's contributed modules and themes ideally follow these principles of cleansing user input, preventing hacking, and checking Drupal permissions. The Drupal project has a volunteer security team, which handles reports of security issues, and every contributor's first module or theme is reviewed before it is allowed to be promoted to "full project" status on *drupal.org*. Your Drupal programming should also follow these principles, and the following sections give you an introduction to making your Drupal code more secure. You will also need to make sure your site permissions are reasonable and take other measures to set up a secure site.

Further reading and reference:

- Securing a Drupal site: *https://www.drupal.org/security/secure-configuration*.
- The Drupal site building section of "Where to Find More Information" on page 199 lists additional resources.
- "Mistake: Saving PHP Code in the Database" on page 81.

Cleansing and Checking User-Provided Input

The philosophy used in Drupal for ensuring security with user-provided input is to store whatever the user typed in the database without alteration, and then cleanse it prior to display. Both of these steps must be done carefully.

In the database storage step, you need to be concerned about SQL injection attacks when queries include user-provided input: a malicious user could input specially constructed text that would change your query so that it updates the database in ways you didn't intend. If you use the Drupal Database API correctly, however, all user-provided input will either be put into the query using placeholders or as arguments to safe methods such as condition(), and the integrity of your database will be protected.

In the output step, the Drupal API provides functions you can use to cleanse or escape data to make it safe for HTML output. Also, in Drupal 8, the rendering and theming process attempts to keep track of which input has been cleansed and which hasn't, and Twig templates will escape all HTML in output that is not marked as having been cleansed. Here are some examples of how you can cleanse data:

- If you are outputting data that is supposed to be plain text (without HTML tags) in Drupal 7, you should pass it through the `check_plain()` function, which will escape the HTML tags. Drupal 8 keeps track of whether text is safe to use or not, and unless you pass it through a function such as `t()` that marks it as safe, the theme and render system will automatically escape text when it is printed out. If you are outputting data via JSON or another means, you will need to sanitize it.

- If you are outputting data that is supposed to contain HTML tags (which should be limited for untrusted users), you should pass it through the `check_markup()` function, which will remove forbidden tags.

- If you are outputting a user-provided URL, you should pass it through `check_url()`.

 Some Drupal API functions, such as `l()` or `\Drupal::l()` (for making links), and `t()` for internationalization, cleanse or escape input themselves, so read the function documentation and don't double-escape.

Examples:

```
// Bad:
$paragraph = '<p>' . $text . '</p>';
$link = '<a href="' . $url . '">' . $text . '</a>';
$link = l(check_plain($text), check_url($url));

// Good, Drupal 7 version:
$paragraph = '<p>' . check_plain($text) . '</p>';
// The l() function sanitizes its input.
$link = l($text, $url);

// Good, Drupal 8 version:
use Drupal;
use Drupal\Core\Url;
// This assumes $url is an external URL.
$url_object = Url::fromUri($url);
$link = Drupal::l($text, $url_object);
```

Further reading and reference:

- Drupal Database API: "Querying the Database with the Database API" on page 58.
- Drupal functions that cleanse data can be found on *https://api.drupal.org* under the "Sanitization functions" topic.
- More about writing secure code: *https://www.drupal.org/writing-secure-code*.
- "Mistake: Saving PHP Code in the Database" on page 81.

Checking Drupal Permissions

Drupal has a rich permission system, which your modules need to interact with properly to ensure that users, including anonymous site visitors, are only allowed to see information and perform actions that they have permission for. There are several systems for permission checking in Drupal core, and some contributed modules have their own permission systems. It is important to understand the permission systems of all modules that your module interacts with.

Drupal core's main permission system

The main system for permission checking in Drupal core works as follows:

- Modules define *permissions* that users can be granted, which allow them to perform the module's tasks or view the module's information.
- In Drupal 7, define permissions by implementing hook_permission() in your *mymodule.module* file, which goes in your main module directory:

```
// Drupal 7:
function mymodule_permission() {
  return array(
    // The array keys are the permissions' machine names.
    'administer mymodule' => array(
      'title' => t('Administer My Module settings'), // Human-readable name.
      'description' => t('Longer description only if it is really necessary.'),
    ),
    // Define additional permissions by adding more array elements.
  );
}
```

- In Drupal 8, define permissions in a *mymodule.permissions.yml* file, which goes in your main module directory:

```
# Drupal 8:
administer mymodule:
```

```
title: 'Administer My Module settings'
description: 'Longer description only if it is really necessary.'
```

- If you have dynamic permissions to define in Drupal 8, you can also define a `permission_callbacks` entry in your *mymodule.permissions.yml* file. The functions or methods listed return permissions in the same format. See the *core/modules/filter/filter.permissions.yml* and *core/modules/filter/src/FilterPermissions.php* files for an example of how to do this.

- In the Drupal user interface, site administrators can define *roles* and grant one or more permissions to each role. A user account can then be assigned to one or more roles, which grants all of the roles' permissions to that user account.

- When Drupal 7 code performs an action on behalf of a user, or displays information to the user, it either directly or indirectly calls `user_access('permission machine name')` to see whether the current user has the needed permission, and only performs the action or displays the information if that is the case. The Drupal 8 equivalent is that there is a `current_user` service, which will return an object implementing `\Drupal\Core\Session\AccountProxyInterface`; you can obtain this service in noncontainer code by calling `\Drupal::currentUser()`. On this object, the `hasPermission()` method checks whether the current user has a given permission.

So, in your programming, you need to be aware of permissions that other modules define, and make sure to use the appropriate permission check when using that module's functions. You also need to determine which actions your module defines that should be restricted, define appropriate permissions for them, and verify those permissions appropriately.

Luckily, in some cases Drupal will make the permission check for you, which makes this system pretty easy to use. For instance, when you are defining routing URLs with `hook_menu()` in Drupal 7, or in a *routing.yml* file in Drupal 8, you can define permissions for that URL, and Drupal will enforce them for you when someone goes directly to the URL, as well as when making lists of links for menus and other purposes. Drupal 8 entity definitions also include permissions for creating, viewing, and other actions, which the entity system enforces.

Further reading and reference:

- General information about programming with hooks: "The Basics of Module and Theme Hook Programming" on page 23

Examples—permission defining and checking:

- URL registration permissions in Drupal 7: "Registering for a URL in Drupal 7" on page 89.

- URL registration permissions in Drupal 8: "Registering for a URL in Drupal 8" on page 92.
- "Defining a Content Entity Type in Drupal 8" on page 139.
- "Defining a Configuration Entity Type in Drupal 8" on page 149.
- Several of the examples in Examples for Developers (*https://www.drupal.org/project/examples*) create or check permissions, such as the Cache example, the Tokens example, and the Menu example.

Permissions and security in forms

The Drupal Form API also has a permission and security system that you can take advantage of. This consists of the following components:

- When you are defining a form array, each form element can be given a Boolean '#access' property—TRUE means the form element is displayed and usable, and FALSE means it is not accessible to the current user. When you are building a form, you can assign the result of an access check call to the '#access' property of an element, to programmatically show/hide form elements.
- Assuming that you use the standard Drupal form functions to display and process the form, Drupal will protect against cross-site forgery form submissions by adding a unique token to the form and validating the token when the form is submitted. URL access permission will also be checked for the form submission URL.
- You should also use *confirmation forms* to prevent hacking attacks that might trick an administrative user into visiting a URL that would maliciously destroy or alter data. For instance, if your module has a URL that triggers deleting a particular database record, have that URL instead display a confirmation form, and only delete the database record if the action is confirmed.

Further reading and reference:

- "Using the Drupal Form API" on page 109

Examples—form security:

- "Form Arrays, Form State Arrays, and Form State Objects" on page 110
- The Form example in Examples for Developers (*https://www.drupal.org/project/examples*)

Permissions in displaying and operating on content

Some Drupal core modules that manage content have complex permission systems that also need to be considered in your module programming. For instance, the core Node module provides hooks that allow other modules to define permission systems for node content, which can be as simple as "Only allow users of role A to view node content of type B," or as complex as allowing access to particular node content items only to certain individual users. If you are writing a module that allows users to operate or view node content, you need to respect whatever permissions other modules may have defined. Similarly, if you are writing a module that deals with core taxonomy terms, comments, or content managed by a contributed module, you need to make sure that your module is complying with the content permission scheme that applies. Luckily, modules that define complex content permission schemes have APIs that make obeying the permissions feasible, without knowing the details of the permissions that are in place on a particular site.

For example, if you are writing a Drupal 7 module that operates on individual node content items, you need to check access permission by calling the node_access() function, passing in the operation you are performing ('view', 'delete', etc.) and the node content item you are operating on. And if you are writing a module that queries the database to make a node content item listing, such as a block that lists content satisfying some criteria, you need to add the node_access tag to your database query. This will ensure that only items the user has permission to view are returned by the query, without having to guess at what particular permissions modules might be in use.

In Drupal 8, this is even easier: as long as you use entity queries to query entities, and the entity storage controller to load entities, view permission will be enforced. Permission for other actions can be checked using the access() method on an individual entity object; this method is provided by the \Drupal\Core\Entity\Entity base class, so it exists on all entity classes.

Further reading and reference:

- "Programming with Entities and Fields" on page 129
- "Avoiding Custom Programming with Fielded Data" on page 75

Examples—content permission:

- Adding tags to queries: "Dynamic queries" on page 59
- The Node Access and Entity examples in Examples for Developers (*https:// www.drupal.org/project/examples*)

Principle: Drupal Code Is Tested and Documented

There was a large effort during the Drupal version 7 development cycle to adopt the SimpleTest automated web testing framework for Drupal core, and to adhere to the development principle that all major functionality should have automated tests. This commitment has been continued and even strengthened in the Drupal 8 development cycle with the addition of the industry-standard PHPUnit framework for unit testing, and it is expected to continue in the future.

To aid in following this principle, a team within the Drupal project maintains a group of servers to run automated tests. Before any proposed change is committed to the Drupal core source code, all of the existing automated tests must pass. Furthermore, if the change adds new functionality or fixes a bug, it must usually be accompanied by new tests to ensure that the new functionality works as expected, or that the bug is really fixed. Many contributed module projects on *drupal.org* have also adopted this principle, at least to some extent.

A related effort in the Drupal project has been to improve the documentation of the code in Drupal core. The project has standards for in-code documentation, which include the principle that each distinct code item (function, class, file, method, etc.) should include a documentation header; these documentation headers are parsed to create the Drupal API reference site, *https://api.drupal.org*. Most of the Drupal 7 code is reasonably well documented, and for the Drupal 8 development cycle, a standard was adopted to say that no change should be committed without its accompanying documentation being complete, which at least made it a critical-priority bug if documentation was omitted.

Adopting the "everything should be tested" and "everything should be documented" principles in your own programming is an excellent idea. Writing formal documentation headers before you start work on the code for a function or class is a great way to ensure that you've thought out what the function or class should do, and it will also help you or the next maintainer of the code to remember what the code was supposed to do. Writing *README* files, API documentation, and end-user documentation for your code is a great way to ensure that the user interface, API, installation procedure, and other aspects of your code design make sense (there's nothing like trying to write coherent documentation for making you realize that something makes no sense or is incomplete). It's also a great way to ensure that you or the next user know how to use or program with your code, and prevent people having to contact you with the same boring questions over and over…or at least if they do, you can politely tell them to read the existing documentation.

In the arena of testing, writing tests for the functionality of your code does take time, and the testing framework takes some time to learn how to use. However, I have found that even basic tests usually find bugs in code that I would not otherwise be aware of, and having tests also greatly lessens the chance that feature additions or bug fixes added later will break existing functionality.

Tests can also be considered to be another form of documentation, as they document the expected functionality of your code by testing that it performs the way it should. The testing frameworks in Drupal allow you to create *unit tests* (low-level tests of specific functions or classes) and *functional tests* (higher-level tests that can involve simulating a browser and checking that pages and forms behave as they should); both can be appropriate for code that you write.

I've also found tests to be very valuable when updating code from one major Drupal version to another, and when developing for a prerelease version of Drupal. For instance, before Drupal 7 was first released, I was already working on updating the contributed modules I maintain from Drupal 6 to Drupal 7. During my first pass, I had some extra work to do, because I had to port both the main module code and the tests I had written from Drupal 6 to Drupal 7. However, once I got to the stage when all of the tests passed, I was pretty confident that my module port had worked. Then, as Drupal 7 continued to evolve, I could rerun my tests and immediately know if any changes to Drupal 7 had affected my module.

I also wrote tests for the code in this book. This was especially important when I started work on the Drupal 8 edition, because the Drupal API was still in quite a state of flux. So besides ensuring that the code worked correctly in the first place, having tests also meant that as Drupal 8 evolved, I could run the tests for the book against the latest Drupal 8 code, and when they failed (which happened many times), I just updated the book's code until the tests passed again. This let me gradually evolve the book's code as Drupal 8's API solidified. I even wrote a test that verified that files, functions, classes, services, etc. that I mentioned in the book still existed, which was great insurance against the many reorganizations and name changes that occurred. There is really no way I could have written this edition of the book without the tests, and the code for both Drupal 7 and 8 would have had many more problems and bugs without the tests.

Further reading and reference:

- How to write and run automated tests: *https://www.drupal.org/simpletest* and *https://www.drupal.org/phpunit*.

- Documentation standards: *https://www.drupal.org/coding-standards/docs*.

- If you want to write tests for the Drupal project, look for issues tagged "needs tests" in a project that interests you (Drupal core or a contributed project). If you want to contribute API documentation to the Drupal project, look for issues in the "documentation" component in a project that interests you, or issues tagged "Needs documentation" or "documentation."

- The module that parses API documentation for *https://api.drupal.org* (you can use it to build your own API documentation site): *https://www.drupal.org/project/api*.

Examples—tests:

- If you download the code for this book from the book website (see "How to Contact Us" on page xii), it includes tests. These can be found in the *tests* directory under the Drupal 7 module directory, and *src/Tests* under the Drupal 8 module directory.
- All of the examples in Examples for Developers (*https://www.drupal.org/project/examples*) have tests.
- There are also many tests in Drupal core. In Drupal 7, test class files have extension *.test*, and they are located in the core module directories. In Drupal 8, each test class is in its own *.php* file. SimpleTest tests are located in *core/modules/<module_name>/src/Tests/* directories, and PHPUnit tests are located under *core/modules/<module_name>/tests/src* directories.
- Contributed modules with tests either follow the same conventions, or in Drupal 7, may put the test files in a *tests* subdirectory under the main module directory.

Examples—documentation:

- If you download the code for this book from the book website (see "How to Contact Us" on page xii), the downloaded code includes more documentation headers than are included in this book.
- The Drupal core files for Drupal 7 and 8 are mostly pretty well documented and mostly adhere to the Drupal documentation standards.

## CHAPTER 3

Common Drupal Programming Mistakes

Experienced programmers have accumulated, through training or the experience of trial and error, a body of knowledge about how to approach problems and build applications. Unfortunately, some of this knowledge may lead them to make mistakes when they start working with Drupal, or to do things in less-than-optimal ways. This chapter covers several (somewhat overlapping) areas where programmers can shift their thinking or their approach in order to become more efficient at using the strengths of the Drupal platform, rather than fighting against it. Of course, following the principles in Chapter 2 will also help you shift your thinking to the Drupal way of doing things, and the suggestions and tools in Chapter 5 can help you avoid mistakes and find the mistakes that you do make.

Mistake: Programming Too Much

Experienced programmers who are new to Drupal often suffer from a variety of the "if all you have is a hammer, everything looks like a nail" syndrome: when faced with a challenge on a website (such as adding a feature or fixing a problem), they always try to solve it with programming. But although Drupal is built on PHP, and you can definitely do a lot of PHP programming when setting up a Drupal site, this is usually not the best approach: it results in a lot of unnecessary (and often tedious) programming. Related to this, experienced programmers coming to Drupal can be in a rush to become Drupal *programmers*, when really it would be better if they started out by becoming more effective Drupal *users* and *site builders* first, and resorted to programming only when necessary. While this goes against all the "solve all problems by programming" instincts of an experienced programmer (at least, speaking from my experience), if you learn advanced Drupal site-building techniques before you dive into Drupal programming, you will reap many benefits:

- You will be in a position to create very complex and interesting websites with Drupal because of your strong site-building skills.
- You'll be doing more interesting programming tasks rather than tedious ones.
- You'll save time by taking advantage of previous efforts by others.
- You can use code that has been reviewed for security problems and tested on many other sites instead of custom code that is for only your site.
- You can take advantage of the internationalization and translation capabilities of built-in Drupal systems.

Of course, some balance is appropriate here. For instance, it may be better to write a few lines of code in a custom module rather than installing an entire contributed module with a lot of functionality that you don't need. Each module you install has code that gets read in by the PHP interpreter on every page load, so efficiency is definitely a consideration. That said, here are some examples of Drupal site-building knowledge you should explore in order to avoid unnecessary and tedious programming:

Customizing fielded content display and editing
The core Fields administrative interface provides a lot of flexibility in defining how fields are displayed and edited in content, including the order of fields, labels and label placement, data formatting, and which fields are shown. If that is not enough, the Display Suite module can be helpful, as can the Panels module. Drupal 8 provides even more flexibility for content editing forms than Drupal 7 does.

Altering other user interface text
Drupal provides hooks and other mechanisms that let you write a module that can alter page content and form elements. These can be quite useful, but often all you really need to do is change some text on a button or a form field label. If so, you don't need to program—use the String Overrides module. If you need to do something to a form beyond what String Overrides covers, you can alter a form in a module.

Content permissions
The Drupal core Node module allows add-on modules to define very flexible content access permissions. So, if you need something beyond the default Node module permissions, your first instinct might be to write a content access module. However, the permissions needed for most sites are covered by the contributed Content Access module, which allows you to define permissions on a per-content-type or per-content-item basis, which can be applied by role or by managing lists of individual users (with the addition of the Access Control Lists, or ACL, module). If you do need a permission system that is more customized

than what Content Access and other contributed content access modules provide, you will need to create a custom module.

Marking and classifying content

If your site needs content classification, use the core Taxonomy module. If users need to mark content (as bookmarked, spam, etc.), the contributed Flag module is the usual choice. There are also voting modules, such as Fivestar, if this is a feature you need on your site. All of these solutions are likely better choices than writing your own custom content classification or marking system, and they are well integrated with the Views and Rules modules.

Placing content on pages

Rather than using PHP code or embedding content directly into custom theme template files or theme functions, use the Drupal core block system to place content into regions on pages. If your theme doesn't have a region that would allow you to put the content where you want it, add a region to your theme. If the block system is not flexible enough, the contributed Context module provides much more flexibility in block placement, although in Drupal 8 the core block system is probably flexible enough to cover the vast majority of cases that required Context in Drupal 7. Many people prefer to use the contributed Panels module instead of Context, which lets you build pages and page types out of blocks, fields, and other pieces; try both Panels and Context and see which one you prefer. You may also find the contributed Delta module (which lets you make theme variations) and its Delta Blocks submodule useful; they integrate well with the Context module.

Web forms

In Drupal 7, the contributed Webform module covers many web form use cases, and you can also learn its API and do a little programming if you need a form field type that is not included (but check to see if someone has already contributed a module that defines the form field that you need). In Drupal 8, the core Contact module allows you to use core fields to build custom web forms. Note, however, that the Drupal 8 Contact module solution is only workable for a site with a small number of forms, each having a relatively small number of fields; if you need large numbers of forms and/or large numbers of fields, the Drupal 8 port of Webform plans to support this use case.

Responding to events

The contributed Rules module allows you to define responses (such as sending email or redirecting to a different page) to various events (such as updating or adding content) on your website, under certain conditions (such as matching a content type or user role). If the events, conditions, or responses defined by the Rules module do not cover your needs, you can extend it, either by using a contributed module or making your own custom module. The Notifications module can also be useful—it lets users subscribe to content updates on a site.

Site navigation

Novice Drupal programmers sometimes want to code site navigation directly into their theme templates, because they have used this approach to ensure uniform navigation on custom-built PHP/MySQL or pure HTML sites in the past. While this is certainly possible, it's much better to use the core Menu module to manage site navigation. If you use the Menu module, you can define different *menus* for the main header navigation, the footer, sidebars, etc., and use CSS to style them appropriately. Drupal will automatically omit navigation items that are not accessible to whoever is viewing the site, and you will be able to manage the menus in the administrative user interface. If you code them into a theme template file, they will be much more difficult to manage, and permissions will not be enforced.

Breadcrumbs

The default Drupal breadcrumbs for content pages are often not what is desired for a site. So, it is tempting to override them by programming. While that is sometimes necessary, many use cases are covered by the contributed Custom Breadcrumbs module, which is quite easy to set up.

Site configuration export

In Drupal 7, the contributed Features module lets you export much of the configuration of a Drupal site to PHP code. For instance, you can export your custom content types and fields, your views, and many other settings; the result is a module, which you can then put into revision control or share with another site. However, note that not all contributed modules support Features export, so not all of your settings can be exported. In Drupal 8, site configuration can easily be exported and imported using core modules.

Further reading and reference:

- "Avoiding Custom Programming with Fielded Data" on page 75
- "Defining Theme Regions for Block Placement" on page 77
- Internationalization capabilities of Drupal: "Principle: Drupal Is International" on page 48
- Configuration export: "Configuration API in Drupal 8" on page 42

Examples—code for strategies in the preceding list:

- The Node Access example in Examples for Developers (*https://www.drupal.org/project/examples*)
- "Creating Rules Module Add-Ons in Drupal 7" on page 185
- "Altering Forms" on page 121

Contributed modules mentioned in this section:

- Access Control Lists: *https://www.drupal.org/project/acl*
- Content Access: *https://www.drupal.org/project/content_access*
- Context: *https://www.drupal.org/project/context*
- Custom Breadcrumbs: *https://www.drupal.org/project/custom_breadcrumbs*
- Delta: *https://www.drupal.org/project/delta*
- Display Suite: *https://www.drupal.org/project/ds*
- Features: *https://www.drupal.org/project/features*
- Fivestar: *https://www.drupal.org/project/fivestar*
- Flag: *https://www.drupal.org/project/flag*
- Notifications: *https://www.drupal.org/project/notifications*
- Panels: *https://www.drupal.org/project/panels*
- Rules: *https://www.drupal.org/project/rules*
- String Overrides: *https://www.drupal.org/project/stringoverrides*
- Webform: *https://www.drupal.org/project/webform*

Avoiding Custom Programming with Fielded Data

While your first instinct, if you need to manage some fielded data on your website, might be to set up a custom database table to store your data, and to display your data using custom queries, you can save yourself a lot of unnecessary programming by instead using *entities*, fields, and the Views module. Entities were a new concept for Drupal version 7: modules define entity types to store information for a website, and the field system allows many different types of data to be attached to the base entity. In Drupal 7, core modules define four basic entity types (node content items, comments, taxonomy terms, and user accounts); Drupal 8 has many more entity types. Both Drupal core and contributed modules define fields to store various types of data (text, numbers, images, etc.).

So, rather than defining a database table in a custom module to store the custom data for your website, your first step should usually be to instead set up a custom node content type and add the fields you need to it. If your data is not semantically "content," you might be better off setting up a taxonomy vocabulary; or if it is semantically very different from the existing entity types provided by Drupal core or contributed modules, you can create your own entity type (this will involve some programming).

Once you have your core or custom entity type set up with its fields, you should not need to do any more programming to query and display the data. Instead, use the Views module, which is basically a very flexible content query and display engine (you may also find the contributed Nodequeue module useful if you are using the node content entity for your data). Examples of pages, blocks, and feeds you can build with Views include:

- A photo gallery, which could include searching by keyword, topic- or user-based galleries, and a block that displays a random image added within the past 24 hours
- A "recent site updates" block
- A News block that detects which section of the site it is being displayed on and chooses news related to that section
- A map of a company's offices or of the site's registered users
- Blog archives with searching and filtering capability

The way that Views works is that its user interface lets you set up the parameters for what is basically a formatted list of content (known as a *view*); these parameters can then be saved to PHP code in Drupal 7, or exported as configuration in Drupal 8. This might not sound very exciting or useful, but when you come to understand that "lists" encompasses grids, clouds, tables, feeds, and other formats; and "content" encompasses node content items, taxonomy terms, files, user account data, and other Drupal entities, you will begin to see how flexible and powerful this module is. Then when you learn how to make *relationships* (basically query table joins) between content types, and how to use static, exposed, and contextual filters to define which content items are shown, you will really become a power Views user. Finally, you can even extend Views by creating custom output formats, data types, fields, filters, and relationships, if the base module and available contributed Views add-on modules do not cover your use case.

So, rather than writing modules to define database tables and using custom database queries to create content lists or displays, instead define content types (or other entities), add fields to them, become a power Views user, and extend Views if you need to. There is help within the Views module (Drupal 7 only) that explains the basics, and countless blog articles, video tutorials, and books covering the subject.

Further reading and reference:

- "Programming with Entities and Fields" on page 129
- Views module for Drupal 7: *https://www.drupal.org/project/views* (Views is part of Drupal 8 core)
- Advanced Help module, for Views version 7 help: *https://www.drupal.org/project/advanced_help*
- Nodequeue module: *https://www.drupal.org/project/nodequeue*

Examples—views programming:

- "Creating Views Module Add-Ons" on page 171

Defining Theme Regions for Block Placement

Blocks in Drupal are placed in *regions* in your theme, which might include the header, footer, left sidebar, right sidebar, and main content region. In most themes, the regions are the same on every page, although the Drupal theme system allows you to define multiple templates, each containing different regions. Drupal core's block system allows you to place each block into a particular region and then define conditions for whether the block should be visible or not on particular pages or for particular users. In Drupal 8, the block placement system lets you make multiple copies of each defined block, with each one having its own visibility conditions and region placement. For some sites, this limited flexibility is not enough, so the contributed Context module or Panels module can be used to gain more flexibility in block placement.

Sometimes all you need to achieve your desired site layout is a new theme region to put blocks in. For instance, maybe your site design calls for a "Call to Action" section on some pages, which would have a contrasting color scheme and appear in the upper-right corner of the main content area of the page. You can use the Drupal core block system to control what appears there on each page, if you add a new region to your theme. Here are the steps:

1. If you were using a Drupal core theme or a theme you downloaded, start by making a custom *sub-theme*. This will let you inherit most of the base theme while overriding just the parts that you want to change. Here are the *mytheme.info* file and *mytheme.info.yml* file that make a theme be a Bartik sub-theme in Drupal 7 or a Classy sub-theme in Drupal 8, respectively:

```
; mytheme.info for Drupal 7
name = My theme
description = Bartik sub-theme
core = 7.x
```

```
base theme = bartik

# mytheme.info.yml for Drupal 8
name: My theme
type: theme
description: Classy sub-theme
core: 8.x
base theme: classy
```

2. Add lines like the following ones to the info file, to tell Drupal about the new region. You will need to give the region both an internal name and a human-readable name for the Blocks administration page:

```
; Regions line for Drupal 7 mytheme.info file.
regions[internal_region_name] = Readable region name

# Regions section of Drupal 8 mytheme.info.yml file.
regions:
  internal_region_name: 'Readable region name'
```

3. If you are making a new sub-theme rather than adding to an existing custom theme, copy in the custom regions from the base theme's info file. Only the Drupal core standard regions are inherited in a sub-theme, not the regions from the base theme.

4. Copy the *page.tpl.php* file (Drupal 7) or *page.html.twig* file (Drupal 8) from the base theme to your theme's *templates* directory. Add markup that displays the region:

```
<?php // Drupal 7 page.tpl.php file. ?>
<?php if ($page['internal_region_name']): ?>
  <div id="internal-region-name">
    <?php print render($page['internal_region_name']); ?>
  </div>
<?php endif; ?>

{# Drupal 8 page.html.twig file. #}
{% if page.internal_region_name %}
  <div id="internal-region-name">
    {{ page.internal_region_name }}
  </div>
{% endif %}
```

5. Clear the Drupal cache so that Drupal will recognize your new region.

As a variation on this process, you could use Drupal's *template suggestions* process of automatic template overrides. For instance, if your theme has a file called *page--front.php* (Drupal 7) or *page--front.html.twig* (Drupal 8), that file will be used in place of the generic *page.tpl.php* or *page.html.twig* template when the home page of your site is being displayed. So if you only needed this new region on the home page, you could put it into the front-page template instead of the generic page template. Using a template suggestion will only control the final printing of your blocks, however, so for performance reasons, you should also make sure that your blocks are configured to show only on the appropriate pages (otherwise, they'll be generated even though they are not printed in the end).

Further reading and reference:

- Creating a sub-theme for Drupal 7: *http://bit.ly/drupal7_sub-themes*
- Creating a sub-theme for Drupal 8: *http://bit.ly/drupal8_sub-themes*
- Template suggestions: *http://bit.ly/template_suggestions*
- "The Drupal Cache" on page 10

Mistake: Overexecuting Code

New Drupal programmers often make the mistake of writing PHP code that is executed more often than is necessary. Two examples of this are covered in this section.

Mistake: Executing Code on Every Page Load

One efficiency mistake that Drupal programmers make is to place code so that it gets executed on every page load:

- In the main body of a module (outside all function definitions): All modules' main module files are loaded on every page load, and any executable code outside of function and class definitions would get run.
- In Drupal 7, in an implementation of hook_boot() or hook_init(): both of these hooks run early in the page-generation process on most or all page loads.
- In Drupal 8, in an event subscriber for Symfony's main request event, which may be invoked multiple times during a typical page load.

While this practice might be a good idea in a custom PHP/MySQL site or in other CMS systems, Drupal generally has a different hook or method that can be used to accomplish the same purpose with less overhead (as it will be executed only when needed) and less programming (as you are taking advantage of Drupal's built-in logic, rather than re-creating it). For example:

- Detecting an unauthorized user and redirecting to an error page: use the Drupal permissions system instead. You may also find the contributed Redirect 403 to User Login module useful.

- Detecting a particular URL and executing custom PHP code to generate output (HTML, Ajax, etc.): use the Drupal routing (URL registration) system instead.

- Overriding behavior that another module has defined for a particular URL: use hook_menu_alter() in Drupal 7, and a routing system subscriber in Drupal 8.

- Processing submitted form input: use the Drupal Form API instead.

Examples—avoiding executing code on every page load:

- "Checking Drupal Permissions" on page 64
- "Registering for URLs and Displaying Content" on page 88
- Altering routing: "Altering a URL Registration in Drupal 7" on page 91 and "Altering Routes and Providing Dynamic Routes in Drupal 8" on page 98
- "Using the Drupal Form API" on page 109
- Redirect 403 to User Login module: *https://www.drupal.org/project/r4032login*

Mistake: Using an Overly General Hook

Another efficiency mistake that many new Drupal programmers make is using an overly general hook when a more specific hook exists. This leads to your hook implementation function being executed more often than necessary. Your hook implementation function most likely will also be longer than necessary, because it will have more logic in it to detect the special case you are trying to handle.

The most common example of this is hook_form_alter(), which you can use to make alterations in forms provided by other modules. Use hook_form_FORM_ID_alter() instead:

```
// Bad - runs whenever any form is generated:
function mymodule_form_alter($form, $form_state, $form_id) {
  if ($form_id == 'othermodule_form') {
    // Alteration code here.
  }
}

// Good - runs when this specific form is generated:
function mymodule_form_othermodule_form_alter($form, $form_state) {
  // Alteration code here.
}
```

Examples—specific hooks instead of general ones:

- "Altering Forms" on page 121
- "Repurposing an existing field widget" on page 167

You can use the generic `hook_form_alter()` during development as a quick way to figure out the form ID of a form you need to alter. For instance, you could put this in the function body, and it will put a message out with the ID of each form on the page:

```
drupal_set_message($form_id);
```

The Drupal For Firebug (*https://www.drupal.org/project/drupalfor firebug*) browser plugin is also helpful.

Mistake: Saving PHP Code in the Database

It is possible, by enabling certain modules and granting certain permissions, for users to include PHP code within the body of page or block content (and in other places), which is stored in the database and executed when the page or block is displayed. While this might seem like a great convenience and a time-saver, it is usually a mistake to allow this because of the following factors:

Security risk

    PHP code can add, change, or delete files and database records (any PHP code run during a page request has full rights to change the database). Thus, granting this permission opens up the possibility of malicious PHP code being added to a block or a page.

Risk of bugs

    Even if you only grant the permission to highly trusted users, they could, through a bug in their PHP code, alter files or database records by mistake (the code would only have to run once to cause problems).

Hard to debug

    Even if the PHP code isn't dangerous, if it has a coding error, the page or block could sometimes produce the wrong output or cause a "White Screen of Death" (completely blank page), which is difficult to debug when it comes from PHP code stored in the database.

Hard to track

    Allowing PHP code to be stored makes it hard to keep track of which page or block does what.

Luckily, there are good alternatives for the common reasons people might want to store PHP code in the database:

Control block visibility

    Use the Context module or the Panels module, which allow you much more flexibility on block placement. Drupal 8's core block system is also a lot more flexible than Drupal 7's, and you could also write a module to add new block visibility plugin.

Database queries
Use the Views module.

Custom page or block output
Create your block or page in a module.

Change how something is displayed
Override a theme function or template.

Calculations for a field
Create your own custom field or formatter.

Examples—alternatives to storing PHP in the database:

- "Avoiding Custom Programming with Fielded Data" on page 75
- "Registering for URLs and Displaying Content" on page 88
- "The Basics of Module and Theme Hook Programming" on page 23
- "Defining a Field Type" on page 161
- "Programming with Field Formatters" on page 168

Contributed modules mentioned in this section:

- Context: *https://www.drupal.org/project/context*
- Panels: *https://www.drupal.org/project/panels*
- Views for Drupal 7: *https://www.drupal.org/project/views* (Views is part of Drupal 8 core)

Mistake: Working Alone

One of the great strengths of the Drupal software is that it is produced by the Drupal open source project, which is a worldwide community of people who have chosen to come together and donate their time and money toward making Drupal better. The software has been around since 2001 or so, in which time the community of contributors has grown from one person (the founder and continuing leader of the Drupal project, Dries Buytaert) to thousands of people. And although it does have its dysfunctional moments, the Drupal community often works together pretty well to create the core Drupal software and add-ons, write the documentation, and support Drupal users.

As a Drupal programmer, and especially when you're getting started with Drupal programming, if you try to work alone without connecting to the Drupal community, you are making a mistake: engaging with the community will almost certainly directly help you become more effective and skillful in your Drupal endeavors. But if you engage with the Drupal community by thinking only about what you can get from the community, you are also making a mistake. Instead, engaging in a thoughtful and respectful way and thinking about how you can contribute to the Drupal community and project as well as meeting your own needs will get you better results (people are more likely to help someone who has this type of attitude). Furthermore, if you are able to engage in ways that contribute to the Drupal project and community, you will end up with better Drupal software to use as well as improved skills.

Participating in Groups and IRC

One of the best ways to connect to the Drupal community is to join a local or regional Drupal user group and participate in meetings and events that members of the group organize. At these events, you may learn techniques that you can apply to your own work, or you may be inspired by seeing what others have done with Drupal; many local Drupal groups also encourage members to ask one another questions using forums or online IRC chats.

If you do not live in or near a city with a local group, or if your local group does not have meetings, you could also consider organizing a meeting, which could be as simple as choosing a coffee shop and setting a time for people to gather to talk about Drupal or show off the projects they are working on. There are also worldwide groups organized around topics and languages, which come together primarily on forums and on IRC. And if you don't have a particular topic to gravitate toward, you can always chat with the global Drupal community on the general Drupal IRC channels.

Next steps:

- Find a geographical or topical group to join: *https://groups.drupal.org*.
- Learn about IRC and local, topical, and general channels: *https://www.drupal.org/irc*.

Reporting Issues and Contributing Code to the Drupal Community

Another key way to connect to the Drupal community is to use the Drupal *issue queues* (known as bug databases or ticket systems in other projects) to report software bugs and request new features. Each project (Drupal core, contributed modules, contributed themes, and contributed Drupal distributions) has its own issue queue, so the first step in reporting an issue is to narrow down exactly what project the issue pertains to. Then, visit that project's home page on *drupal.org*, and search to make sure the issue has not already been reported (you will need to log in to *drupal.org* in order to search issues). If the issue has already been reported, you can "follow" (subscribe to) the existing issue. You might also add a comment to the issue if you are seeing the same problem from a slightly different cause or in a slightly different environment than previously reported, or if it was reported a long time ago and you've discovered that it is still a problem in a newer version. Finally, if what you would like to report is a new issue, click the "Create a new issue" link on the project's issue search results page, and fill in the issue details.

Subscribing to Issues

The *drupal.org* website allows you to subscribe to individual issues or to entire projects' issues (you'll need to log in to do any of these actions):

- To subscribe to an individual issue, click on the Follow button on the issue page.

- To subscribe to an entire project's issues, click the E-mail notifications link when viewing the issue list for the project.

- You can see a paginated list of all the issues you have followed on the Your issues tab of your user profile page.

- On your user Dashboard, you can add blocks that show the issues you have followed, or statistics and links for the issues of individual projects.

- By default, you should receive email for individual issues and projects that you have followed (an email message is generated for each comment or issue update). To change your email notification settings, visit your user profile page and click on Notifications. You can also subscribe to issues for entire projects on this page.

To ensure that your issue reports are well received, consider these points:

Be polite and respectful
Drupal is open source, community-produced software, so for the most part it is created by volunteers. Sounding angry or disgusted in your issue report is not likely to inspire the volunteer who created the software that has the bug to fix it.

Be constructive
If possible, suggest a solution rather than just pointing out the problem.

Be clear and complete
If you report a vague problem like "This doesn't work," without details of what you were doing, what you observed happening, and why you think what you observed was not correct, your report is likely to be ignored or marked "cannot reproduce." You'll also find that your issue is better received if you have selected appropriate values for status, component, and the other "issue meta-data" fields; there are links on the issue reporting page that will take you to explanations of these fields.

Be attentive

Often, the maintainers of the component or project you are reporting the issue on will have questions for you, such as whether you have certain other modules installed on your site. They will ask the questions as comment replies to your original issue; your quick response to questions will expedite action to resolve the issue.

Issues are also the starting point for contributing code to the Drupal project, as most (ideally, all) code changes in Drupal core and add-on projects are coordinated on issues. To contribute suggested code changes, first file an issue report, and then create and attach a *patch* file to the issue. After attaching a patch, be attentive—it's highly unlikely that your patch will be accepted without some changes, and it's much more likely that your patch will eventually be accepted if you follow the issue and make the requested changes, rather than just dropping the patch on the issue and hoping that someone else will finalize it. Keep in mind these additional points:

- It is in your interest to get the code *committed* (added to the project): presumably you want the new feature or want to have the bug fixed. So, do everything you can to get it committed (make changes suggested by reviewers).

- Patches that don't follow the Drupal coding standards, that have security problems, or that don't follow standard Drupal programming practices are unlikely to be committed.

- The priorities of the project maintainers may be different from yours, but they do have final say. For instance, they may decide that they don't want to add complexity to their module, if you propose a new feature, or they may suggest that you submit your patch (or idea) to a different project. So, be prepared to be flexible.

Further reading and reference:

- Novice contributor guide to patches: *https://www.drupal.org/novice*
- Git revision control system: *https://www.drupal.org/documentation/git*
- Drupal project coding standards: *https://www.drupal.org/coding-standards*

Contributing to the Drupal Community in Other Ways

Programmers naturally think about contributing code to the project, but there are many other ways to contribute to the project and to the community, which are all valuable. Some ideas:

- Write or edit Drupal documentation: see *https://www.drupal.org/contribute/docu mentation*.

- Attend a DrupalCon or regional conference and make a presentation to share your Drupal knowledge: see *https://groups.drupal.org/calendar*.

- Answer questions in the *#drupal* or *#drupal-support* IRC channels, the *drupal.org* Forums, or *http://drupal.stackexchange.com*.

- If you speak a non-English language, translate Drupal software into your language: see *https://localize.drupal.org*.

- Find many more ideas for volunteering your time at: *https://www.drupal.org/new-contributors*.

- Join or donate targeted money to the Drupal Association, the nonprofit organization that keeps the *drupal.org* servers running, organizes DrupalCon events, and generally works for the benefit of the Drupal project: see *https://association.drupal.org*.

## CHAPTER 4

Drupal Programming Examples

Now that you have learned the basic principles of Drupal programming and how to avoid making common Drupal programming mistakes, it's time to put your programming skills to work! This chapter covers special topics in Drupal programming that you can use to enhance websites built with Drupal; they're all things I've actually needed to do either in my freelance work as a Drupal site builder or my volunteer work programming for the Drupal project (for Drupal core and contributed modules). My advice is to skim this chapter now so you know what it covers and then read individual sections in more detail when you need them.

Other places to look for programming examples:

- The Drupal core code itself, which includes extensive documentation and tests
- Examples for Developers (*https://www.drupal.org/project/examples*), which has comprehensive coverage of the Drupal core APIs and how to use them in your own modules
- Thousands of GPL-licensed contributed modules you can download from *https://www.drupal.org/project/modules* and then adapt for your own work
- The API reference site, *https://api.drupal.org*; see also "Using api.drupal.org" on page 201

Registering for URLs and Displaying Content

"How Drupal Handles HTTP Requests" on page 7 contains overviews of how Drupal 7 and Drupal 8 handle URL requests and return content to a web browser or other requester. This section goes into more detail about how a module you write can be part of that process, by registering with Drupal to handle specific URLs and by providing page and block content.

 Given that Drupal has many hooks and that it is written in PHP, there are many ways that you could consider writing code for Drupal that would return output in response to a URL request, or that would place content in a region on a page or set of pages. Most of these ways would, however, amount to subverting Drupal's standard processes, rather than working within the Drupal framework. Use the methods in this section of the book for best results.

Assuming that you have decided you need your module to output some content, the first choice you need to make is whether to provide a *router* entry or a *block*. A router entry allows you to respond to a URL request by providing the main HTML content for that page or, in some cases, the entire output for the URL (such as XML output that is used by a Flash script on your site, an RSS feed, or an Ajax response). A block allows you to provide a chunk of output that can be placed on one or more of a site's HTML-based pages. In either case, you will need to register with Drupal for the block or URL, and then write a function or class to generate the output; in the case of a router entry, you will also need to define permissions for accessing the URL. All of these steps are described in the following sections.

Note that you should write code to provide blocks and router entries only if there is some logic or programming needed to generate the content of the block or page. If you want to display static content on a website, you can create a block or content item using Drupal's user interface, and if you need to employ complicated logic to decide where or when to show the block, use the Context module or Panels module. Also, keep in mind that using the Views module is a better choice than making a custom module in many cases.

Further reading and reference:

- "Mistake: Programming Too Much" on page 71 (which also lists the modules mentioned here)
- "Avoiding Custom Programming with Fielded Data" on page 75

Registering for a URL in Drupal 7

To register to provide the main page content for a URL in Drupal 7, you will need to define a router entry by implementing hook_menu() in your *mymodule.module* file, which is covered in this section, and then you will need to write a function to generate your page content, which is covered in "Creating Render Arrays for Page and Block Output" on page 102 (the functions to generate the actual page and block output are quite similar, so they are covered together).

To define your router entry, first you will need to choose a URL. All URLs are relative to your base site URL, and in Drupal terms, the suffix of the URL, after your base site URL and possibly a language code, is known as a *path*. Here are some considerations when choosing a URL path for your page:

- If you are providing an administrative page, the path should be chosen to place the page in an appropriate, existing section of the Drupal core administration screens. For instance, if it's "structural," it should start with *admin/structure/*, and if it's for use by developers, it should start with *admin/config/development/*. You can see a complete list of the sections in the system_menu() function in the *modules/system/system.module* file that comes with Drupal (paths that start with *admin*).

- Make sure your path does not conflict with a path that another module might provide. Normally, prefixing with or including your module's machine name is a good idea (mymodule in this example).

- Make your path like others in Drupal. For instance, if you are defining an autocomplete responder for a form, choose the *mymodule/autocomplete* path, similar to the *user/autocomplete* path defined by the core User module.

- The path can contain *placeholders*. For example, the core Node module defines a path *node/* followed by the node content item's ID number.

After choosing your path, implement hook_menu() to tell Drupal about it:

```
function mymodule_menu() {
  $items = array();

  // Put the chosen path here. Do not start it with /.
  $items['mymodule/mypath'] = array(
    // Do not translate this!
    'title' => 'My page title',
    // Function that will generate the content.
    'page callback' => 'mymodule_page_generate',
    // Function used to check permissions. This defaults to user_access(),
    // which is provided here as an illustration -- you can omit this line
    // if you want to use the user_access() function. Put the name of your
    // custom access check function here if you have one.
    'access callback' => 'user_access',
```

```
    // Arguments needed for your access callback function. If using the
    // default user_access() function, the argument is the name of the
    // permission a user must have to access the page.
    'access arguments' => array('administer mymodule'),
  );

  return $items;
}
```

Notes:

- hook_menu() is invoked rarely, and its output is cached.

- Strings such as the page title in hook_menu() implementations are not translated using t(). The menu and routing systems translate the strings when necessary on output.

- The hook_menu() implementation references a page-generating function (mymodule_page_generate() in this example). Because block-generating functions are very similar to page-generating functions, the details of what this function should return are covered in a separate section, "Creating Render Arrays for Page and Block Output" on page 102.

- There is no need to explicitly check for access permissions in your page-generating function or elsewhere, assuming that you set up an access callback in your hook_menu() implementation. Drupal will verify and run this access check for you automatically and return a 403 access denied response for unauthorized users.

- If you use the default user_access() callback, the permission name needs to be registered in a hook_permission() implementation.

Autoloading, Arguments, and Placeholders in hook_menu()

The routing system in Drupal 7 is fairly powerful, and one of the powerful features that new Drupal programmers often don't know about is the ability to autoload objects. Using this feature takes several steps:

1. Use a placeholder in the path you are registering for and give it a name. Placeholders in hook_menu() paths start with %, so for instance you could register for a path like *mymodule/%mymodule_object*.

2. Define a function of the same name as your placeholder with a load suffix: mymodule_object_load() in this example. It should load your object and return it, or return FALSE if it cannot be loaded, which will trigger a 404 Not Found response.

---

3. When someone goes to a specific URL matching your pattern, such as *example.com/mymodule/123*, your load function will be called with the corresponding piece of the URL as its first argument (`'123'` in this example). You can tell Drupal to pass additional arguments to this function by adding a `'load arguments'` element to your hook_menu() implementation.

4. In `'page arguments'`, `'access arguments'`, and related elements of your hook_menu() implementation, you can pass the loaded object by using the numeric index of your placeholder in the path. In the *mymodule/%mymodule_object* path, for example, the 0 placeholder would have value `'mymodule'` and the 1 placeholder would have your loaded object. So if your page-generating function has two arguments, the object and a view mode, you might put:

       'page arguments' => array(1, 'full'),

   into your hook_menu() implementation to indicate this.

There is an example that uses an autoloading placeholder in Step 4 of "Defining an Entity Type in Drupal 7" on page 132.

Further reading and reference:

- "The Basics of Module and Theme Hook Programming" on page 23
- "Drupal core's main permission system" on page 64

Examples—hook_menu() implementations:

- "Basic Form Generation and Processing in Drupal 7" on page 112.
- "Adding Autocomplete to Forms" on page 119.
- "Defining an Entity Type in Drupal 7" on page 132.
- The Page example in Examples for Developers (*https://www.drupal.org/project/examples*).
- Look up hook_menu() on *https://api.drupal.org* for complete documentation of all its return value options and to find many examples of Drupal core implementations.

Altering a URL Registration in Drupal 7

A related task that you may need to do in a Drupal 7 module is to alter how another module has registered for a URL. One common reason would be that you want to use a different access permission system for the URL. To do this, implement hook_menu_alter() in your *mymodule.module* file. For example:

```
function mymodule_menu_alter(&$items) {
  // $items contains all items from hook_menu() implementations.
  $items['other/module/path']['access callback'] = 'mymodule_check_access';
}

function mymodule_check_access() {
  // The user who is trying to access the page.
  global $user;

  // Calculate whether this user should get access or not,
  // and return TRUE or FALSE.
}
```

Further reading and reference:

- Look up hook_menu() on *https://api.drupal.org* for complete documentation of all its return value options. The combined return values from all modules' hook_menu() implementations are passed into hook_menu_alter() implementations.
- "The Basics of Module and Theme Hook Programming" on page 23.
- "Drupal core's main permission system" on page 64.

Registering for a URL in Drupal 8

To register to provide the main page content for a URL in Drupal 8, you will need to register for the URL in a *routing.yml* file and define a class method to provide the actual page output. These steps are covered in this section.

To register the URL, create a file called *mymodule.routing.yml* in your main module directory. As in Drupal 7, first you will need to choose a URL. All URLs are relative to your base site URL, and in Drupal terms, the suffix of the URL, after your base site URL and possibly a language code, is known as a *path*. Here are some considerations when choosing a URL path for your page:

- If you are providing an administrative page, the path should be chosen to place the page in an appropriate, existing section of the Drupal core administration screens. For instance, if it's "structural," it should start with *admin/structure/*, and if it's for use by developers, it should start with *admin/config/development/*. The Drupal core hierarchy can be found in the *core/modules/system/system.routing.yml* file, in the paths that start with *admin*.
- Make sure your path does not conflict with a path that another module might provide. Normally, prefixing with or including your module's machine name is a good idea (mymodule in this example).

- Make your path like others in Drupal. For instance, if you are defining an auto-complete responder for a form, make the path *mymodule/autocomplete*, similar to the *block-category/autocomplete* path defined by the core Block module.

- The path can contain *placeholders*. For example, the core Node module defines a path of *node/* followed by the node content item's ID number.

After choosing your path, register it as a *route* with Drupal's routing framework by creating a file called *mymodule.routing.yml* in your main module directory, which contains:

```
mymodule.mydescription:
  path: '/mymodule/mypath'
  defaults:
    _controller: '\Drupal\mymodule\Controller\MyUrlController::generateMyPage'
    _title: 'My page title'
  requirements:
    _permission: 'administer mymodule'
```

Notes:

- The first line is a *route identifier*, which must be unique. By convention, it should start with your module's machine name, followed by a period.

- The `path` line gives the URL path that you have chosen, starting with /. It can also contain placeholders. For instance, this entry would register for a set of URL paths containing an ID:

```
path: '/mymodule/mypath/{id}'
```

- The `defaults` section tells what method on what class should be used to generate the content for the path and provides other defaults. You have a few choices for specifying the content generator, which is known as the route *controller*. Specifying it with `_controller`, as in this example, means that it is a generic page. Another possibility is `_form`, if your page contains a form. You can also provide default argument values for your page-generating method, by adding lines to this section. For instance, if your method had an argument `$foo`, you could define its default value using:

```
foo: 'bar'
```

- The `_title` line within `defaults` gives the page title.

- The `requirements` section defines the permission needed to access the page. It must be registered in your *mymodule.permissions.yml* file.

After registering the route in the routing file, you need to define a page-controller class to provide the actual page output. This class should usually extend the

\Drupal\Core\Controller\ControllerBase class; by convention, it should be part of the \Drupal\mymodule\Controller namespace and thus must be located in the *src/Controller* subdirectory under your module directory. In our example, the class is called MyUrlController, so the file must be called *MyUrlController.php* and it contains:

```
namespace Drupal\mymodule\Controller;

use Drupal\Core\Controller\ControllerBase;
use Drupal\Core\Database\Connection;
use Drupal\Core\DependencyInjection\ContainerInjectionInterface;
use Symfony\Component\DependencyInjection\ContainerInterface;

class MyUrlController extends ControllerBase {

  // Database service, obtained through dependency injection.
  // This is needed for the pager sample output in a later section.
  protected $database;

  public static function create(ContainerInterface $container) {
    return new static($container->get('database'));
  }

  public function __construct(Connection $database) {
    $this->database = $database;
  }

  // Page-generating method.
  public function generateMyPage() {
    // Function body will be defined later.
  }
}
```

The page-generating method on your controller either needs to return a Symfony response object of class \Symfony\Component\HttpFoundation\Response, or a *render array*; a render array is the usual choice for generic pages. Because block-generating functions also return render arrays, they are covered in a separate section: "Creating Render Arrays for Page and Block Output" on page 102.

Further reading and reference:

- "The Basics of Module and Theme Hook Programming" on page 23
- "Automatic Class Loading in Drupal" on page 12
- "Drupal core's main permission system" on page 64

Examples—routing:

- "Basic Form Generation and Processing in Drupal 8" on page 114

- "Creating Confirmation Forms" on page 116
- "Adding Autocomplete to Forms" on page 119
- "Defining a Content Entity Type in Drupal 8" on page 139
- "Defining a Configuration Entity Type in Drupal 8" on page 149

Providing Administrative Links

In Drupal 7, when you use hook_menu() to register for a path under *admin*, you will also automatically be creating an administrative menu link. For instance, if you register a path *admin/structure/mymodule* and navigate to the Structure administrative page at *admin/structure*, your page will be listed; you'll also be able to see it in the Management menu hierarchy.

In Drupal 8, menu-entry creation has been decoupled from route registration, so using a **.routing.yml* file to register a route does not automatically register an administrative menu link. In order to register an administrative menu link for a route you've already defined, you'll need to create a *mymodule.links.menu.yml* file in your main module directory. In this file, you'll tell Drupal where to place the menu entry (by giving the machine name of the parent link—not the route name of the parent link, although they are often the same). You'll also need to provide your route machine name (which will tell Drupal the URL path of your link), the link title, and the description. For instance, you could make the route defined in the previous section appear in the Structure menu section with this entry in *mymodule.links.menu.yml*:

```
mymodule.mydescription:
  title: 'Configure My Module'
  description: 'Longer description goes here'
  parent: system.admin_structure
  route_name: mymodule.mydescription
```

In some cases, you'll want to provide a local task (tab) for an existing administrative page, rather than adding your own administrative menu entry. In Drupal 7, this is also taken care of in hook_menu(), by making an entry that is of type MENU_LOCAL_TASK instead of the default MENU_NORMAL_ITEM. Here's an example from the core User module, which makes the Permissions page be a local task for the People list page:

```
$items['admin/people/permissions'] = array(
    'title' => 'Permissions',
    'description' => 'Determine access to features.',
    'page callback' => 'drupal_get_form',
    'page arguments' => array('user_admin_permissions'),
    'access arguments' => array('administer permissions'),
    'file' => 'user.admin.inc',
```

```
    'type' => MENU_LOCAL_TASK,
  );
```

In Drupal 8, the creation of a local task to be displayed on a given page is accomplished by creating a *mymodule.links.task.yml* file in your main module directory, giving the route name for the task page, the tab title, and the base route name (the route name of the page that should display the task). For this same User module Permissions page, the *core/modules/user/user.links.task.yml* file contains:

```
user.admin_permissions:
  title: Permissions
  route_name: user.admin_permissions
  base_route: entity.user.collection
```

Besides local tasks, there are also local actions. Local tasks are usually rendered as tabs at the tops of pages, while local actions are usually rendered as buttons. A typical use for a local action is an "add" button; for example, the Drupal core User module has an "Add user" button on the People administration page. This is accomplished in Drupal 7 with the following code in its hook_menu() implementation:

```
$items['admin/people/create'] = array(
  'title' => 'Add user',
  'page arguments' => array('create'),
  'access arguments' => array('administer users'),
  'type' => MENU_LOCAL_ACTION,
);
```

In Drupal 8, local actions are defined in the *mymodule.links.action.yml* file in the main module directory. For this same Add user button, the *core/modules/user/user.links.action.yml* file contains:

```
user_admin_create:
  route_name: user.admin_create
  title: 'Add user'
  appears_on:
    - entity.user.collection
```

Note that the appears_on entry is the name of the route for the page the local action should appear on.

The final type of administration link that you can define is a contextual link, which gives users context-based operations. They are a little bit more complex to implement than local tasks and actions, because they operate on some specific piece of data and have to be collected and added to administrative pages that display that type of data.

In Drupal 7, again contextual links are part of the hook_menu() system, specified by giving a context element to a local task entry. Here's the section of block_menu() from the core Block module that sets up the Configure link for a block:

```
$items['admin/structure/block/manage/%/%/configure'] = array(
  'title' => 'Configure block',
```

```
   'type' => MENU_DEFAULT_LOCAL_TASK,
   'context' => MENU_CONTEXT_INLINE,
);
```

In Drupal 8, the entity system sets up contextual links automatically for content entities; if you want to have contextual links for non-entity data, here are the steps that Drupal core uses to provide this same contextual link.

First, choose a *group* name for your contextual links, which needs to be unique and should describe what type of data the links operate on. In our Block module example, there is a group called block for contextual links that operate on blocks.

Second, in your *mymodule.links.contextual.yml* file, define the operations on either a group that your module has defined or one from another module. In the Block example, the Configure link is defined in its *block.links.contextual.yml* file:

```
block_configure:
  title: 'Configure block'
  route_name: 'entity.block.edit_form'
  group: 'block'
```

Here, the first line defines the machine name of the contextual link, and the other lines give the group machine name, the link title, and the route name for making the link.

Third, on the administrative page that displays your data, add a #contextual_links element to a render array, to render the links. In the Block example, \Drupal\block \BlockViewBuilder::viewMultiple() has these lines:

```
$build[$entity_id]['#contextual_links'] => array(
  'block' => array(
    'route_parameters' => array('block' => $entity->id()),
  ),
);
```

This tells the Contextual Links module (if installed) to collect all the contextual links in the block group and render them, passing in the route parameter from the current block to construct each link. If the Contextual Links module is not installed, this part of the render array will be ignored.

If you want to alter the menu links, local tasks, contextual links, or local actions defined by another module, you can do that with an alter hook. In Drupal 7, all of these are defined in hook_menu(), so use hook_menu_alter() to alter them. In Drupal 8, use hook_menu_links_discovered_alter() to alter the administrative menu links, hook_menu_local_tasks_alter() to alter the local tasks, hook_menu_local_actions_alter() to alter the local actions, and hook_contextual_links_alter() to alter contextual links. For local tasks, you can also implement hook_menu_local_tasks() to provide additional, dynamic local tasks; this hook runs before the alter hook.

Further reading and reference:

- "The Basics of Module and Theme Hook Programming" on page 23
- hook_menu_alter() in Drupal 7: "Altering a URL Registration in Drupal 7" on page 91

Examples—administrative links:

- "Defining a Content Entity Type in Drupal 8" on page 139
- "Defining a Configuration Entity Type in Drupal 8" on page 149

Altering Routes and Providing Dynamic Routes in Drupal 8

Drupal 8's event system is used for *dynamic routes* and *route altering*:

- Dynamic routes are for URL paths that cannot be set up as static routes in a *routing.yml* file. For example, the core Field UI module provides field management pages (Manage Fields, Manage Display, and Manage Form Display) for each entity type and subtype that supports fields and administrative management. Because the Field UI module does not know what entity types will be available on a given Drupal site, and because each entity type has full flexibility and control over its administrative URL path, there is no way for the Field UI module to set these up as static routes in a YAML file. Instead, at runtime, it needs to set up the needed routes for defined entity types.
- Route altering is when a module changes some aspect of a route that another module has set up. As an example, if the core Editor module is enabled, it changes the names and descriptions of the Filters administrative page, because editors are managed on the same page.

To provide dynamic routes or alter other modules' routes:

1. Create an event subscriber class. This class must implement \Symfony\Component \EventDispatcher\EventSubscriberInterface; the easiest way to do that is to extend \Drupal\Core\Routing\RouteSubscriberBase, as it sets up all of the needed framework for you. Put it into the \Drupal\mymodule\Routing namespace, so if the class name is MyModuleRouting, it must go into the *src/Routing/MyModuleRouting.php* file under your main module directory. Be sure to include use statements for the \Symfony\Component\Routing\Route, \Symfony\Component\Routing\RouteCollection, and \Drupal\Core\Routing \RouteSubscriberBase classes.

2. In your class, override the `alterRoutes()` method, which operates on the *route collection* (the list of all of the routes that are set up by all modules). Here are some examples:

```
protected function alterRoutes(RouteCollection $collection) {
  // Alter the title of the People administration page (admin/people).
  $route = $collection->get('entity.user.collection');
  $route->setDefault('_title', 'User accounts');
  // Make sure that the title text is translatable.
  $foo = t('User accounts');

  // Add a dynamic route at admin/people/mymodule, which could have been
  // a static route in this case.
  $path = $route->getPath();
  // Constructor parameters: path, defaults, requirements, as you would have
  // in a routing.yml file.
  $newroute = new Route($path . '/mymodule', array(
      '_controller' =>
        '\Drupal\mymodule\Controller\MyUrlController::generateMyPage',
      '_title' => 'New page title',
    ), array(
      '_permission' => 'administer mymodule',
    ));
  // Make sure that the title text is translatable.
  $foo = t('New page title');
  $collection->add('mymodule.newroutename', $newroute);
}
```

3. Because this example is altering routes from the User module, declare a dependency on this module in the *mymodule.info.yml* file:

```
dependencies:
  - user
```

4. Put these lines into the *mymodule.services.yml* file in the main module directory (omit the first line if you already have services in the file):

```
services:
  mymodule.subscriber:
    class: Drupal\mymodule\Routing\MyModuleRouting
    tags:
    - { name: event_subscriber }
```

5. After adding a new route subscriber, or after updating what it does, you will need to clear the Drupal cache so that Drupal will rebuild its cached routing information.

Further reading and reference:

- "The Drupal Cache" on page 10
- "Drupal 8 Services and Dependency Injection" on page 35
- "Interacting with the Drupal 8 Event System" on page 38

Registering a Block in Drupal 7

If you want to provide content that can be displayed on multiple pages, you should register for a block rather than for a path in your module. To register for a block in Drupal 7, you need to implement hook_block_info() in your *mymodule.module* file to tell Drupal about the existence of your block, and then implement hook_block_view() to generate the block content. For example:

```
// Tell Drupal about your block.
function mymodule_block_info() {
  $blocks = array();

  // The array key is known as the block "delta" (a unique identifier
  // within your module), and is used in other block hooks. Choose
  // something descriptive.
  $blocks['first_block'] = array(
    // The name shown on the Blocks administration page.
    // Be descriptive and unique across all blocks.
    'info' => t('First block from My Module'),
  );

  return $blocks;
}

// Generate the block content. Note that the $delta value passed in
// is the same as the array key you returned in your hook_block_info()
// implementation.
function mymodule_block_view($delta = '') {
  if ($delta == 'first_block') {
    return array(
      // The block's default title.
      'subject' => t('First block'),
      // The block's content.
      'content' => mymodule_block_generate(),
    );
  }
}
```

Notes:

- Implementations of hook_block_info() can be more complex than this: they can specify cache parameters (block output is cached by default for efficiency) and default placement.

- Blocks can also have configuration settings. These are provided by implementing hook_block_configure() and hook_block_save().

- The hook_block_view() implementation here calls a function (in this example, mymodule_block_generate()) to provide the actual block content. Because block-generating functions are very similar to page-generating functions, the details of what this function should return are covered in a separate section: "Creating Render Arrays for Page and Block Output" on page 102.

- After adding a new block to a hook_block_info() implementation, you will need to clear the Drupal cache to make it visible on the Blocks page.

Further reading and reference:

- "The Basics of Module and Theme Hook Programming" on page 23
- "The Drupal Cache" on page 10

Examples—blocks:

- Look up hook_block_info() on *https://api.drupal.org* to find all the options and links to the Drupal core functions that implement it.

- The Block example in Examples for Developers (*https://www.drupal.org/project/ examples*) and many Drupal core blocks include configuration options, cache settings, and other options.

Registering a Block in Drupal 8

In Drupal 8 (as in Drupal 7), if you want to provide content that can be displayed on multiple pages, you should register for a block rather than for a route in your module. Drupal 8 uses a plugin system for blocks, so all you have to do to register a block in Drupal 8 is properly define a Block plugin class. Block plugin classes should either extend the \Drupal\Core\Block\BlockBase class or implement the \Drupal\Core \Block\BlockPluginInterface interface, and they need to have Block plugin annotation from the \Drupal\Core\Block\Annotation\Block annotation class. They must be in the \Drupal\mymodule\Plugin\Block namespace and thus must be located in the *src/Plugin/Block* subdirectory under your module directory.

To define the same block as in "Registering a Block in Drupal 7" on page 100, a good name for the class would be MyModuleFirstBlock, making the file *src/Plugin/Block/ MyModuleFirstBlock.php*:

```
namespace Drupal\mymodule\Plugin\Block;

use Drupal\Core\Block\BlockBase;

/**
 * Provides a sample block.
 *
 * @Block(
 *   id = "mymodule_first_block",
 *   admin_label = @Translation("First block from My Module")
 * )
 */
class MyModuleFirstBlock extends BlockBase {
  public function build() {
    // Function body will be defined later.
  }
}
```

Notes:

- The @Block annotation provides a unique identifier for the block, as well as the name for the block that will appear on the Blocks administration page. See "The Basics of Drupal 8 Plugin Programming" on page 28 for more details about plugins and annotation.

- The build() method does the work of providing output for the block. Because block-generating functions are very similar to page-generating functions, the details of what this function should return are covered in "Creating Render Arrays for Page and Block Output" on page 102.

- You can also implement or override additional methods to provide access control, caching control, and configuration settings.

- After defining a new block plugin class, you will need to clear the Drupal cache to make it visible on the Blocks page.

Creating Render Arrays for Page and Block Output

Once your module has registered for a URL or block (see previous sections), you need to write a function or a method that returns the page or block output. In many content management systems, and in Drupal 6 and prior versions, output is generated directly and returned as a string of HTML markup and text. The problem with this philosophy is that when a module (rather than the theme) is making HTML markup decisions, it is difficult for the theme to have full control over how data is presented. Accordingly, Drupal 7 and 8 use a different philosophy, where modules that provide output for site visitors should always return the output data and meta-data properties, rather than rendered markup. This data can then be altered by other modules and finally used by the theme system to render the data into HTML. The structure used to return the output data and properties is known as a *render array*.

Here is the general structure of a render array that you could return from a page- or block-generating function or method:

```
$output = array(
  'sensible_identifier_1' => array(
    '#type' => 'element_identifier',
    // Other properties and data here.
  ),
  'sensible_identifier_2' => array(
    '#theme' => 'theme_hook',
    // Other properties and data here.
  ),
  // Other pieces of output here.
);
```

Notes:

- The outermost array keys are arbitrary: choose sensible identifiers that will remind you of what each piece of your block or page is.

- At the next level of arrays, keys starting with '#' are *property* keys that are recognized by the Render API. You can also provide properties on the outermost array.

- A render array should contain one or more of the following:

  — A '#type' property, whose value is the machine name of a *render element*; see "What Is a Render Element?" on page 104.

  — A '#theme' property, whose value is the name of a theme hook. If used with the '#type' property, it would override the default theme hook for the render element.

  — Keys not starting with '#', whose array values are themselves render arrays. If the parent array does not have a render element type or theme hook specified, each child array will be independently rendered and the output concatenated.

- Theme hooks are defined by modules by implementing hook_theme(), and each theme hook also requires one or more properties to be provided.

- Be sure that all your text is internationalized.

- If there is a '#markup' property and '#type' is not set, a render element type of markup will be assumed.

What Is a Render Element?

A render element represents the attributes and data to be output in one or more HTML elements, such as tables, forms, and form input elements; in principle, render elements can also represent non-HTML output. In practical terms, each render element defined in Drupal has a machine name and an array of default values for its properties; the property names start with '#'. Properties of render elements include '#theme' (for the theme hook that will be used to create the HTML output), other attributes, and the data to be output. When you use a render element in a render array, by giving its machine name in the '#type' property of the array, you will provide property values to override the defaults.

In Drupal 7, render elements are defined in implementations of hook_element_info(), and the common ones are defined by the System module in system_element_info(). You can discover available element types by looking at the hook implementations; the machine names for elements are the array keys in the return values, and the default properties for each element are the array values.

In Drupal 8, render elements are plugins annotated with \Drupal\Core\Render\Annotation\RenderElement or \Drupal\Core\Render\Annotation\FormElement annotation, whose classes implement \Drupal\Core\Render\Element\ElementInterface or \Drupal\Core\Render\Element\FormElementInterface. You can look for classes that implement either of these interfaces to discover element types; the machine names for the render elements are given in the plugin annotation, and the default properties are in the getInfo() class methods.

Here's an example of a render array that has an informational paragraph, followed by a list of items, followed by a table (the paragraph uses a 'markup' render element; the list and table use the 'item_list' and 'table' theme hooks):

```
$output = array(
  'introduction' => array(
    '#type' => 'markup',
    '#markup' => '<p>' . t('General information goes here.') . '</p>',
  ),
  'colors' => array(
    '#theme' => 'item_list',
    '#items' => array(t('Red'), t('Blue'), t('Green')),
    '#title' => t('Colors'),
  ),
  'materials' => array(
    '#theme' => 'table',
```

```
      '#caption' => t('Materials'),
      '#header' => array(t('Material'), t('Characteristic')),
      '#rows' => array(
        array(t('Steel'), t('Strong')),
        array(t('Aluminum'), t('Light')),
      ),
    ),
  );
```

Generic JavaScript code and files can be added to a render array by using the `'#attached'` property. In Drupal 7, the jQuery library will be attached by default on every page, so you can make use of that when writing your JavaScript. Here are some Drupal 7 examples:

```
// Attach a JavaScript file.
$output['#attached']['js'][] =
  drupal_get_path('module', 'mymodule') . '/mymodule.js';

// Attach some in-line JavaScript code.
$output['#attached']['js'][] = array(
  'type' => 'inline',
  'data' => $my_code,
);
```

CSS attachment works the same way, with the `'css'` array element. You can also define a *library* that contains one or more JavaScript and CSS files, and it can depend on other libraries. Look up `hook_library_info()` on *https://api.drupal.org* for more information on that.

Further reading and reference:

- The general structure and many of the details of render arrays are the same between Drupal 7 and Drupal 8. Drupal 8 specifics are covered in "Render Arrays in Drupal 8" on page 106.

- More about theme hooks: "Making Your Module Output Themeable" on page 25.

- Internationalizing text: "Principle: Drupal Is International" on page 48.

- Find Drupal core theme hooks on the "Default theme implementations" (Drupal 7) or "Theme system overview" (Drupal 8) topic on *https://api.drupal.org*.

- CSS and JavaScript libraries in Drupal 7: *http://bit.ly/js_in_drupal7*.

- CSS and JavaScript libraries in Drupal 8: *http://bit.ly/css_js_in_drupal8*.

Examples—render arrays:

- "Generating Paged Output" on page 107

- "Form Arrays, Form State Arrays, and Form State Objects" on page 110

- "Wrapper-Based Ajax Callback Functions" on page 127

- "Defining a field formatter in Drupal 7" on page 168
- "Defining a field formatter in Drupal 8" on page 169

 It is still possible in Drupal 7 to return strings from your page and block content functions instead of render arrays. Using render arrays is preferred, however, because:

- They are self-documenting.
- They allow modules to use hook_page_alter() to alter the page before it is rendered.
- They leave final rendering until late in the page-generation process, so unnecessary rendering can be avoided if a particular section of the page is not actually displayed.

Render Arrays in Drupal 8

As noted in the previous section, both the general concept and nearly all of the details of render arrays are the same in Drupal 7 and 8. Here are some differences:

- If your render array is being generated in a class that has a t() method, you should call this method in place of the global t() function, to internationalize user-interface text.
- In Drupal 8, attaching CSS and JavaScript files has to be done via a library. You'll need to put all of your JavaScript and CSS into files, and then define a library in a *mymodule.libraries.yml* file in your main module directory that looks like this:

```
myjslib:
  version: 1.x
  js:
    mymodule.js : {}
```

- Once you have a library defined, you can attach it to a render array like this:

```
$form['#attached']['library'][] = 'mymodule/myjslib';
```

- Data caching in Drupal 8 is more sophisticated and granular than in Drupal 7, and page caching is done on a more granular level. To enable this, render array elements need to include information about what cache tags and cache contexts they depend on, so that the Drupal rendering system can decide whether to render them during a page load or use a cached version.

Further reading and reference:

- "Drupal 8 Cache API" on page 11

Generating Paged Output

If a page or block you are generating output for is listing data, you need to think about what should happen if the list of data gets long; usually you would want the output to be separated into pages. If you are using a database query to generate the list, Drupal's Database API and theme system make separating the output into pages very easy. Here are the steps:

1. Use a dynamic query with db_select(), rather than a static query with db_query(). In Drupal 8, the select() method on a database service object is preferable to using db_select(), if you have dependency injection available.

2. In Drupal 7, add the PagerDefault *extender* to your database query. In Drupal 8, it is the \Drupal\Core\Database\Query\PagerSelectExtender extender.

3. Add an entry with '#theme' set to pager to your output render array in Drupal 7, or '#type' set to pager in Drupal 8. This will add a section to your page containing links to the pages of output. Each link will take you to your base page URL, with the URL query parameter *?page=N* appended (*N* starts at 0 for the first page, 1 for the second, etc.). The pager query extender will automatically read this URL query parameter to figure out what page of output the user is on and return the appropriate rows in the database query.

As an example, assume you want to show the titles of the most recently created node content items, and you want to show 10 items per page. You should really use the Views module to do this, but for purposes of illustration, here is the code you would need to put into your output-generating function for the block or page in Drupal 7:

```
// Find the most recently created nodes.
$query = db_select('node', 'n')
  ->fields('n', array('title'))
  ->orderBy('n.created', 'DESC')
  // Be sure to check permissions, and only show published items.
  ->addTag('node_access')
  ->condition('n.status', 1)
  // Put this last, because the return value is a new object.
  ->extend('PagerDefault');
// This only applies with the PagerDefault extender.
$query->limit(10);
$result = $query->execute();

// Extract the information from the query result.
$titles = array();
```

```
  foreach ($result as $row) {
    $titles[] = check_plain($row->title);
  }

  // Make the render array for a paged list of titles.
  $build = array();
  // The list of titles.
  $build['items'] = array(
    '#theme' => 'item_list',
    '#items' => $titles,
  );
  // The pager.
  $build['item_pager'] = array('#theme' => 'pager');

  return $build;
```

In Drupal 8, you should also use the Views module to accomplish this, or an entity query. But for illustration purposes, here is the equivalent code in Drupal 8:

```
  // If you have a database connection object $database:
  $query = $database->select('node', 'n');
  // Otherwise:
  $query = db_select('node', 'n');

  // Continuing on...
  $query->innerJoin('node_field_data', 'nd', 'n.nid = nd.nid AND n.vid = nd.vid');
  $query = $query
    ->extend('Drupal\Core\Database\Query\PagerSelectExtender') // Add pager.
    ->addMetaData('base_table', 'node') // Needed for join queries.
    ->limit(10) // 10 items per page.
    ->fields('nd', array('title', 'nid')) // Get the title field.
    ->orderBy('nd.created', 'DESC') // Sort by last updated.
    ->addTag('node_access') // Enforce node access.
    ->condition('nd.status', 1);

  $result = $query->execute();

  // Extract and sanitize the information from the query result.
  $titles = array();
  foreach ($result as $row) {
    $titles[] = $row->title;
  }

  // Make the render array for a paged list of titles.
  $build = array();
  $build['items'] = array(
    '#theme' => 'item_list',
    '#items' => $titles,
  );
  // Add the pager.
  $build['item_pager'] = array('#type' => 'pager');

  return $build;
```

Further reading and reference:

- "Dynamic queries" on page 59.
- "Cleansing and Checking User-Provided Input" on page 62.
- It is usually better to use the Views module rather than doing your own page queries: "Avoiding Custom Programming with Fielded Data" on page 75.
- "Querying and Loading Entities in Drupal 8" on page 160.

Using the Drupal Form API

One of the real strengths of Drupal for programmers is the Form API, which is a vast improvement over the process you would see in a standard reference on PHP programming for output and processing of web forms. The first step in using the Drupal Form API is to create a form-generating function (Drupal 7) or a form class with a form-generating method (Drupal 8); this function or method generates a structured *form array* containing information about the form elements and other markup to be displayed. Then, you will write form validation and submission functions or methods, which are called automatically by Drupal when your form is submitted, allowing you to securely process the submitted data. The advantages of using the Form API over doing all of this in raw HTML and PHP are:

- You can write a lot less code, as you're letting Drupal handle all of the standard parts of form creation and submission. For instance, you do not have to write code to read the $_GET or $_POST variable, and you do not have to create a dedicated PHP file with root-level code for the form's `action` attribute.
- Your code will be easier to read and maintain: Drupal's form arrays are much easier to deal with than raw HTML forms.
- As with other parts of Drupal, your form will be alterable by other modules, and the exact rendering is controlled by the theme system.
- When the form is rendered, Drupal adds a unique token to protect against cross-site scripting, and this is validated during form submission.
- Other security checks are also performed on form submission, such as matching up submitted values to allowed fields, omitting submissions to disabled form elements, and so on.
- The HTML output of the Drupal Form API is set up to be accessible, with no extra effort required on your part.

Form Arrays, Form State Arrays, and Form State Objects

Form arrays have the same general structure as the render arrays discussed in "Creating Render Arrays for Page and Block Output" on page 102—they are a specialized type of render array. (Actually, form arrays predate render arrays in Drupal history, so you could also say that render arrays are a generalization of form arrays.) There are special render element types that should only be used in form arrays, representing HTML form input elements or groups of input elements. Here is an example of a form array:

```
$form = array();

// Plain text input element for first name.
$form['first_name'] = array(
  '#type' => 'textfield',
  '#title' => t('First name'),
);

// Plain text element for company name, only visible to some
// users.
$form['company'] = array(
  '#type' => 'textfield',
  '#title' => t('Company'),
  // This assumes permission 'use company field' has been defined.
  '#access' => user_access('use company field'),
);

$my_information = 'stuff';

// Some hidden information to be used later.
$form['information'] = array(
  '#type' => 'value',
  '#value' => $my_information,
);

// Submit button.
$form['submit'] = array(
  '#type' => 'submit',
  '#value' => t('Submit'),
);
```

Notes:

- The preceding code is for Drupal 7. In Drupal 8, only one line changes: user_access() is replaced by \Drupal::currentUser()->hasPermission(), or the equivalent call on a dependency-injected current_user service.

- The type of element is specified in the '#type' property. The types supported by Drupal are listed in the Drupal Form API Reference, which also tells which prop-

---

erties each element uses. You can find the Drupal-version-specific Form API Reference on *https://api.drupal.org*.

- The value form element type can be used to pass information to form validation and submission functions. This information is not rendered at all into the form's HTML, and no input is accepted from these elements (in contrast to form elements of type hidden, which render as HTML input elements with type="hidden"), so they are more secure and can contain any PHP data structure.

- Most elements have '#title' properties, which are displayed as form element labels.

- All form elements have an '#access' property. If it evaluates to TRUE or is omitted, the element is shown; if it evaluates to FALSE, the element is not displayed. In Drupal 8, you can alternatively provide an '#access_callback' property, which is a PHP callable (or function name), which is called to determine access (the element being access checked is passed in as the sole argument).

- You can include markup and other render elements in your form arrays.

The form generation, validation, and submission functions or methods receive information about the form submission in a *form state* variable, $form_state, which is retained through the whole process. In Drupal 7, $form_state is an array; in Drupal 8, it is an object that implements \Drupal\Core\Form\FormStateInterface. You can add custom information to the form state during any step for later use. In Drupal 7, add information directly as array elements in $form_state, and retrieve it later from the array. In Drupal 8, use the set() method to add information and get() to retrieve it later.

The main piece of information you will use from $form_state is the values entered in the form elements by the user, which are in $form_state['values'] in Drupal 7, and retrieved by a call to the getValues() method in Drupal 8. Either way, the submitted values are an array, keyed by the same keys used in the form array for the form input elements.

One difficulty in the values array is that if the form has a nested structure, the values can be either nested or flat, depending on the '#tree' property of the form as a whole, or any parent subarray. Because this would make extracting form values complicated, after the initial processing step Drupal's Form API provides a '#parents' property, on each element or subelement in a form array, which is an array giving the nested parents needed to find the submitted values in the values array. Assuming that $parents holds this property for the element you're trying to get the value of, you can extract the value by calling:

```
// Drupal 7
$value = drupal_array_get_nested_value($form_state['values'], $parents);
// Drupal 8
$values = $form_state->getValues();
$value = \Drupal\Component\Utility\NestedArray::getValue($values, $parents);
```

Further reading and reference:

- "Drupal 8 Services and Dependency Injection" on page 35
- "Creating Render Arrays for Page and Block Output" on page 102

Examples—form arrays (besides the rest of the form section):

- "Programming with Ajax in Drupal" on page 123
- "Defining an Entity Type in Drupal 7" on page 132
- "Defining a Content Entity Type in Drupal 8" on page 139
- "Defining a Configuration Entity Type in Drupal 8" on page 149
- "Defining a field widget in Drupal 7" on page 164
- "Defining a field widget in Drupal 8" on page 165

Basic Form Generation and Processing in Drupal 7

Here are the steps needed to generate and process a form in Drupal 7:

1. Choose an ID for your form, which is a string that should typically start with your module name. For example, you might choose `mymodule_personal_data_form`.

2. In your *mymodule.module* file, define a form-generating function (also known as a *form constructor*) with the same name as the form ID, which returns the form array (see "Form Arrays, Form State Arrays, and Form State Objects" on page 110):

```
function mymodule_personal_data_form($form, &$form_state) {
  // Generate your form array here.

  return $form;
}
```

3. If you need to perform any data validation steps on form submissions, create a form validation function called `mymodule_personal_data_form_validate()`. This function should call `form_set_error()` if the submission is invalid, and it should do nothing if all is well.

4. Create a form-submission function called `mymodule_personal_data_form_submit()` to process the form submissions (for instance, to save information to the database). Here is an example of a form submission function:

```
function mymodule_personal_data_form_submit(&$form, &$form_state) {
  // The values submitted by the user are in $form_state['values'].
  $name = $form_state['values']['first_name'];
  // Values you stored in the form array are also available.
  $info = $form_state['values']['information'];

  // Your processing code goes here, such as saving this to the database.
  // Sanitize values before display, but not before storing to the database!
}
```

5. Call `drupal_get_form('mymodule_personal_data_form')` to build the form—do not call your form-generating function directly. Your validation and submission functions will be called automatically when a user submits the form. If your form is the sole content of a page whose path you are registering for in a `hook_menu()` implementation, you can use `drupal_get_form()` as the page-generating function:

```
// Inside your hook_menu() implementation:
$items['mymodule/my_form_page'] = array(
  'page callback' => 'drupal_get_form',
  'page arguments' => array('mymodule_personal_data_form'),
  // Don't forget the access information, title, etc.!
);
```

Further reading and reference:

- `hook_menu()`: "Registering for a URL in Drupal 7" on page 89

Examples—form processing (besides the rest of the form section):

- "Defining a field widget in Drupal 7" on page 164.
- "Defining an Entity Type in Drupal 7" on page 132.
- Form-generating functions in Drupal core are listed in the "Form builder functions" topic on *https://api.drupal.org*.
- The Form example in Examples for Developers (*https://www.drupal.org/project/examples*).

Be careful about caching form output, because `drupal_get_form()` adds verification information to the form output, and this information is invalid after some time has passed. If your form is displayed in a block, be sure that the block is not cached; this is not a problem if the form is part of the main page content.

Basic Form Generation and Processing in Drupal 8

In Drupal 8, to generate and process a form, create a form class. By convention, form classes usually go into the \Drupal\mymodule\Form namespace, and of course you should pick a class name that describes the form. You'll also need to choose a unique ID for your form, which should generally start with your module's machine name.

Here is a simple example of a form class for a personal data form; this needs to go into the *src/Form/PersonalDataForm.php* file under your module directory:

```php
namespace Drupal\mymodule\Form;

use Drupal\Core\Form\FormBase;
use Drupal\Core\Form\FormStateInterface;

class PersonalDataForm extends FormBase {

  // getFormId() returns the form ID you chose, which must be unique.
  public function getFormId() {
    return 'mymodule_personal_data_form';
  }

  // buildForm() generates the form array.
  public function buildForm(array $form, FormStateInterface $form_state) {
    // Generate your form array here.

    return $form;
  }

  // submitForm() processes the form submission.
  public function submitForm(array &$form, FormStateInterface $form_state) {
    // Extract the values submitted by the user.
    $values = $form_state->getValues();
    $name = $values['first_name'];
    // Values you stored in the form array are also available.
    $info = $values['information'];

    // Your processing code goes here, such as saving this to the database.
    // Sanitize values if you are displaying them, but do not sanitize before
    // saving to the database!
  }
}
```

Notes:

- The three methods defined here are essential. `getFormID()` returns the unique ID you chose for your form. `buildForm()` returns the form array; see "Form Arrays, Form State Arrays, and Form State Objects" on page 110 for details. `submit Form()` processes the form submission.

- You can also include a `validateForm()` method, if your form needs validation. If you find a validation error, call the `setErrorByName()` method on `$form_state`; if there are no validation errors, just return.

- In a form class, in place of calling the `t()` function to translate user interface text, use the `t()` method from the `FormBase` class.

- If you are creating a form for simple (non-entity) configuration, you should extend `\Drupal\Core\Form\ConfigFormBase` instead of the generic `FormBase` class.

Once you have a form class defined, you need to do one of the following to display your form:

- If your form is the sole content of a page, you can put the class name into your *mymodule.routing.yml* file. For example, to make the personal data form appear on path *mymodule/my_form_page*, visible to anyone, you would use the following entry:

```
mymodule.personal_data_form:
  path: '/mymodule/my_form_page'
  defaults:
    _form: '\Drupal\mymodule\Form\PersonalDataForm'
    _title: 'Personal data form'
  requirements:
    _access: 'TRUE'
```

- If your form is to appear in a block or inside some other content you are generating, you can add it to a render array as follows:

```
// Code without dependency injection or $container variable:
$my_render_array['personal_data_form'] =
  \Drupal::formBuilder()->getForm('Drupal\mymodule\Form\PersonalDataForm');

// With $container variable (dependency injection):
$builder = $container->get('form_builder');
$my_render_array['personal_data_form'] =
  $builder->getForm('Drupal\mymodule\Form\PersonalDataForm');
```

Further reading and reference:

- "Registering for a URL in Drupal 8" on page 92

- "Creating Render Arrays for Page and Block Output" on page 102
- "Drupal 8 Services and Dependency Injection" on page 35

Examples—form processing (besides the rest of the form section):

- "Defining a field widget in Drupal 8" on page 165
- "Defining a Content Entity Type in Drupal 8" on page 139
- "Defining a Configuration Entity Type in Drupal 8" on page 149

Creating Confirmation Forms

For security reasons, it is important to verify destructive actions connected with a URL. For instance, if your module has a URL that allows an administrative user to delete some data or a file, you should confirm this intention before deleting the data. One reason is that the user could have been tricked into visiting that URL by a cross-site scripting attack; also, sometimes people click links by mistake, and confirming before destroying all their data is the polite thing to do.

Drupal makes this type of confirmation easy. Here are the steps for Drupal 7:

1. Instead of registering your path with a function that performs the deletion directly, use `drupal_get_form()` as the page callback, passing in the name of a form-generating function.

2. Have your form-generating function call `confirm_form()` to generate a confirmation form.

3. Perform the data deletion in the form-submission function, which will only be called if the action is confirmed (which also means that the unique form token will be validated).

Here's an example of the code:

```
// The menu router registration.
function mymodule_menu() {
  // ...

  // Assume there is a content ID number.
  $items['admin/content/mycontent/delete/%'] = array(
    'title' => 'Delete content item?',
    'page callback' => 'drupal_get_form',
    // Pass the content ID number to the form-generating function.
    // It is position 4 in the path (starting from 0).
    'page arguments' => array('mymodule_confirm_delete', 4),
    // Permission needs to be defined by the module.
    'access arguments' => array('delete mycontent items'),
  );
```

```
  // ...
}

// Form-generating function.
function mymodule_confirm_delete($form, $form_state, $id) {
  // Save the ID for the submission function.
  $form['mycontent_id'] = array(
    '#type' => 'value',
    '#value' => $id,
  );

  return confirm_form($form,
    // You could load the item and display the title here.
    t('Are you sure you want to delete content item %id?',
      array('%id' => $id)),
    // The URL path to return to if the user cancels.
    'mymodule/mypath');
}

// Form-submission function.
function mymodule_confirm_delete_submit($form, $form_state) {
  // Read the ID saved in the form.
  $id = $form_state['values']['mycontent_id'];

  // Sanitize.
  $id = (int) $id;

  // Perform the data deletion.
  // ...

  // Redirect somewhere.
  drupal_goto('mymodule/my_form_page');
}
```

In Drupal 8, this same form can be generated by the following class, which needs to go into the *src/Form/ConfirmDeleteForm.php* file under the main module directory:

```
namespace Drupal\mymodule\Form;

use Drupal\Core\Form\ConfirmFormBase;
use Drupal\Core\Form\FormStateInterface;
use Drupal\Core\Url;

class ConfirmDeleteForm extends ConfirmFormBase {

  protected $to_delete_id;

  public function getFormId() {
    return 'mymodule_confirm_delete';
  }

  // Note that when adding arguments to buildForm(), you need to give
```

```
// them default values, to avoid PHP errors.
public function buildForm(array $form, FormStateInterface $form_state,
  $id = '') {
  // Sanitize and save the ID.
  $id = (int) $id;
  $this->to_delete_id = $id;

  $form = parent::buildForm($form, $form_state);
  return $form;
}

public function getQuestion() {
  return  t('Are you sure you want to delete content item %id?',
    array('%id' => $this->to_delete_id));
}

public function getCancelUrl() {
  return new Url('mymodule.mydescription');
}

public function submitForm(array &$form, FormStateInterface $form_state) {
  $id = $this->to_delete_id;

  // Perform the data deletion.
  // ...

  // Redirect somewhere.
  $form_state->setRedirect('mymodule.personal_data_form');
}
}
```

You'll also need to display this form on a page. Here's a *mymodule.routing.yml* entry, with a placeholder corresponding to the form builder input variable name $id:

```
mymodule.delete_confirm:
  path: '/admin/content/mycontent/delete/{id}'
  defaults:
    _form: '\Drupal\mymodule\Form\ConfirmDeleteForm'
    _title: 'Delete content item?'
  requirements:
    _permission: 'delete mycontent items'
```

Further reading and reference:

- "Form Arrays, Form State Arrays, and Form State Objects" on page 110
- "Basic Form Generation and Processing in Drupal 7" on page 112
- "Basic Form Generation and Processing in Drupal 8" on page 114
- "Principle: Drupal Is Secure; User Input Is Insecure" on page 61
- "Registering for a URL in Drupal 7" on page 89

- "Registering for a URL in Drupal 8" on page 92

Examples—confirmation forms:

- "Defining a Content Entity Type in Drupal 8" on page 139
- "Defining a Configuration Entity Type in Drupal 8" on page 149

Adding Autocomplete to Forms

If you have a form where a user needs to select a value from several choices, there are several ways to do it:

- If there are fewer than about seven choices, you should use checkboxes if the user can select multiple items, and radio buttons if the user can only select one item.
- If there are more than seven choices, you should use a select list.
- However, if you have a very large number of choices, select lists do not perform well in browsers; in this case, you should use an autocomplete text field: choices pop up as the user begins to enter text.
- You may also want to use an autocomplete text field if the user is free to make an entry that was not one of the suggested choices. This will let users see existing choices, prompting them to select one if it exists, while still letting them create a new entry.

To make a text input field have autocomplete behavior in Drupal, here are the steps:

1. In Drupal 7, add an '#autocomplete_path' property to your 'textfield' form element array, with a URL path in it. In Drupal 8, the property is '#autocomplete_route_name', and the value is a route machine name. Or to autocomplete on an entity in Drupal 8, add an 'entity_autocomplete' render element to your array. This looks like:

   ```
   // In a form-generating function:
   $form['my_autocomplete_field'] = array(
     '#type' => 'textfield',
     '#title' => t('Autocomplete field'),
     // Drupal 7:
     '#autocomplete_path' => 'mymodule/autocomplete',
     // Drupal 8:
     '#autocomplete_route_name' => 'mymodule.autocomplete',
   );

   // For an entity autocomplete in Drupal 8 for Nodes:
   $form['my_node_element'] = array(
     '#type' => 'entity_autocomplete',
   ```

```
  '#target_type' => 'node',
  // Limit this to just Articles.
  '#selection_settings' => array(
    'target_bundles' => array('article'),
  ),
);
```

2. Register for this URL path in your hook_menu() implementation (Drupal 7) or
   for the route in your *mymodule.routing.yml* file (Drupal 8). This looks like:

```
// Inside Drupal 7 hook_menu() implementation:
$items['mymodule/autocomplete'] = array(
  'page callback' => 'mymodule_autocomplete',
  'access arguments' => array('use company field'),
  'type' => MENU_CALLBACK,
);
```

```
# Inside Drupal 8 mymodule.routing.yml file:
mymodule.autocomplete:
  path: '/mymodule/autocomplete'
  defaults:
    _controller: '\Drupal\mymodule\Controller\MyUrlController::autocomplete'
  requirements:
    _permission: 'use company field'
```

3. Define the page-callback function or page-generation method. In Drupal 7, it will
   take one argument (the string the user has typed); in Drupal 8, the argument will
   be the Symfony request. In either case, it should return an array of responses in
   JSON format, as in these examples:

```
// Drupal 7:
function mymodule_autocomplete($string = '') {
  $matches = array();
  if ($string) {
    // Sanitize $string and find appropriate matches -- about 10 or fewer.
    // Put them into $matches as $key => $visible text.
    // ...
  }

  drupal_json_output($matches);
}
```

```
// Drupal 8, top of MyUrlController class file:

use Symfony\Component\HttpFoundation\JsonResponse;
use Symfony\Component\HttpFoundation\Request;

// Drupal 8, new method in MyUrlController class:

public function autocomplete(Request $request) {
  $string = $request->query->get('q');
```

```
    $matches = array();
    if ($string) {
      // Sanitize $string and find appropriate matches -- about 10 or fewer.
      // Put them into $matches as items, each an array with
      // 'value' and 'label' elements.
      // ...
    }

    return new JsonResponse($matches);
}
```

Further reading and reference:

- "Registering for a URL in Drupal 7" on page 89.
- "Registering for a URL in Drupal 8" on page 92.
- Autocomplete is a special case of Ajax (see "Programming with Ajax in Drupal" on page 123). Autocomplete is covered here because in Drupal it is handled in a completely different manner from other Ajax responses.

Examples—autocomplete:

- There are several examples of autocompletes in Drupal core version 7, such as the author name field in node_form(), which auto-completes on user names at path *user/autocomplete*. This path is registered in user_menu(), and its page-callback function is user_autocomplete().
- In Drupal 8, most ad-hoc autocomplete functionality has been removed in favor of the generic entity autocomplete described in the preceding text. But the Block module still has a special autocomplete controller for block categories. The routing is in *core/modules/block/block.routing.yml* (route name block.category_autocomplete) with the \Drupal\block\Controller \CategoryAutocompleteController::autocomplete() page-controller method.
- There is a complete standalone autocomplete example in the Ajax example in Examples for Developers (*https://www.drupal.org/project/examples*).

Altering Forms

One of the more common reasons that someone building a Drupal site would decide to create a custom module is to alter a form that is displayed by Drupal core or another module. Typically, the reason is that the site owner or site designer decides that some of the text on the form is confusing, wants some part of the form hidden, wants to change the order of fields on a form, or wants some additional validation to be done on form submissions. All of these alterations can be done by implementing a form alter hook.

Before deciding you need a custom form-altering module, however, you should check to see if you can alter the form in a different way. Some core and contributed modules, for example, have configuration options that will let you alter labels on forms, and you can also use the String Overrides contributed module to make global text changes (such as changing all Submit buttons to say Send). If you want to add text at the top of a form, you might be able to use a block. Also, content-editing forms are configurable in the administrative user interface: you can add help text to fields, change field labels, change the order of fields, add and remove fields from content types, and change the displayed name of the content type, among other settings. In Drupal 8, you can also define *form modes*, which allow you to make different content editing forms for different situations, in the user interface, with different subsets of fields displayed, different labels, and different ordering. Each content type also has several settings for comments that affect the comment form, and there are many other examples of configuration options—so be sure to investigate before you start programming.

If you do need to alter a form via an alter hook in your custom module, here are the steps (in Drupal 7 or 8):

1. Figure out the form ID of the form you are altering. The easiest way to do this is to look at the HTML source of the page with the form—the ID will be the id attribute of the HTML form tag. For this example, let's assume the ID is the_form_id.

2. Implement hook_form_FORM_ID_alter() by declaring a function called mymodule_form_the_form_id_alter() in your *mymodule.module* file. Some forms, like field widget forms, use a different alter hook, such as hook_field_widget_form_alter(); these hooks work the same way as hook_form_FORM_ID_alter().

3. Alter the form array in this function.

Implementing hook_form_FORM_ID_alter() can sometimes lead to some crazy-looking function names. For instance, in both Drupal 7 and 8, there is a module used for testing called *form_test.module*. This module defines a form whose ID is form_test_alter_form, and then it implements hook_form_FORM_ID_alter() to test form alteration hook functionality. The name of the implementing function is therefore composed of the module's machine name, then form, then the form ID, then alter, resulting in form_test_form_form_test_alter_form_alter()—kind of a mouthful!

As an example, assume that you want to change the user-registration form on a site so that it only allows people to register using email addresses within your company's domain. The form ID in this case is `user_register_form`, and here is the alter function you would need to define:

```
// Form alteration in Drupal 7. Drupal 8 is the same except the
// function signature, see below.
function mymodule_form_user_register_form_alter(&$form, &$form_state, $form_id) {
  // Change the label on the email address field.
  $form['account']['mail']['#title'] = t('Company e-mail address');

  // Add a validation function.
  $form['#validate'][] = 'mymodule_validate_register_email';
}

// Drupal 8 use statement needed:
use Drupal\Core\Form\FormStateInterface;

// Drupal 8 function signature:
function mymodule_form_user_register_form_alter(&$form,
  FormStateInterface $form_state, $form_id)

// Validation function in Drupal 7.
function mymodule_validate_register_email($form, $form_state) {
  $email = $form_state['values']['mail'];

  // Check that the email is within the company domain.
  // If not, call form_set_error('mail', t('message goes here'));
}

// Validation function in Drupal 8.
function mymodule_validate_register_email($form,
    FormStateInterface $form_state) {
  $values = $form_state->getValues();
  $email = $values['mail'];

  // Check that the email is within the company domain.
  // If not, call $form_state->setErrorByName('mail', t('message goes here'));
}
```

Further reading and reference:

- "Repurposing an existing field widget" on page 167

Programming with Ajax in Drupal

Ajax is a technique whereby a web page can make an asynchronous (background) request to a URL without a full page load, in response to a JavaScript event (mouse click, typing, etc.) on an HTML element. When the request finishes, JavaScript commands are run, typically updating part of the page. Autocomplete text fields in forms, covered in "Adding Autocomplete to Forms" on page 119, are one example of Ajax handling in Drupal; generic Ajax responses in forms work differently and are covered in this section.

 Ajax was formerly known as AJAX, or Asynchronous JavaScript and XML. However, these days few people actually work with XML when doing their asynchronous requests, so what was once the acronym AJAX has become Ajax, and it is used to mean any kind of asynchronous JavaScript request (whether or not XML is involved).

Like many aspects of Drupal, because Drupal is written in PHP and browsers support JavaScript, you can technically use any Ajax programming techniques you know to accomplish your Ajax requirements. However, you should use the Drupal Ajax framework instead, which provides several benefits:

- Defining the Ajax responses for HTML elements is done in the form array, as part of the Drupal Form API, which is much easier than doing it from scratch.

- Drupal performs its standard security checks for forms and HTTP requests.

- In place of completely handling the server end (the URL request), you can let Drupal use its standard Ajax URL and just provide the PHP function to be called to handle the processing. You can also use your own URL if you wish; in that case, you would use the standard Drupal routing system to set up your Ajax URL.

- In place of writing all the JavaScript commands for the browser when the response is returned, the Drupal Ajax framework provides an easy and flexible way to define the browser actions.

The remainder of this section describes how to use the Drupal Ajax framework.

Setting Up a Form for Ajax

Drupal Ajax responses are specified in forms. To set up an Ajax response in a form, the main thing you need to do is add the #ajax property (an array) to the form element that should trigger the response. In the #ajax array, provide values for one or more of the following keys:

- callback: The name of the PHP function or method to call when the event occurs.

- In place of callback, if you want to use your own URL, in Drupal 7 you can instead define a value for the path key (a URL path string), and register for the URL in the standard Drupal way. In Drupal 8, you'd use the url key and its value would be a \Drupal\Core\Url object.

- wrapper: If you want the browser response to replace part of the page markup on return, set up a <div> with an id attribute, and provide this ID. By default, the entire <div> will be *completely* replaced with returned content (including the <div> tags), but you can also supply a value for method, equal to 'append', 'prepend', 'before', 'after', or the name of another JQuery manipulation function to change this. Omit wrapper if your response is more complex than just replacing markup.

- event: Form elements have default events to respond to, but you can override the default by specifying the name of a JavaScript event.

- prevent: Optionally, specify an event to prevent from being triggered (e.g., if you respond to 'mousedown' events, you might want to prevent 'click' events from being triggered when the mouse comes back up).

- There are additional Ajax elements governing effect speeds, progress indicators, and other factors of the Ajax response.

If you are using your own URL for Ajax, via the path (Drupal 7) or url (Drupal 8) element in your #ajax property instead of callback, you'll need to construct your URL so that all the information you need is part of the HTTP request (generally, you'll put the information into URL query parameters); it is usually simpler to use callback.

As the start of an example (continued in the rest of this section), here's a form array with two Ajax-triggering elements, and two HTML <div> elements to put responses in:

```
$form['ajax_output_1'] = array(
  '#type' => 'markup',
  '#markup' => '<div id="ajax-output-spot"></div>',
);

$form['text_trigger'] = array(
  '#type' => 'textfield',
  '#title' => t('Type here to trigger Ajax'),
  '#ajax' => array(
    'event' => 'keyup',
    'wrapper' => 'ajax-output-spot',
    'callback' => 'mymodule_ajax_text_callback',
  ),
);

$form['ajax_output_2'] = array(
  '#type' => 'markup',
  '#markup' => '<div id="other-ajax-response-spot"></div>',
```

```
  );

  $form['button_trigger'] = array(
    '#type' => 'button',
    '#value' => t('Click here to trigger Ajax'),
    '#ajax' => array(
      'callback' => 'mymodule_ajax_button_callback',
    ),
  );
```

If you are doing this in Drupal 8, the callbacks could also be public static class methods on the form class, such as:

```
'callback' => 'Drupal\mymodule\Form\PersonalDataForm::ajaxTextCallback',

'callback' => 'Drupal\mymodule\Form\PersonalDataForm::ajaxButtonCallback',
```

The Ajax callback specified in the `callback` element of the `#ajax` property on a form element is a PHP function that receives `$form` and `$form_state` as arguments. `$form_state['triggering_element']` (Drupal 7) or `$form_state->get('triggering_element')` (Drupal 8) will tell you which form element triggered the Ajax response, so you can use the same callback to handle Ajax responses to several different form elements, if you wish. You can also retrieve all of the currently entered form values in `$form_state` as you would in any other form processing. The following sections give a few examples of these callbacks.

In most cases, the other thing you need to do for Ajax to work properly is to make sure that the form is rebuilt properly during Ajax handling. To do that, you'll need to set `$form_state['rebuild']` to `TRUE` in your form submit handler function (Drupal 7), or call the `setRebuild()` method on the form state object in Drupal 8.

Further reading and reference:

- "Form Arrays, Form State Arrays, and Form State Objects" on page 110
- "Basic Form Generation and Processing in Drupal 8" on page 114
- "Registering for a URL in Drupal 7" on page 89
- "Registering for a URL in Drupal 8" on page 92
- JQuery manipulation functions: *http://bit.ly/jquery_manipulation*
- Online documentation for Ajax in Drupal 7 (also mostly applies to Drupal 8): *http://bit.ly/js_api_in_drupal7*

Examples—Ajax (besides the rest of this section):

- The Ajax example in Examples for Developers (*https://www.drupal.org/project/examples*)

Wrapper-Based Ajax Callback Functions

If you use the `wrapper` element of the `#ajax` property, your callback returns the HTML markup to replace the wrapper `<div>`, or (preferably) a render array that generates the desired HTML markup. In addition, any calls to `drupal_set_message()` during processing will result in messages being prepended to the returned markup. Here's an example callback function for Drupal 7:

```
function mymodule_ajax_text_callback($form, &$form_state) {
  // Read the text from the text field.
  $text = $form_state['values']['text_trigger'];
  if (!$text) {
    $text = t('nothing');
  }

  // Set a message.
  drupal_set_message(t('You have triggered Ajax'));

  // Return a render array for markup to replace the wrapper <div> contents.
  return array(
    '#type' => 'markup',
    // Text was not sanitized, so use @variable in t() to sanitize.
    // Be sure to include the wrapper div!
    '#markup' => '<div id="ajax-output-spot">' .
      t('You typed @text', array('@text' => $text)) . '</div>',
  );
}
```

Only the first few lines are different in Drupal 8, to make it a static method on the `PersonalDataForm` class defined in "Basic Form Generation and Processing in Drupal 8" on page 114 and use the Drupal 8 `$form_state` interface:

```
public static function ajaxTextCallback(array $form,
  FormStateInterface $form_state) {
  // Read the text from the text field.
  $text = $form_state->getValues()['text_trigger'];
```

Further reading and reference:

- "Form Arrays, Form State Arrays, and Form State Objects" on page 110
- "Creating Render Arrays for Page and Block Output" on page 102

Command-Based Ajax Callback Functions in Drupal 7

If you are not using a `wrapper` element in your `#ajax` property, your Drupal 7 Ajax callback function should return a set of Ajax commands from the Drupal Ajax framework. Note that unlike when using `wrapper`, if you are using a command-based callback, drupal_set_message() does not automatically trigger messages to be displayed. Here's an example of a callback using commands for Drupal 7:

```
function mymodule_ajax_button_callback($form, &$form_state) {
  $commands = array();

  // Replace HTML markup inside the div via a selector.
  $text = t('The button has been clicked');
  $commands[] = ajax_command_html('div#other-ajax-spot', $text);

  // Add some CSS to the div.
  $css = array('background-color' => '#ddffdd', 'color' => '#000000');
  $commands[] = ajax_command_css('div#other-ajax-spot', $css);

  return array('#type' => 'ajax', '#commands' => $commands);
}
```

Each command in the returned array is the return value of one of the Drupal Ajax command functions. You can find all of these functions listed in the "Ajax framework commands" topic on *https://api.drupal.org*.

Command-Based Ajax Callback Functions in Drupal 8

If you are not using a wrapper element in your #ajax property, your Drupal 8 Ajax callback function should return a set of Ajax commands from the Drupal Ajax framework, in the form of an object of class \Drupal\Core\Ajax\AjaxResponse. Note that unlike when using wrapper, if you are using a command-based callback, drupal_set_message() does not automatically trigger messages to be displayed. Here is an example of a callback using commands, as a method on the PersonalDataForm class defined in "Basic Form Generation and Processing in Drupal 8" on page 114:

```
use Drupal\Core\Ajax\AjaxResponse;
use Drupal\Core\Ajax\HtmlCommand;
use Drupal\Core\Ajax\CssCommand;

public static function ajaxButtonCallback(array $form,
  FormStateInterface $form_state) {

  $response = new AjaxResponse();

  // Replace HTML markup inside the div via a selector.
  $text = t('The button has been clicked');
  $response->addCommand(
    new HtmlCommand('div#other-ajax-spot', $text));

  // Add some CSS to the div.
  $css = array('background-color' => '#ddffdd', 'color' => '#000000');
  $response->addCommand(
    new CssCommand('div#other-ajax-spot', $css));
```

```
    return $response;
  }
```

Each command you add to the AjaxResponse object via the AjaxResponse :: add
Command() method is an object that implements \Drupal\Core\Ajax\CommandInter
face. The available commands can be found in the *core/lib/Drupal/Core/Ajax* directory in the Drupal source code (find classes there whose names end in Command).

Programming with Entities and Fields

This section covers programming with Drupal entities and fields. The sections on
defining entity types, field types, widgets, and formatters are independent of one
another, so skim the terminology section first, and then you can skip to the section
you need. The code samples in this section complement, but do not duplicate, the
well-documented Entity and Field examples in the Examples for Developers project.

Further reading and reference:

- "Avoiding Custom Programming with Fielded Data" on page 75

Examples—entity and field programming (besides the rest of this section):

- The Drupal core entities and fields are all good to look at; Drupal 8 has even
  more Drupal core examples than Drupal 7.
- Entity example in Examples for Developers (*https://www.drupal.org/project/exam
  ples*). Note that the Drupal 7 example is a bit different from the example in this
  section, because it does not make use of the contributed Entity API module.
- Field example in Examples for Developers.
- The Node example in Examples for Developers shows how to create a content
  type for the core Node entity in a module.

There is sometimes confusion between entity fields and database
table fields. Within this section, the term *field* will always mean an
entity field as defined in this section, and any references to database
table fields will be clearly noted as such.

Terminology of Entities and Fields

The Drupal entity and field systems introduced quite a bit of terminology that you'll
need to be familiar with if you're planning on doing any entity or field programming.
Here's a list of terms and other background information:

Entity

As of Drupal version 7, Drupal core defines the concept of an *entity*, which stores data (such as content or settings) for a Drupal website.

Entity type

Each *entity type* represents a particular kind of data, and comes with a small number of properties, such as an ID, a universal identifier (UUID), and a label or title.

Content and configuration entities

Drupal 8 formally divides entities into *content entities* (for content that should be displayed to site visitors) and *configuration entities* (for site configuration). This distinction is not explicit in Drupal 7, and entities in Drupal 7 are really meant only for content.

Drupal core entity types

Drupal core version 7 defines five main user-visible entity types: *node* (for basic content), *taxonomy_term* and *taxonomy_vocabulary* (for classification of content), *comment* (for comments attached to nodes), and *user* (for user account information). Drupal 7 core also defines the *file* entity type, which is used internally to manage uploaded files. Drupal 8 core defines many additional entity types, most of which are configuration entities. Also, in Drupal 8, the comment entity type is generalized: comments can be attached to any entity type, not just nodes.

Module-defined entity types

The Drupal API allows modules to define additional entity types. The API is quite different for Drupal 7 and Drupal 8 and is described in the following sections.

Bundle

Each content entity type can have one or more *bundles*, which are groupings of the entity objects within a given entity type. For instance, the bundles of the node entity type are *content types*, which an administrator can define within the Drupal user interface (modules can define them too); examples of content types are basic pages, news items, blog posts, and forum posts. The bundles of the taxonomy entity type are *vocabularies*, and the objects are the individual taxonomy terms. The user entity type doesn't use bundles, and its objects are user accounts. Each entity object belongs to exactly one bundle (assuming that you count entities that don't use bundles as having all objects belonging to the same, default bundle).

Fields, base fields, and properties

Most content entity types are *fieldable*, meaning that *fields* can be added to each bundle of the entity type (the fields can be different for each bundle within an entity type). In Drupal 7, fields supplement the intrinsic *properties* of the entity type; in Drupal 8, the entity properties are actually fields themselves (they're known as *base fields* in Drupal 8). Fields and intrinsic properties both store information, which could be text, numbers, attached files, images, media URLs, or other data, and fields can be single- or multiple-valued. Some entity types are not fieldable or do not allow administrators to change their fields; for example, configuration entity types are normally not fieldable.

Field type

Each field has a *field type*, which defines what type of data the field stores; Drupal core defines several field types—including one-line text, formatted long text, and images—and modules can define additional field types. A field type can be used to create one or more individual fields, which have machine names and other settings pertaining to data storage (such as how many values they can store); the settings cannot be changed after the field is created.

Field instance

Once a field is created, it can be attached to one or more bundles; each field/bundle combination is known as a *field instance*. In Drupal 7, fields can be shared across entity types; in Drupal 8, fields are specific to each entity type, so for instance, if you needed a first-name field for both Nodes and Comments, you'd have to create it twice. Field instances have settings such as whether the field is required and a label; these settings can be different for each bundle and can be changed later.

Widgets and form modes

When a user is creating or editing an entity object, a field *widget* is used to edit the field data on the entity editing form. For instance, a field storing text can use a normal HTML text field as its widget, or if its values are restricted to a small set, it could use an HTML select, radio buttons, or checkboxes. Drupal core defines the common widgets needed to edit its fields in standard ways, and modules can define widgets for their fields or other modules' fields. In Drupal 7, widgets are assigned to each field instance when the field is attached to the bundle. In Drupal 8, each bundle can have one or more *form modes*, which allow entity objects and their fields to be edited differently under different circumstances. In each form mode, some fields can be hidden, display order can be chosen, and a widget can be chosen for each visible field.

Formatters and view modes

When an entity object is being displayed, field *formatters* are used to display the field data. For instance, a long text field could be formatted as plain text (with all HTML tags stripped out), passed through a text filter, or truncated to a particular length. Modules can define field formatters for their own or other modules' field types. Each bundle can have one or more *view modes* (such as *full page* and *teaser* for the node entity type); fields can be hidden or shown, ordered, and assigned different formatters in each view mode. View modes allow entity objects and their fields to be displayed differently under different circumstances; this is mostly useful for fieldable content entity types.

Translations and revisions

The data in entity objects and their fields can be edited and translated, and many entity types keep track of *revisions*, making it possible to revert entity and field data to a prior version.

If your data storage needs are similar to an existing entity type, it is a good idea to use it instead of defining your own entity type. This will be a lot less work, because existing entity types include administrative screens and other functionality, and it will also allow you to use the many add-on modules that work with existing entity types.

Defining your own entity type is a good idea for these circumstances:

- In Drupal 7, to store groups of settings for a module, to allow them to be translated with the Entity Translation module.

- In Drupal 8, to store configuration that has multiple copies, as described in "Defining a Configuration Entity Type in Drupal 8" on page 149.

- In either Drupal 7 or 8, to define storage for a set of content for a site that needs a completely different permissions system and display mechanism from the Drupal core node entity type (and from other existing entity types). Define your own entity when the additional programming that would be needed to coerce an existing entity type into doing what you want would be more work than the programming needed to define a separate entity type.

Defining an Entity Type in Drupal 7

This section shows how to define a new entity type in Drupal 7, which could be used to store a special type of content, or for module settings. You might want to download the Entity example from Examples for Developers (*https://www.drupal.org/project/examples*) and follow along there, or perhaps look at the code for one of the Drupal core entities.

Step 1: Implement hook_entity_info()

The first step in defining a new entity type is to implement hook_entity_info() in your module. In Drupal 7, it is advisable to make use of the contributed Entity API module, as it takes care of many standard operations for you; you may also want to make use of the Entity Construction Kit module. To use the Entity API module, you'll need your module to have a dependency in its *mymodule.info* file:

```
dependencies[] = entity
```

With that taken care of, to define an entity type whose machine name is myentity, declare the following function in your *mymodule.module* file:

```php
// Simple internal-use entity.
function mymodule_entity_info() {
  $return = array();

  $return['myentity'] = array(

    // Define basic information.
    'label' => t('Settings for My Module'),
    'plural label' => t('Settings for My Module'),
    'fieldable' => TRUE,

    // Provide information about the database table.
    'base table' => 'mymodule_myentity',
    'entity keys' => array(
      'id' => 'myentity_id',
      'label' => 'title',
    ),

    // Use classes from the Entity API module.
    'entity class' => 'Entity',
    'controller class' => 'EntityAPIController',

    // Have Entity API set up an administrative UI.
    'admin ui' => array(
        'path' => 'admin/myentity',
    ),
    'module' => 'mymodule',
    'access callback' => 'mymodule_myentity_access',

    // For content-type entities only, define the callback that
    // returns the URL for the entity.
    'uri callback' => 'mymodule_myentity_uri',
  );

  return $return;
}

// For content-type entities, return the URI for an entity.
function mymodule_myentity_uri($entity) {
```

```
      return array(
        'path' => 'myentity/' . $entity->myentity_id,
      );
    }
```

Note about the URI callback: if your entity is for settings, you probably just need a way to edit the settings, rather than a dedicated page to display them. So, you probably do not need a URL for each entity (akin to *node/1* for a node entity). In this case, you can leave out the URI callback and the hook_menu() entry defined in a later step.

Further reading and reference:

- "The Basics of Module and Theme Hook Programming" on page 23
- Entity API module: *https://www.drupal.org/project/entity*
- Entity Construction Kit module: *https://www.drupal.org/project/eck*

Step 2: Implement hook_schema()

The next step, for both settings and content entity types, is to implement hook_schema() in your *mymodule.install* file, to set up the database table for storing your entity information. The table name and some of the database field names need to match what you put into your hook_entity_info() implementation, and you'll also want a database field for language (assuming that you want your entity objects to be translatable), and possibly additional database fields to keep track of when entity objects are created and last updated. Here's the schema for the settings entity type example:

```
function mymodule_schema() {
  $schema = array();

  $schema['mymodule_myentity'] = array(
    'description' => 'Storage for myentity entity: settings for mymodule',
    'fields' => array(
      'myentity_id' => array(
        'description' => 'Primary key: settings ID.',
        'type' => 'serial',
        'unsigned' => TRUE,
        'not null' => TRUE,
      ),
      'title' => array(
        'description' => 'Label assigned to this set of settings',
        'type' => 'varchar',
        'length' => 200,
        'default' => '',
      ),
      'language' => array(
        'description' => 'Language of this set of settings',
        'type' => 'varchar',
```

```
        'length' => 12,
        'not null' => TRUE,
        'default' => '',
      ),
      // Consider adding additional fields for time created, time updated.
    ),
    'primary key' => array('myentity_id'),
    'indexes' => array(
      'language' => array('language'),
      // Add indexes for created/updated here too.
    ),
  );

  return $schema;
}
```

Further reading and reference:

- "Setting Up Database Tables: Schema API and hook_update_N()" on page 55

Step 3: Add predefined fields in hook_install()

If you are defining an entity type to use for settings, the next step is to attach fields to your entity bundle to store the settings you need. For a content-type entity, you may want to just let administrators add the fields in the administrative user interface (the Entity API module provides the URLs and screens), in which case you can skip this step. To add fields programmatically, implement hook_install() in your *mymodule.install* file, using Drupal core Field API functions:

```
function mymodule_install() {
  // Create a plain text field for a setting.
  $field = field_create_field(array(
    'field_name' => 'myentity_setting_1',
    'type' => 'text',
    'entity_types' => array('myentity'),
    'locked' => TRUE,
    'translatable' => TRUE,
  ));

  // Attach the field to the entity bundle.
  $instance = field_create_instance(array(
    'field_name' => 'myentity_setting_1',
    'entity_type' => 'myentity',
    'bundle' => 'myentity',
    'label' => t('Setting 1'),
    'description' => t('Help for this setting'),
    'required' => TRUE,
    'widget' => array(
      'type' => 'text_textfield',
    ),
```

```
          'display' => array(
            'default' => array(
              'label' => 'above',
              'type' => 'text_default',
            ),
          ),
        ));

        // Repeat these two function calls for each additional field.
      }
```

Further reading and reference:

- "The Basics of Module and Theme Hook Programming" on page 23

Step 4: Set up display

The next step is to set up your entity type so that its objects can be displayed, which is only necessary for a content-type entity. Given the `mymodule_myentity_uri()` URL callback function that was declared in "Step 1: Implement hook_entity_info()" on page 133, you need to register for the URL it returns and tell Drupal to use the Entity API module's `entity_view()` function to display the entity:

```
function mymodule_menu() {
  $items = array();

  // Register for the URL that mymodule_myentity_uri() returns.
  // The placeholder %entity_object in the URL is handled by the Entity
  // API function entity_object_load().
  $items['myentity/%entity_object'] = array(
    // entity_object_load() needs to know what the entity type is.
    'load arguments' => array('myentity'),

    // Use a callback for the page title, not a static title.
    'title callback' => 'mymodule_myentity_page_title',
    'title arguments' => array(1),

    // Callback to display the entity.
    'page callback' => 'entity_ui_entity_page_view',
    'page arguments' => array(1),

    // Access callback.
    'access callback' => 'mymodule_myentity_access',
    'access arguments' => array('view', array(1)),
  );

  return $items;
}

// Title callback function registered above.
function mymodule_myentity_page_title($entity) {
```

```
    return $entity->title;
  }
```

Further reading and reference:

- "Registering for a URL in Drupal 7" on page 89
- "Autoloading, Arguments, and Placeholders in hook_menu()" on page 90
- "Checking Drupal Permissions" on page 64

Step 5: Set up editing and management

Both settings and content entity types need management pages and forms for creating and editing entity objects. The Entity API module sets these up for you using the information that you provided in your hook_entity_info() implementation (in "Step 1: Implement hook_entity_info()" on page 133). There are several functions that you do need to define, however:

- An access callback (which defines access permissions for your entity type). The function name is provided in your hook_entity_info() and hook_menu() implementations. You'll also need to implement hook_permission() to define permissions.
- A function to generate the entity object editing form, which must be called myentity_form(). A corresponding form-submission handler is also needed. Your form needs to handle editing the title and the language, and then it needs to call field_attach_form() to let the Field module add the other fields to the form.

Here is the code for these functions:

```
// Define the permissions.
function mymodule_permission() {
  return array(
    'view myentity' => array(
      'title' => t('View my entity content'),
    ),
    'administer myentity' => array(
      'title' => t('Administer my entities'),
    ),
  );
}

// Access callback for Entity API.
function mymodule_myentity_access($op, $entity, $account = NULL) {
  // $op is 'view', 'update', 'create', etc.
  // $entity could be NULL (to check access for all entity objects)
  // or it could be a single entity object.
```

```
  // $account is either NULL or a user object.

  // In this simple example, just check permissions for
  // viewing or administering the entity type generically.
  if ($op == 'view') {
    return user_access('view myentity', $account);
  }
  return user_access('administer myentity', $account);
}

// Form-generating function for the editing form.
function myentity_form($form, $form_state, $entity) {
  $form['title'] = array(
    '#title' => t('Title'),
    '#type' => 'textfield',
    '#default_value' => isset($entity->title) ? $entity->title : '',
  );

  // Build language options list.
  $default = language_default();
  $options = array($default->language => $default->name);
  if (module_exists('locale')) {
    $options = array(LANGUAGE_NONE => t('All languages')) +
      locale_language_list('name');
  }

  // Add language selector or value to the form.
  $langcode = isset($entity->language) ? $entity->language : '';
  if (count($options) > 1) {
    $form['language'] = array(
      '#type' => 'select',
      '#title' => t('Language'),
      '#options' => $options,
      '#default_value' => $langcode,
    );
  }
  else {
    $form['language'] = array(
      '#type' => 'value',
      '#value' => $langcode,
    );
  }

  $form['actions'] = array('#type' => 'actions');
  $form['actions']['submit'] = array(
    '#type' => 'submit',
    '#value' => t('Save'),
    '#weight' => 999,
  );

  field_attach_form('myentity', $entity, $form, $form_state, $langcode);
```

```
      return $form;
  }

  // Form submission handler for editing form.
  function myentity_form_submit($form, &$form_state) {
    // Make use of Entity API class.
    $entity = entity_ui_form_submit_build_entity($form, $form_state);
    $entity->save();

    // Redirect to the management page.
    $form_state['redirect'] = 'admin/myentity';
  }
```

Further reading and reference:

- "Checking Drupal Permissions" on page 64
- "Using the Drupal Form API" on page 109

Step 6: Enable your module

If you have followed all of these steps, you should be able to enable your module and see your entity type's administration pages at *example.com/admin/myentity* (as given in the hook_entity_info() implementation). If you had previously installed your module, you'll probably need to uninstall (losing all your data) and then reenable. You may be able to just disable and enable, if you also define an update hook that adds the necessary database tables.

Defining a Content Entity Type in Drupal 8

Entity types in Drupal 8 are a type of plugin, so they use the plugin system described in "Implementing a plugin in a module" on page 33. This section describes how to define a content entity type, and the following section ("Defining a Configuration Entity Type in Drupal 8" on page 149) describes how to define a configuration entity type.

Before you start, you will need to choose a machine name for your entity type, which should be short but unique; in this example, myentity is the machine name. The maximum length for an entity type machine name is 32 characters.

Step 1: Define the entity interface and class

The first steps in defining an entity in Drupal 8 are to define an entity interface and entity class. The interface should define the get* and set* methods for the base properties of your entity (such as getTitle() and setTitle() for the title property), and should extend \Drupal\Core\Entity\ContentEntityInterface. The class should implement your interface and normally extends \Drupal\Core\Entity

\ContentEntityBase; it will need to implement any methods you put on the class, plus `ContentEntityInterface::baseFieldDefinitions()`. The interface should either go in the top-level namespace of your module, or in the `Entity` namespace underneath; the entity class needs to be in the `Entity` namespace and needs to have `\Drupal\Core\Entity\Annotation\ContentEntityType` annotation in its documentation header to be recognized as an entity type definition plugin.

The interface can usually be pretty simple, because normally there are only a few base properties (most of the data goes in fields). Here is an example (minus documentation headers), which goes in *src/Entity/MyEntityInterface.php* under the module directory:

```
namespace Drupal\mymodule\Entity;
use Drupal\Core\Entity\ContentEntityInterface;

interface MyEntityInterface extends ContentEntityInterface {
  public function getTitle();
  public function setTitle($title);
}
```

The class is a bit more complicated, because of the necessary annotation in the documentation header. Here is a fairly minimal example, which goes in *src/Entity/MyEntity.php* under the module directory:

```
namespace Drupal\mymodule\Entity;
use Drupal\mymodule\Entity\MyEntityInterface;
use Drupal\Core\Entity\ContentEntityBase;
use Drupal\Core\Entity\EntityTypeInterface;
use Drupal\Core\Field\BaseFieldDefinition;

/**
 * Represents a MyEntity entity object.
 *
 * @ContentEntityType(
 *   id = "myentity",
 *   label = @Translation("My entity"),
 *   bundle_label = @Translation("My entity subtype"),
 *   fieldable = TRUE,
 *   handlers = {
 *     "view_builder" = "Drupal\Core\Entity\EntityViewBuilder",
 *     "list_builder" = "Drupal\Core\Entity\EntityListBuilder",
 *     "views_data" = "Drupal\mymodule\Entity\MyEntityViewsData",
 *     "form" = {
 *       "default" = "Drupal\mymodule\Entity\MyEntityForm",
 *       "edit" = "Drupal\mymodule\Entity\MyEntityForm",
 *       "delete" = "Drupal\Core\Entity\ContentEntityDeleteForm",
 *     }
 *   },
 *   admin_permission = "administer my entities",
 *   base_table = "myentity",
 *   data_table = "myentity_field_data",
```

```
 *    translatable = TRUE,
 *    entity_keys = {
 *      "id" = "eid",
 *      "bundle" = "subtype",
 *      "label" = "title",
 *      "langcode" = "langcode",
 *      "uuid" = "uuid",
 *    },
 *    links = {
 *      "canonical" = "/myentity/{myentity}",
 *      "delete-form" = "/myentity/{myentity}/delete",
 *      "edit-form" = "/myentity/{myentity}/edit",
 *    },
 *    field_ui_base_route = "entity.myentity_type.edit_form",
 *    bundle_entity_type = "myentity_type",
 * )
 */
class MyEntity extends ContentEntityBase implements MyEntityInterface {

  public function getTitle() {
    return $this->get('title')->value;
  }

  public function setTitle($title) {
    $this->set('title', $title);
    return $this;
  }

  public static function baseFieldDefinitions(EntityTypeInterface $entity_type) {
    // Define base fields for the items in the entity_keys
    // annotation. Note that as this is a static method, you cannot use
    // $this->t() here; use t() for translation instead.
    // Also note that the reason for the redundant descriptions is that
    // Views displays errors if they are missing.
    $fields['eid'] = BaseFieldDefinition::create('integer')
      ->setLabel(t('My entity ID'))
      ->setDescription(t('My entity ID'))
      ->setReadOnly(TRUE)
      ->setSetting('unsigned', TRUE);

    $fields['subtype'] = BaseFieldDefinition::create('entity_reference')
      ->setLabel(t('Subtype'))
      ->setDescription(t('Subtype'))
      ->setSetting('target_type', 'myentity_type');

    // Add a language code field so the entity can be translated.
    $fields['langcode'] = BaseFieldDefinition::create('language')
      ->setLabel(t('Language'))
      ->setDescription(t('Language code'))
      ->setTranslatable(TRUE)
      ->setDisplayOptions('view', array(
        'type' => 'hidden',
```

```
  ))
  ->setDisplayOptions('form', array(
    'type' => 'language_select',
    'weight' => 2,
  ));

// The title field is the only editable field in the base
// data. Set it up to be configurable in Manage Form Display
// and Manage Display.
$fields['title'] = BaseFieldDefinition::create('string')
  ->setLabel(t('Title'))
  ->setDescription(t('Title'))
  ->setTranslatable(TRUE)
  ->setRequired(TRUE)
  ->setDisplayOptions('view', array(
      'label' => 'hidden',
      'type' => 'string',
      'weight' => 5,
    ))
  ->setDisplayConfigurable('view', TRUE)
  ->setDisplayOptions('form', array(
      'type' => 'string_textfield',
      'weight' => 5,
    ))
  ->setDisplayConfigurable('form', TRUE);

$fields['uuid'] = BaseFieldDefinition::create('uuid')
  ->setLabel(t('UUID'))
  ->setDescription(t('Universally Unique ID'))
  ->setReadOnly(TRUE);

return $fields;
  }
}
```

A few notes on the annotation lines:

- The first few lines of the annotation give the ID you chose, whether the entity is fieldable or not, and a human-readable label for the entity and its bundles. If your entity does not use bundles, leave out everything in this example that refers to them.

- The permission defined in the admin_permission annotation must be defined in your *mymodule.permissions.yml* file. See "Drupal core's main permission system" on page 64.

- The base_table and entity_keys annotation sections define the database table and database table fields for the basic entity data. data_table is used for translations. You can also indicate revision_table if your entity type should store revisions, in which case you should also add a revision key to the entity_keys section. Assuming your entity uses the default entity storage controller as your entity storage mechanism, these tables will be automatically set up for you.

- If your entity supports bundles, each bundle definition is a configuration entity. So, you'll need to define a configuration entity type for your bundles and put its machine name (ID) in the `bundle_entity_type` annotation. To find out how to do this, see "Defining a Configuration Entity Type in Drupal 8" on page 149, which uses this exact example.

- "Implementing a plugin in a module" on page 33 has more information about annotations in general.

The rest of the steps in the entity definition process create the classes that are referred to in the annotation header of your entity class, and set up other necessary data, functions, and so on.

Step 2: Define handlers

The `handlers` section of the annotation lists the classes that govern storage, access, and other operations on your entity objects. Drupal provides default handlers for most of the operations; you can override the defaults by adding entries to this part of the annotation. You'll need to define the classes for each specific handler you designate; most entities, like this example, will at least need custom edit and delete confirm forms.

The edit form should extend `\Drupal\Core\Entity\ContentEntityForm`. In this example, the annotation gives the class as `\Drupal\mymodule\Entity\MyEntityForm`, so it needs to go into the *src/Entity/MyEntityForm.php* file under the main module directory. Typically, entity forms will need to override the `form()`, `save()`, and possibly `validateForm()` methods; you may also need to override other methods for special cases, such as `buildEntity()` if taking form values and making an entity is special. Here's a basic example (look for Drupal core classes that extend `Content EntityForm` for others); in this case, the base method for `form()` is sufficient, as it will take care of the title and all of the added fields:

```
namespace Drupal\mymodule\Entity;
use Drupal\Core\Entity\ContentEntityForm;
use Drupal\Core\Form\FormStateInterface;
use Drupal\Core\Url;

class MyEntityForm extends ContentEntityForm {

  public function save(array $form, FormStateInterface $form_state) {
    $entity = $this->entity;
    $entity->save();
    // You could do some logging here, set a message, and so on.

    // Redirect to the entity display page.
```

```
    $form_state->setRedirect('entity.myentity.canonical',
        array('myentity' => $entity->id( )));
    }
}
```

The delete form should confirm that the user wants to delete the entity object. The default class of \Drupal\Core\Entity\ContentEntityDeleteForm is sufficient for this entity; if not, you could extend this class (for instance, to override the confirmation message).

This entity type is set up to use the default \Drupal\Core\Entity\EntityView Builder to build render arrays for viewing entities with view modes. This relies on the existence of a theme hook named 'myentity', which should render the base properties of the entity. So, you'll need to add this to the hook_theme() implementation, the mymodule_theme() function in *mymodule.module*:

```
function mymodule_theme($existing, $type, $theme, $path) {
  return array(
    'myentity' => array(
      'render element' => 'elements',
      'template' => 'myentity',
    ),
  );
}
```

Then you'll also need to create the *templates/myentity.html.twig* file to do the rendering:

```
<article{{ attributes }}>
  {% if not page %}
    <h2{{ title_attributes }}>
      <a href="{{ url }}" rel="bookmark">{{ title }}</a>
    </h2>
  {% endif %}

  <div {{ content_attributes }}>
    {{ content }}
  </div>
</article>
```

And you'll need a preprocess function to set up the template variables, which goes into the *mymodule.module* file:

```
use Drupal\Core\Render\Element;
use Drupal\Core\Url;

function template_preprocess_myentity(&$variables) {
  $variables['view_mode'] = $variables['elements']['#view_mode'];
  $entity = $variables['elements']['#myentity'];
  $variables['entity'] = $entity;
  $variables['title'] = $variables['entity']->getTitle();
```

```
    // See if the entity is being viewed on its own page.
    $route_match = \Drupal::routeMatch();
    $page = FALSE;
    if ($variables['view_mode'] == 'full' &&
        $route_match->getRouteName() == 'entity.myentity.canonical') {
      $page_entity = $route_match->getParameter('myentity');
      if ($page_entity && $page_entity->id() == $entity->id()) {
        $page = TRUE;
      }
    }
    $variables['page'] = $page;

    // Set up content variable for templates.
    $variables += array('content' => array());
    foreach (Element::children($variables['elements']) as $key) {
      $variables['content'][$key] = $variables['elements'][$key];
    }

    // Set up attributes.
    $variables['attributes']['class'][] = 'myentity';
}
```

The `list_builder` and `views_data` handlers are for Views integration, which is covered in "Step 4: Add Views integration" on page 147.

Further reading and reference:

- "Basic Form Generation and Processing in Drupal 8" on page 114
- "Creating Confirmation Forms" on page 116
- "Making Your Module Output Themeable" on page 25

Step 3: Set up routing and links

The `links` annotation section lists the URL paths for the basic operations; the corresponding routes need to have names like `entity.myentity.canonical` and need to be defined in your *mymodule.routing.yml* file. If your entity can be displayed on its own page, you'll need to define the `canonical` link to be the viewing page; otherwise, your canonical link should probably be the edit page. Most content entities also need `delete-form` and `edit-form` links. If your entity type is fieldable, then you also need to define the `field_ui_base_route` annotation property (outside of the links section), because this route is used by the Field UI module to set up the management pages for fields, forms, and display modes. For nonbundle entities, it should be a page for the settings for the entity type; for entities with bundles, it should be the page where you edit the bundle. This example uses bundles, so the route it uses is defined later, as part of defining the bundle configuration entity type.

Given the annotation in this entity example, the *mymodule.routing.yml* file needs to contain:

```
entity.myentity.canonical:
  path: '/myentity/{myentity}'
  defaults:
    _entity_view: 'myentity.full'
  requirements:
    _entity_access: 'myentity.view'

entity.myentity.delete_form:
  path: '/myentity/{myentity}/delete'
  defaults:
    _entity_form: 'myentity.delete'
    _title: 'Delete'
  requirements:
    _entity_access: 'myentity.delete'

entity.myentity.edit_form:
  path: '/myentity/{myentity}/edit'
  defaults:
    _entity_form: 'myentity.edit'
    _title: 'Edit my entity'
  requirements:
    _entity_access: 'myentity.edit'
```

 Instead of defining routes as shown here in your *mymodule.routing.yml* file, you can use an entity route provider class, which covers the canonical, edit, and delete routes. The API for this is still in flux as of September 2015, so it is not described here. Check the "Entity API" topic on *https://api.drupal.org* to learn more.

The classes for the entity forms have already been defined, and this example uses the default entity viewer for the entity page, with a placeholder that loads the entity. You could also override the default class to define your own view handler.

For most entities, if you are on the entity viewing page, you would want to see a tab or link to edit the entity. This can be accomplished via a local task set, which goes into the *mymodule.links.task.yml* file:

```
entity.myentity.canonical:
  title: 'View'
  route_name: entity.myentity.canonical
  base_route: entity.myentity.canonical

entity.myentity.edit_form:
  title: 'Edit'
  route_name: entity.myentity.edit_form
  base_route: entity.myentity.canonical
```

You'll also need to think about the process for adding a new entity of this type. For instance, to add a node, you need to choose which type (bundle) of node you're adding, and then visit *example.com/node/add/thetypename*. Taxonomy terms work in a similar way, with an add page that depends on the vocabulary (bundle). But you don't add a comment by bundle—comments are added to a specific entity object. For this example, we'll make it so that you add a new entity object from the entity subtype (bundle) management page, so that will be explained in conjunction with defining the bundle configuration entity type, in "Defining a Configuration Entity Type in Drupal 8" on page 149.

Further reading and reference:

- "Registering for a URL in Drupal 8" on page 92
- Parameter upcasting in routes: *http://bit.ly/parameter_upcasting*
- "Providing Administrative Links" on page 95

Step 4: Add Views integration

Your content entity type will probably also need to have an administrative page, which would presumably list existing entities with edit and delete links, and allow you to add new entities. The best way to create an administrative page is by providing a default view. In order to do that, you'll need to provide Views integration for your entity, as well as a list builder.

Both the Views integration and the list builder are specified in the `handlers` section of your entity annotation, as `views_data` and `list_builder`. The entity here uses the default entity list builder class but has its own views data class `\Drupal\mymodule\Entity\MyEntityViewsData`. This class provides the same kind of output as `hook_views_data()` (see "Providing a New Views Data Source" on page 175), but most of it is provided in an automated way by the base class. In this case, the class goes in *src/Entity/MyEntityViewsData.php* under the module directory:

```
namespace Drupal\mymodule\Entity;
use Drupal\views\EntityViewsData;

class MyEntityViewsData extends EntityViewsData {
  public function getViewsData() {
    // Start with the Views information provided by the base class.
    $data = parent::getViewsData();

    // Override a few things...

    // Define a wizard.
    $data['myentity_field_data']['table']['wizard_id'] = 'myentity';

    // You could also override labels or put in a custom field
```

```
    // or filter handler.

    return $data;
  }
}
```

This class, in turn, refers to a wizard plugin, which is a plugin class that enables a user to go to the "Add new view" page at *admin/structure/views/add* and choose your entity from the list to create a new view. The preceding code tells Views that the plugin ID for this wizard is `myentity`. For Views to find the plugin, it needs to be in the *src/Plugins/views/wizard* directory (and corresponding namespace). Let's call the class `MyEntityViewsWizard` and just accept the default behavior of a Views wizard:

```
namespace Drupal\mymodule\Plugin\views\wizard;

use Drupal\Core\Form\FormStateInterface;
use Drupal\views\Plugin\views\wizard\WizardPluginBase;

/**
 * Provides a views wizard for My Entity entities.
 *
 * @ViewsWizard(
 *   id = "myentity",
 *   base_table = "myentity_field_data",
 *   title = @Translation("My Entity")
 * )
 */
class MyEntityViewsWizard extends WizardPluginBase {
}
```

This is sufficient to provide Views integration for the entity. So, to provide an administrative interface for managing the My Entity content, you'd also need to:

- Define a view using the Views user interface. It should include exposed filters; sorting (usually via table headers); and links to add, edit, and delete your entities.

- Export the view as a YAML configuration file. Edit the file manually and remove the UUID line, because the export will contain a UUID, but supplied configuration shouldn't. Place the configuration file in your module's *config/install* or *config/optional* directory. See "Configuration file format and schema in Drupal 8" on page 42.

Note that if the only available management page for your entity uses Views, you might want to make the Views module a dependency of your module, because if Views is not enabled, users will not be able to manage their entities.

Step 5: Enable your module

If you are using bundles, your content entity type will not work until you've also defined the configuration entity type for the bundle (see "Defining a Configuration Entity Type in Drupal 8" on page 149).

If you are not using bundles, enable your module and the entity type should be defined. If your module is already enabled, you should be able to get by with a container rebuild (see "Rebuilding the container" on page 38), but you may need to uninstall your module and reinstall it. You should probably test your entity type module in a test installation of Drupal until you've verified that it's working, though, or at least make frequent database backups, because you may get Drupal into an unrecoverable state during the debugging phase.

Defining a Configuration Entity Type in Drupal 8

Defining a configuration entity type is somewhat similar to defining a content entity type (described in the previous section, "Defining a Content Entity Type in Drupal 8" on page 139), but the process has several differences. The basic steps are listed in this section; as an example, we'll define the content entity bundle configuration entity needed for the content entity type defined "Defining a Content Entity Type in Drupal 8" on page 139.

If you need to define a configuration entity for a generic configuration purpose rather than as a bundle for a content entity, a good example to look at is the entity for date format configuration in the Drupal core DateTime library. Accordingly, this section also points out which classes and files are used to define this entity, so that you can follow along with that example as well.

Before you start, you will need to choose a machine name for your configuration entity, and a configuration prefix for configuration data storage. The configuration prefix defaults to `$module_name.$machine_name`, or `core.$machine_name` for entities defined in Drupal core outside of modules, but you can shorten the suffix (after the module name) if you want, by adding `config_prefix` to the annotation to your configuration entity class header. For our bundle example, the machine name `myentity_type` was specified in the content entity type annotation, and we'll leave the configuration prefix as `mymodule.myentity_type`. For the date format entity, the machine name is `date_format` and the prefix is `core.date_format`.

The maximum length for an entity type machine name or configuration prefix is 32 characters.

Further reading and reference:

- *http://bit.ly/config_entitites* has some more documentation about configuration entities.

Step 1: Define the configuration schema

The first step in defining a configuration entity type is to define a configuration schema for `mymodule.myentity_type.*` in the *config/schema/mymodule.schema.yml* file that defines the fields for your configuration data. For the date format example, see the `core.date_format` section of *core/config/schema/core.data_types.schema.yml*; for our bundle example:

```
mymodule.myentity_type.*:
  type: config_entity
  label: 'My entity subtype'
  mapping:
    id:
      type: string
      label: 'Machine-readable name'
    label:
      type: label
      label: 'Name'
    description:
      type: text
      label: 'Description'
    settings:
      label: 'Settings'
      type: mymodule.settings.myentity

mymodule.settings.myentity:
  type: mapping
  label: 'My entity subtype settings'
  mapping:
    default_status:
      type: boolean
      label: 'Published by default'
```

Note that the `'Published by default'` setting is just for illustration; the content entity does not actually have a `'published'` property.

Further reading and reference:

- "Configuration file format and schema in Drupal 8" on page 42

Step 2: Define the entity interface and class

The next step is to define an entity interface and class for your configuration entity. The interface should extend `\Drupal\Core\Config\Entity\ConfigEntityInterface` and may define a few additional methods that your configuration entities will need. In the date format example, this interface is `\Drupal\Core\Datetime\DateFormat Interface`; in our bundle example, it's `\Drupal\mymodule\Entity\MyEntityType Interface`, which goes in the *src/Entity/MyEntityTypeInterface.php* file under the module directory:

```
namespace Drupal\mymodule\Entity;
use Drupal\Core\Config\Entity\ConfigEntityInterface;

interface MyEntityTypeInterface extends ConfigEntityInterface {
  public function getDescription();
}
```

Note that even if you do not need to define additional methods, it is still a good idea to define an interface, so that you can declare objects to be of that type (leading to better self-documenting code).

The entity class should extend `\Drupal\Core\Config\Entity\ConfigEntityBase` and implement your entity interface. For a configuration entity being used as an entity bundle, there is another base class to use: `Drupal\Core\Config\Entity\Con figEntityBundleBase`, which contains some additional helper code. Whichever base class is used, your class also needs to be annotated with `\Drupal\Core\Entity\Anno tation\ConfigEntityType` annotation in its documentation header. In the date format example, this class is `\Drupal\Core\Datetime\Entity\DateFormat`; in our bundle example, the class is `\Drupal\mymodule\Entity\MyEntityType`, which goes in the *src/Entity/MyEntityType.php* file under the module directory:

```
namespace Drupal\mymodule\Entity;

use Drupal\Core\Config\ConfigException;
use Drupal\Core\Config\Entity\ConfigEntityBundleBase;
use Drupal\Core\Entity\EntityStorageInterface;
use Drupal\mymodule\Entity\MyEntityTypeInterface;

/**
 * Defines the My Entity bundle configuration entity.
 *
 * @ConfigEntityType(
 *   id = "myentity_type",
 *   label = @Translation("My entity subtype"),
 *   handlers = {
 *     "form" = {
 *       "add" = "Drupal\mymodule\Entity\MyEntityTypeForm",
 *       "edit" = "Drupal\mymodule\Entity\MyEntityTypeForm",
 *       "delete" = "Drupal\mymodule\Entity\MyEntityTypeDeleteForm",
```

```
 *     },
 *       "list_builder" = "Drupal\mymodule\Entity\MyEntityTypeListBuilder",
 *     },
 *     admin_permission = "administer my entities",
 *     bundle_of = "myentity",
 *     entity_keys = {
 *       "id" = "id",
 *       "label" = "label",
 *     },
 *     links = {
 *       "add-form" = "/admin/structure/myentity_type/add",
 *       "edit-form" = "/admin/structure/myentity_type/manage/{myentity_type}",
 *       "delete-form" = "/admin/structure/myentity_type/delete/{myentity_type}",
 *     }
 * )
 */
class MyEntityType extends ConfigEntityBundleBase implements MyEntityTypeInterface {
  // Machine name or ID of the entity bundle.
  public $id;

  // Human-readable name of the entity bundle.
  public $label;

  // Description of the entity bundle.
  public $description;

  // Settings for the entity bundle.
  public $settings = array();

  public function getDescription() {
    return $this->description;
  }

  public function preSave(EntityStorageInterface $storage) {
    parent::preSave($storage);

   if (!$this->isNew() && ($this->getOriginalId() != $this->id())) {
      throw new ConfigException('Cannot change machine name');
    }
  }
}
```

A few notes on the annotation lines:

- The first few lines of the annotation give the ID you chose and a human-readable label for the entity.

- For some configuration entities, you will need to define permissions for administering your entity in your *mymodule.permissions.yml* file. This permission is referenced in the annotation on your entity class; you can also use an existing permission from another module (if so, make sure that this module is listed as a dependency of your module).

- The `bundle_of` annotation gives the machine name of the entity that this entity is a bundle type for. Omit for generic configuration entities.

- The `entity_keys` annotation section lists the mapping between the entity ID and label to the configuration schema fields that you've defined.

- The rest of the annotation is discussed in the following steps.

- "Implementing a plugin in a module" on page 33 has more information about annotations.

Step 3: Define handlers

The `handlers` section of the annotation lists classes that handle storage, access, and other operations on your entity objects. Drupal provides default handler classes for most of the operations; you can override the defaults by adding entries to this list. For configuration entities, you will need to define the form for adding and editing, the confirmation form for deleting, and the list builder, which is used to build an administrative screen to manage your configuration items.

The editing form should extend `\Drupal\Core\Entity\EntityForm`; usually, the only methods you need to override are `form()`, `save()`, and possibly `validateForm()`. In the date format example, this class is `\Drupal\system\Form\DateFormatEditForm`; in our bundle example, the class is given in the annotation as `\Drupal\mymodule\Entity\MyEntityTypeForm`, so it needs to go in file *src/Entity/MyEntityType-Form.php* under the main module directory:

```
namespace Drupal\mymodule\Entity;
use Drupal\Core\Entity\EntityForm;
use Drupal\Core\Form\FormStateInterface;
use Drupal\Core\Url;

class MyEntityTypeForm extends EntityForm {
  public function form(array $form, FormStateInterface $form_state) {
    $form = parent::form($form, $form_state);

    $form['id'] = array(
      '#title' => $this->t('Machine-readable name'),
      '#type' => 'textfield',
      '#required' => TRUE,
    );

    // If we are editing an existing entity, show the current ID and
    // do not allow it to be changed.
    if ($this->entity->id()) {
      $form['id']['#default_value'] = $this->entity->id();
```

```
      $form['id']['#disabled'] = TRUE;
    }

    $form['label'] = array(
      '#title' => $this->t('Label'),
      '#type' => 'textfield',
      '#default_value' => $this->entity->label,
    );

    $form['description'] = array(
      '#title' => $this->t('Description'),
      '#type' => 'textfield',
      '#default_value' => $this->entity->description,
    );

    $form['settings'] = array(
      '#type' => 'details',
      '#title' => t('Settings'),
      '#open' => TRUE,
    );

    $settings = $this->entity->settings;
    $form['settings']['default_status'] = array(
      '#title' => t('Published by default'),
      '#type' => 'checkbox',
    );
    if (isset($settings['default_status']) && $settings['default_status']) {
      $form['settings']['default_status']['#default_value'] = TRUE;
    }

    return $form;
  }

  public function validateForm(array &$form, FormStateInterface $form_state) {
    parent::validateForm($form, $form_state);

    $values = $form_state->getValues();

    // Require non-empty ID.
    $id = trim($values['id']);
    if (empty($id)) {
      $form_state->setErrorByName('id', $this->t('Subtype names must not be empty'));
    }
  }

  public function save(array $form, FormStateInterface $form_state) {
    $type = $this->entity;
    $type->save();
    // You could do some logging here, set a message, and so on.

    // Redirect to admin page.
    $form_state->setRedirect(new Url('mymodule.my_entity_type_list'));
```

```
      }
    }
```

The delete form should confirm that the user wants to delete the configuration item and should extend \Drupal\Core\Entity\EntityConfirmFormBase. For this class, you will need to specify (in methods) the text for the question to ask the user, what to do if delete is confirmed, and the URL (route) to go to if the action is canceled. In the date format example, this class is \Drupal\system\Form\DateFormatDeleteForm.

Our example is a bit more complicated: you should not delete an entity bundle if there would be any corresponding entity objects left over. Some entity types (such as node—see \Drupal\node\Form\NodeTypeDeleteConfirm) handle this by disallowing bundle deletion if entities exist of that type, and others delete the corresponding entities (of course, warning the user). For this example, in order to illustrate how to do it, we'll take the latter tactic and delete the entities. The delete form class is given in the annotation as \Drupal\mymodule\Entity\MyEntityTypeDeleteForm, and it needs to go in the *src/Entity/MyEntityTypeDeleteForm.php* file under the main module directory:

```
namespace Drupal\mymodule\Entity;

use Drupal\Core\Entity\EntityConfirmFormBase;
use Drupal\Core\Entity\EntityManagerInterface;
use Drupal\Core\Entity\Query\QueryFactory;
use Drupal\Core\Form\FormStateInterface;
use Drupal\Core\Url;
use Symfony\Component\DependencyInjection\ContainerInterface;

class MyEntityTypeDeleteForm extends EntityConfirmFormBase {
  protected $manager;
  protected $queryFactory;

  public function __construct(QueryFactory $query_factory,
    EntityManagerInterface $manager) {
    $this->queryFactory = $query_factory;
    $this->manager = $manager;
  }

  public static function create(ContainerInterface $container) {
    return new static(
      $container->get('entity.query'),
      $container->get('entity.manager')
    );
  }

  public function getQuestion() {
    return $this->t('Are you sure you want to delete %label?',
      array('%label' => $this->entity->label()));
  }
```

```
  public function getDescription() {
    return $this->t('All entities of this type will also be deleted!');
  }

  public function getCancelUrl() {
    return new Url('mymodule.myentity_type.list');
  }

  public function submitForm(array &$form, FormStateInterface $form_state) {

    // Find all the entities of this type, using an entity query.
    $query = $this->queryFactory->get('myentity');
    $query->condition('subtype', $this->entity->id());
    $ids = $query->execute();

    // Delete the found entities, using the storage handler.
    // You may actually need to use a batch here, if there could be
    // many entities.
    $storage = $this->manager->getStorage('myentity');
    $entities = $storage->loadMultiple($ids);
    $storage->delete($entities);

    // Delete the bundle entity itself.
    $this->entity->delete();

    $form_state->setRedirectUrl($this->getCancelUrl());
  }
}
```

The list builder class makes an administration overview page for managing your configuration data; it should usually extend \Drupal\Core\Config\Entity\ConfigEntityListBuilder. In the date format example, this class is \Drupal\system\DateFormatListBuilder; in our bundle example, the annotation gives the class name as \Drupal\mymodule\Entity\MyEntityTypeListBuilder, so it needs to go in the *src/Entity/MyEntityTypeListBuilder.php* file under the main module directory:

```
namespace Drupal\mymodule\Entity;

use Drupal\Core\Config\Entity\ConfigEntityListBuilder;
use Drupal\Core\Entity\EntityInterface;
use Drupal\Component\Utility\Xss;

class MyEntityTypeListBuilder extends ConfigEntityListBuilder {

  public function buildHeader() {
    $header['label'] = $this->t('Label');

    $header['description'] = array(
      'data' => $this->t('Description'),
    );

    return $header + parent::buildHeader();
```

```
      }

      public function buildRow(EntityInterface $entity) {
        $row['label'] = array(
          'data' => $this->getLabel($entity),
        );

        $row['description'] = Xss::filterAdmin($entity->description);

        return $row + parent::buildRow($entity);
      }
    }
```

Further reading and reference:

- "Basic Form Generation and Processing in Drupal 8" on page 114
- "Creating Confirmation Forms" on page 116
- "Querying and Loading Entities in Drupal 8" on page 160

Step 4: Define routing and route controllers

Finally, in your module's routing file, you will need to define administrative routes for managing your configuration entity: for the paths in the links annotation and various classes. You'll also probably want to add an administrative menu entry for your overview page, so users will be able to find it. In the date format example, the administrative routes are defined in *core/modules/system/system.routing.yml*, the menu entry is in *core/modules/system/system.links.menu.yml*, and there are local actions and tasks defined in *core/modules/system/system.links.action.yml* and *core/modules/system/system.links.task.yml*, respectively.

For the bundle example, the following routes go into the *mymodule.routing.yml* file for the administrative actions on the entity subtypes:

```
mymodule.myentity_type.list:
  path: '/admin/structure/myentity_type'
  defaults:
    _entity_list: 'myentity_type'
    _title: 'My entity subtypes'
  requirements:
    _permission: 'administer my entities'

entity.myentity_type.add_form:
  path: '/admin/structure/myentity_type/add'
  defaults:
    _entity_form: 'myentity_type.add'
    _title: 'Add my entity subtype'
  requirements:
    _entity_create_access: 'myentity_type'
```

```
entity.myentity_type.edit_form:
  path: '/admin/structure/myentity_type/manage/{myentity_type}'
  defaults:
    _entity_form: 'myentity_type.edit'
    _title: 'Edit my entity subtype'
  requirements:
    _entity_access: 'myentity_type.edit'

entity.myentity_type.delete_form:
  path: '/admin/structure/myentity_type/delete/{myentity_type}'
  defaults:
    _entity_form: 'myentity_type.delete'
    _title: 'Delete my entity subtype'
  requirements:
    _entity_access: 'myentity_type.delete'
```

 Instead of defining routes as shown here in your *mymodule.routing.yml* file, you can use an entity route provider class, which covers the canonical, edit, and delete routes. The API for this is still in flux as of September 2015, so it is not described here. Check the "Entity API" topic on *https://api.drupal.org* to learn more.

Also, this menu link entry goes into *mymodule.links.menu.yml*, to make the administration page visible in the Structure administrative section:

```
mymodule.myentity_type.list:
  title: My entity subtypes
  description: Manage my entity subtypes and their fields, display, etc.
  route_name: mymodule.myentity_type.list
  parent: system.admin_structure
```

In order to make an Add link visible on the list page, the following goes into the *mymodule.links.action.yml* file:

```
entity.myentity_type.add_form:
  route_name: entity.myentity_type.add_form
  title: 'Add my entity subtype'
  appears_on:
    - mymodule.myentity_type.list
```

The Field UI module makes a set of local tasks for managing fields, view modes, and form modes on fieldable entities. In order to make the entity subtype editing form part of this set of tasks, the following goes into the *mymodule.links.task.yml* file:

```
entity.myentity_type.edit_form:
  title: 'Edit'
  route_name: entity.myentity_type.edit_form
  base_route: entity.myentity_type.edit_form
```

And finally, during definition of the content entity, we decided that we'd handle adding new content entity objects from the entity subtype bundle management page.

So what we want to happen is that once you have an entity subtype defined, one of the actions available to you (besides Edit, Delete, Manage fields, etc.) would be to add a new entity object.

To accomplish this, we need this route in the *mymodule.routing.yml* file:

```
mymodule.myentity.add:
  path: '/myentity/add/{myentity_type}'
  defaults:
    _controller: '\Drupal\mymodule\Controller\MyUrlController::addEntityPage'
    _title: 'Add new my entity'
  requirements:
    _entity_create_access: 'myentity'
```

We also need to define the controller method to put up the page, which goes into *src/Controller/MyUrlController.php*:

```
namespace Drupal\mymodule\Controller;
use Drupal\mymodule\Entity\MyEntityTypeInterface;

class MyUrlController extends ControllerBase {
  public function addEntityPage(MyEntityTypeInterface $type) {
    // Create a stub entity of this type.
    $entity = $this->entityManager()
      ->getStorage('myentity')
      ->create(array('subtype' => $type->id()));

    // You might want to set other values on the stub entity.

    // Return the entity editing form for the stub entity.
    return $this->entityFormBuilder()->getForm($entity);
  }
}
```

To make this appear in the operations list for the entity subtype, we need to override the getDefaultOperations() method in the MyEntityListBuilder list builder class defined earlier and add a new use statement at the top:

```
// At the top.
use Drupal\Core\Url;

// New method.
public function getDefaultOperations(EntityInterface $entity) {
  $operations = parent::getDefaultOperations($entity);

  // Add an operation for adding a new entity object of this type.
  $url = new Url('mymodule.myentity.add',
    array('myentity_type' => $entity->id()));

  $operations['add_new'] = array(
    'title' => $this->t('Add new My Entity'),
    'weight' => 11,
    'url' => $url,
```

```
    );

    return $operations;
}
```

Further reading and reference:

- "Registering for a URL in Drupal 8" on page 92
- "Providing Administrative Links" on page 95

Step 5: Enable your module

Once you have all of these files created and code written, enable your module and your entity type should be defined. If your module is already enabled, you may be able to get by with a container rebuild (see "Rebuilding the container" on page 38), but you may need to uninstall your module and reinstall it. You should probably test your entity type module in a test installation of Drupal until you've verified that it's working, though, or at least make frequent database backups, because you may get Drupal into an unrecoverable state during the debugging phase.

Querying and Loading Entities in Drupal 8

Although you can technically use the basic Database API described in "Querying the Database with the Database API" on page 58 to query entities—or, worse yet, you could use the base PHP functions for MySQL queries—in Drupal 8 this is strongly discouraged. The reason is that content entity storage is a service in Drupal 8, to allow sites (in principle, anyway) to use alternative storage mechanisms, such as MongoDB or other non-SQL methods, to store entities. So although the default content entity storage is in the main Drupal database, it is a good idea to use entity queries to query entities, rather than the basic Database API.

Entity queries are objects that implement \Drupal\Core\Entity\Query\QueryInter face (for regular queries), or \Drupal\Core\Entity\Query\QueryAggregateInter face (for aggregate queries). You can retrieve the appropriate query object from the entity.query service, as follows:

```
// Code without dependency injection or $container variable:
$query = \Drupal::entityQuery('myentity');
$query = \Drupal::entityQueryAggregate('myentity');

// Using dependency injection or a $container variable in a class:
$query_service = $container->get('entity.query');
$query = $query_service->get('myentity');
$query = $query_service->getAggregate('myentity');
```

Once you have a query object, you can use the `condition()` method to add field or base data conditions, and then execute the query. For example, to find all the entities of a given bundle:

```
// Generic entities with 'bundle' property:
$query->condition('bundle', 'mybundle');
// Node entities:
$query->condition('type', 'mytype');
$ids = $query->execute();
```

The result of a query will be a list of the matching entity IDs. To load them, you should use the entity storage manager, which is an object that implements `\Drupal\Core\Entity\EntityStorageInterface`, which you can retrieve from the `entity.manager` service:

```
// Code without dependency injection or $container variable:
$storage = \Drupal::entityManager()->getStorage('myentity');
// Dependency injection or $container variable:
$storage = $container->get('entity.manager')->getStorage('myentity');

// Load entities:
$entities = $storage->loadMultiple($ids);
```

The result will be an array of loaded entity objects, keyed by the entity IDs.

Further reading and reference:

- "Drupal 8 Services and Dependency Injection" on page 35

Defining a Field Type

If you need to attach data to nodes or other entity types, you need to find a field type that stores this type of data. Between Drupal core and contributed modules, there are field types available for most of the common use cases for fielded content (plain text, numbers, formatted text, dates, images, media attachments, etc.), so if you are building a website, and you need to store a particular type of data that is not covered by the fields in Drupal core, start by searching contributed modules for a field type that will suit your needs.

Keep in mind that the field type only defines the stored *data*, while the formatter defines the display of the data and the widget defines the method for data input. So instead of defining a field, you may only need a custom widget or formatter for your use case. Here are several examples:

- You need to store plain text data, based on clicking in a region on an image or using a Flash-based custom input method. For this use case, use a core Text field for storage, and create a custom widget for data input.

- You need to select one of several predefined choices on input, and display a predefined icon or canned text on output based on that choice. For this use case, use a core Number field for storage, and a core Select widget for input (with text labels; you could also use a core Text field for storage). Create a custom formatter for display.

- You are creating a website that displays company profiles, using a Company node content type. For each company content item, you need to attach several office locations. For this use case, use the contributed Geofield, Location, Address Field, or another geographical information field module rather than defining your own custom field (try module category "Location" to find more).

- For this same Company content type, you need several related fields to be grouped together on input and display; for instance, you might want to group the company size, annual revenue, and other similar fields together under Statistics. For this use case, use the Field Group contributed module to group the fields rather than creating a custom field type module.

- For this same Company content type, you need to keep track of staff people, where each staff person has a profile with several fields. For this use case, create a separate Staff node content type, and use the contributed Entity Reference or Relation module to relate staff people to companies or companies to staff people; the Entity Reference field is included in Drupal core version 8. Or, use the Field Collection contributed module to create a staff field collection that is attached to the Company content type.

- You have a field collection use case similar to the Staff of Company example, but you feel that it is general enough that many other websites would want to use this same field collection. In this case, it may make sense to create a custom field module and contribute it to *drupal.org* so that others can use it. Alternatively, you could use a the Field Collection contributed module, and export your collection configuration using the Features module (Drupal 7) or Drupal core configuration export (Drupal 8).

See "Finding Drupal add-ons" on page 4 for hints on locating contributed modules. Note that some of the modules mentioned here may not yet be available for Drupal 8.

The remainder of this section describes how to define a new field type, if you've decided that this is what you need. Widgets and formatters are covered in "Programming with Field Widgets" on page 164 and "Programming with Field Formatters" on page 168, respectively.

Defining a field type in Drupal 7

Assuming that you have decided you need a custom field module, here is an overview of how to define a field type in Drupal 7:

1. Implement `hook_field_info()` in your *mymodule.module* file to provide basic information about your field type (such as the label used to select it when attaching a field to an entity bundle in the administrative user interface).

2. Implement `hook_field_schema()` in your *mymodule.install* file to provide information about the data stored in your field. This defines database fields in a way similar to `hook_schema()`, but it is not exactly the same.

3. Set up a widget for editing the field, and a formatter for displaying it (see the following sections).

There are many fields defined by Drupal core and contributed modules, so rather than providing another programming example here, I'll just suggest that you use one of the following as a starting point:

- A Drupal core field module (Image, File, Text, List, Number, or Taxonomy).
- The documentation for the two field hooks. These are part of Drupal core, in the *modules/field/field.api.php* file (or look them up on *https://api.drupal.org*).
- Date, Link, or another contributed field module (search modules for category "Fields").
- The Field example in Examples for Developers (*https://www.drupal.org/project/examples*), which has some extra documentation explaining what is going on.

Further reading and reference:

- "The Basics of Module and Theme Hook Programming" on page 23
- "Finding Drupal add-ons" on page 4

Defining a field type in Drupal 8

In Drupal 8, field types are plugins. So, to define one in a module, you need to:

- Define a class in the `Plugin\Field\FieldType` namespace under your module's namespace, therefore located in the *src/Plugin/Field/FieldType* directory. The class needs to implement `\Drupal\Core\Field\FieldItemInterface`, and typically extends `\Drupal\Core\Field\FieldItemBase`. You'll usually just need to define methods `propertyDefinitions()` and `schema()`.
- Annotate it with `\Drupal\Core\Field\Annotation\FieldType` annotation.

See "The Basics of Drupal 8 Plugin Programming" on page 28 for a more detailed overview of the plugin system.

There are many good examples in Drupal core of field types, and they're fairly simple to do, so I have not provided another one here. You can find them listed on the Field-Type annotation class page on *https://api.drupal.org*.

Programming with Field Widgets

There are several reasons that you may need to do some programming with field widgets:

- If you have defined your own custom field type, you will need to define a widget for entering data for that field or repurpose an existing widget for use on your field.
- You may need to define a custom input method for an existing field type.
- You may be want to repurpose an existing widget for use on a different field type.

This section covers both how to define a new widget and how to repurpose an existing widget.

Defining a field widget in Drupal 7

To define a field widget in Drupal 7, you need to implement two hooks in your *mymodule.module* file: hook_field_widget_info() and hook_field_widget_form(); the latter uses the Form API. If you're defining a field widget for a custom field type that you've defined, I suggest going back to the field type module you used as a starting point and using that module's widget as a starting point for your widget.

If you're defining a new widget for an existing field, the following example may be helpful. Assume that you want to define a widget for the core Text field that provides a custom method for input of plain text data, which could use Flash, JavaScript, or an image map to let users click on a region on an image or map, and store their choice as a predefined text string in the field. As a proxy for the custom input method, this example just uses an HTML select element; if you really just need an HTML select for your site, you could use a Drupal core "List (text)" field and choose the "Select list" widget.

Here are the two hook implementations:

```
// Provide information about the widget.
function mymodule_field_widget_info() {
  return array(
    // Machine name of the widget.
    'mymodule_mywidget' => array(
      // Label for the administrative UI.
      'label' => t('Custom text input'),
      // Field types it supports.
      'field types' => array('text'),
    ),
```

```
    // Define additional widgets here, if desired.
  );
}

// Set up an editing form.
// Return a Form API form array.
function mymodule_field_widget_form(&$form, &$form_state, $field,
  $instance, $langcode, $items, $delta, $element) {

  // Verify the widget type. Only needed if you define more than one widget.
  if ($instance['widget']['type'] == 'mymodule_mywidget') {
    // Find the current text field value.
    $value = isset($items[$delta]['value']) ? $items[$delta]['value'] : NULL;

    // Set up the editing form element. Substitute your custom
    // code here, instead of using an HTML select.
    $element['value'] = array(
      '#type' => 'select',
      '#options' => array('x_stored' => t('x label'), 'y_stored' => t('y label')),
      '#default_value' => $value,
    );
  }

  return $element;
}
```

Further reading and reference:

- "The Basics of Module and Theme Hook Programming" on page 23
- "Using the Drupal Form API" on page 109

Defining a field widget in Drupal 8

In Drupal 8, field widgets are plugins. So, to define one in a module, you need to:

- Define a class in the `Plugin\Field\FieldWidget` namespace under your module's namespace, therefore located in the *src/Plugin/Field/FieldWidget* directory. The class needs to implement `\Drupal\Core\Field\WidgetInterface`, and it typically extends `\Drupal\Core\Field\WidgetBase` or a more specific base class that extends it. You'll need to define the `formElement()` method (which gives the widget editing form), and you may need to override additional default methods on the base class.

- Annotate it with `\Drupal\Core\Field\Annotation\FieldWidget` annotation.

If you're defining a field widget for a custom field type that you've defined, I suggest going back to the field type module you used as a starting point and using that module's widget as a starting point for your widget.

If you're defining a new widget for an existing field, the following example may be helpful. Assume that you want to define a widget for the core plain Text field that provides a custom method for input of plain text data, which could use Flash, JavaScript, or an image map to let the user click on a region on an image or map, and store their choice as a predefined text string in the field. As a proxy for the custom input method, this example just uses an HTML select element; if you really just need an HTML select for your site, you could use a Drupal core "List (text)" field and choose the "Select list" widget.

Here is the widget class, which needs to go into the *src/Plugin/Field/FieldWidget/MyCustomText.php* file under the main module directory:

```php
namespace Drupal\mymodule\Plugin\Field\FieldWidget;

use Drupal\Core\Field\WidgetBase;
use Drupal\Core\Field\FieldItemListInterface;
use Drupal\Core\Form\FormStateInterface;

/**
 * Custom widget for choosing an option from a map.
 *
 * @FieldWidget(
 *   id = "mymodule_mywidget",
 *   label = @Translation("Custom text input"),
 *   field_types = {
 *     "string"
 *   }
 * )
 */
class MyCustomText extends WidgetBase {
  public function formElement(FieldItemListInterface $items, $delta,
    array $element, array &$form, FormStateInterface $form_state) {

    $value = isset($items[$delta]->value) ? $items[$delta]->value : NULL;

    // Set up the editing form element. Substitute your custom
    // code here, instead of using an HTML select.
    $element['value'] = $element + array(
      '#type' => 'select',
      '#options' => array(
        'x_stored' => $this->t('x label'),
        'y_stored' => $this->t('y label'),
      ),
      '#default_value' => $value,
    );

    return $element;
  }
}
```

Further reading and reference:

- "The Basics of Drupal 8 Plugin Programming" on page 28

Examples—field widgets:

- There are many good examples of field widgets in Drupal core. You can find them listed on *https://api.drupal.org* on the page for the `FieldWidget` annotation class.

Repurposing an existing field widget

Because the module that defines the widget tells Drupal what field types it supports in its `hook_field_widget_info()` implementation (Drupal 7) or plugin annotation (Drupal 8), if you want to repurpose an existing widget to apply to a different field type, you need to implement `hook_field_widget_info_alter()` in your *mymodule.module* file. This hook allows you to alter the information collected from all other modules' hooks or plugins. For example:

```
function mymodule_field_widget_info_alter(&$info) {
  // Add another field type to a widget.
  $info['widget_machine_name']['field types'][] = 'another_field_type';
}
```

This example works in both Drupal 7 and Drupal 8. The only difference is that the widget machine name comes from `hook_field_widget_info()` (return value array key) in Drupal 7, and the plugin annotation (`id` annotation key) in Drupal 8.

You may also need to alter the widget form so that the widget will work correctly with the new field type. There are two "form alter" hooks that you can use for this: `hook_field_widget_form_alter()`, which gets called for all widget forms, and the more specific `hook_field_widget_WIDGET_TYPE_form_alter()`, which gets called only for the widget you are interested in (and is therefore preferable). These hooks are present in both Drupal 7 and 8.

Further reading and reference:

- "The Basics of Module and Theme Hook Programming" on page 23.
- "Using the Drupal Form API" on page 109.
- "Altering Forms" on page 121.
- *https://api.drupal.org* is the best place to look up details of any of the hooks mentioned here.

Programming with Field Formatters

There are two reasons you might need to do some programming with field formatters:

- If you have defined your own custom field type, you will need to define a formatter that displays the data for that field, or repurpose an existing field formatter.
- You may need to define a custom formatting method for an existing field type.

If you need to repurpose an existing field formatter for a different field type, use `hook_field_formatter_info_alter()`, which works the same as `hook_field_widget_info_alter()` described in the preceding section. The following sections detail how to define new field formatters in Drupal 7 and 8.

Defining a field formatter in Drupal 7

To define a field formatter in Drupal 7, you need to implement two hooks in your *mymodule.module* file: `hook_field_formatter_info()` and `hook_field_format ter_view()`. If you're defining a field formatter for a custom field type that you've defined, I suggest going back to the field type module you used as a starting point and using that module's formatter as a starting point for your formatter.

If you're defining a new formatter for an existing field, the following example may be helpful. Assume that you have set up a Text field with several preselected values, and on output you want to display an icon or some predefined text that corresponds to the preselected value.

Here are the hook implementations for this formatter example:

```
// Provide information about the formatter.
function mymodule_field_formatter_info() {
  return array(
    // Machine name of the formatter.
    'mymodule_myformatter' => array(
      // Label for the administrative UI.
      'label' => t('Custom text output'),
      // Field types it supports.
      'field types' => array('text'),
    ),
    // Define additional formatters here.
  );
}

// Define how the field information is displayed.
// Return a render array.
function mymodule_field_formatter_view($entity_type, $entity,
    $field, $instance, $langcode, $items, $display) {
  $output = array();
```

```
// Verify the formatter type.
if ($display['type'] == 'mymodule_myformatter') {
  // Handle multi-valued fields.
  foreach ($items as $delta => $item) {
    // See which option was selected.
    switch ($item['value']) {
      case 'x_stored':
        // Output the corresponding text or icon.
        $output[$delta] = array('#markup' => '<p>' .
          t('Predefined output text x') . '</p>');
        break;

      case 'y_stored':
        // Output the corresponding text or icon.
        $output[$delta] = array('#markup' => '<p>' .
          t('Predefined output text y') . '</p>');
        break;

      // Handle other options here.
    }
  }
}

return $output;
}
```

Further reading and reference:

- Render arrays: "Creating Render Arrays for Page and Block Output" on page 102

Examples—field formatters:

- There are many Drupal core examples of field formatters. You can find the core implementations of hook_field_formatter_info() on the hook page on *https:// api.drupal.org*.
- A contributed module that I wrote, Simple Google Maps (*https://www.drupal.org/ project/simple_gmap*) is another example to look at. It's a formatter for a plain text field, which assumes the text is an address and formats it as an embedded Google map.
- The Field example in Examples for Developers (*https://www.drupal.org/project/ examples*) is also good.

Defining a field formatter in Drupal 8

In Drupal 8, field formatters are plugins. So, to define one in a module, you need to:

- Define a class in the `Plugin\Field\FieldFormatter` namespace under your module's namespace, therefore located in the *src/Plugin/Field/FieldFormatter* directory. The class needs to implement `\Drupal\Core\Field\FormatterInter face`, and it typically extends `\Drupal\Core\Field\FormatterBase`. You'll need to define method `viewElements()` (which builds a render array for the output), and you may need to override additional default methods on the base class.

- Annotate it with `\Drupal\Core\Field\Annotation\FieldFormatter` annotation.

If you're defining a field formatter for a custom field type that you've defined, I suggest going back to the field type module you used as a starting point and using that module's formatter as a starting point for your formatter.

If you're defining a new formatter for an existing field, the following example may be helpful. Assume that you have set up a plain Text field with several preselected values, and on output you want to display an icon or some predefined text that corresponds to the preselected value.

Here is the plugin class (which goes in file *src/Plugin/Field/FieldFormatter/MyCustom-Text.php* under the main module directory):

```php
namespace Drupal\mymodule\Plugin\Field\FieldFormatter;

use Drupal\Core\Field\FormatterBase;
use Drupal\Core\Field\FieldItemListInterface;

/**
 * Custom text field formatter.
 *
 * @FieldFormatter(
 *   id = "mymodule_myformatter",
 *   label = @Translation("Custom text output"),
 *   field_types = {
 *     "string",
 *   }
 * )
 */
class MyCustomText extends FormatterBase {

  public function viewElements(FieldItemListInterface $items) {
    $output = array();

    foreach ($items as $delta => $item) {
      // See which option was selected.
      switch ($item->value) {

        case 'x_stored':
          // Output the corresponding text or icon.
          $output[$delta] = array('#markup' => '<p>' .
            t('Predefined output text x') . '</p>');
```

```
      break;

    case 'y_stored':
      // Output the corresponding text or icon.
      $output[$delta] = array('#markup' => '<p>' .
        t('Predefined output text y') . '</p>');
      break;

      // Handle other options here.
    }
  }
  return $output;
 }
}
```

Further reading and reference:

- "The Basics of Drupal 8 Plugin Programming" on page 28

Examples—field formatters:

- There are many good examples of field formatters in Drupal core. You can find them listed on *https://api.drupal.org* on the page for the `FieldFormatter` annotation class.

Creating Views Module Add-Ons

The Views module (a contributed module in Drupal 7 and part of Drupal core in Drupal 8) is, at its heart, a query engine for Drupal that can be used to make formatted lists of pretty much any type of data. The base Views module and other contributed Views add-on modules provide the ability to query Node module content items, comments, taxonomy terms, users, and other data; to filter and sort the data in various ways; to relate one type of data to another; and to display the data using a list, grid, table, map, and other formats. In addition, custom entities and fields that you have defined are well supported by Views, and Views uses the Field system's formatters to display field data. But even with all of that ability, you may sometime have needs not covered by Views and existing add-on modules.

This section provides an overview of how to create your own Views module add-ons for the following purposes:

- Querying additional types of data
- Relating new data to existing data types
- Formatting the output in additional ways

- Providing default views that site builders can use directly or adapt to their needs

Aside from the background information in "Views Programming Terminology and Output Construction" on page 172, which you should read or at least skim, each topic in this section is independent. However, if you are programming in Drupal 7, you'll need to follow the steps in "Setting Up Your Module for Views in Drupal 7" on page 174 in order to accomplish all other Views tasks. Also note that some of the topics in this section assume knowledge of advanced usage of the Views user interface, such as relationships and contextual filters.

Further reading and reference:

- Views module for Drupal 7: *https://www.drupal.org/project/views*.
- "Avoiding Custom Programming with Fielded Data" on page 75.
- "Programming with Entities and Fields" on page 129.
- If you use the Views Bulk Operations module and you need a custom bulk operation: they are actually Rules components. You can create these in the Rules user interface; see also "Creating Rules Module Add-Ons in Drupal 7" on page 185.
- For Views programming not covered in this book, there is documentation in the *views.api.php* file in the main Views module download for Drupal 7, as well as in the Advanced Help provided by the module. For Drupal 8, the API is documented in a series of topics that you can find on *https://api.drupal.org*—start with the "Views overview" topic and go from there.

Views Programming Terminology and Output Construction

There are several pieces of background knowledge you'll need before you start programming for the Views module.

First, some terminology. Views makes use of a number of PHP classes, which in the Drupal 7 version are separated into several groups:

- Classes known as *handlers* take care of field display, sorting, filtering, contextual filtering, and relationships.
- Classes known as *plugins* take care of the overall display of the view, access restrictions, paging, and default values for contextual filters.
- Other classes that are neither plugins nor handlers take care of assembling and performing the database query and other Views functionality.

The distinction among handlers, plugins, and other classes is somewhat arbitrary, but because they're declared and defined differently, it's important to know about if you are programming for Drupal 7. In Drupal 8, the distinction among these types of classes doesn't hold—nearly all of them are plugins in Drupal 8, using the standard Drupal 8 plugin API; however, you'll still see some of these plugins referred to as handlers in Drupal 8 documentation.

 Some Views code and documentation use the term *argument* for what is called a *contextual filter* in the Drupal 7 and 8 user interface (in Drupal 6 and prior versions of Views, it was also called an argument in the user interface). The terms are basically interchangeable in Views.

In order to program effectively with Views, you also need to understand how Views uses handlers and plugins to construct its output. Here is a conceptual overview (the actual order of Views performing these steps may be a bit different):

1. Views takes all of the field, relationship, filter, contextual filter, and sort definitions in the view and creates and executes a database query. This process involves a number of handlers, such as *relationship handlers*, *field handlers*, *filter handlers*, and *sort handlers*. Fields defined using the Drupal Field API are not added directly to the query unless they are used in relationships, sorts, or filters; they are instead loaded during the display process.

2. If the view uses fields in its display, each field is run through its field handler's display routines to render the fields.

3. Each row in the database query result is run through a *row plugin* (known as *row style plugin* in Drupal 7), if one is in use. Row plugins format the rows, as a combination of rendered fields and/or raw query output.

4. The formatted rows and/or fields are handed off to the *style plugin*, which combines the rows and fields into a larger output. The base Views module includes style plugins for HTML tables, HTML unordered lists, and so on, and each style plugin is compatible with a certain subset of row plugins (for instance, an HTML list can use either a field row plugin or a row plugin that displays the entire entity, whereas an HTML table does not use a row plugin).

5. The formatted output is handed off to the overall *display plugin*; examples of display plugins are the standard Views Page, Block, and Feed displays.

Note that Views caches information about what hooks, handlers, and plugins exist (and their properties), so whenever you add or modify the properties of a Views hook implementation, handler class, or plugin class, you will most likely need to clear the Views cache. You can do this on the Views advanced settings page, where you can also disable Views caching while you're developing. The Views cache is also cleared when you clear the main Drupal cache.

Further reading and reference:

- "The Basics of Drupal 8 Plugin Programming" on page 28
- "The Drupal Cache" on page 10

Setting Up Your Module for Views in Drupal 7

In Drupal 7, several steps are necessary to make sure that Views will recognize your module as a valid provider of default views, handlers, and/or plugins; none of these steps is needed for Drupal 8 Views programming. The first step for Drupal 7 is to implement the Views hook_views_api() hook in your *mymodule.module* file. To do that, you'll need to choose a location for some additional files; typically, you make a subdirectory called *views* in your module directory to hold all of the Views files, and if you are doing a lot of output formatting, optionally another subdirectory for the theme template files. Alternatively, you can just put all the Views files in your main module directory. The hook_views_api() implementation tells Views this information. For example:

```
function mymodule_views_api() {
  return array(
    // Which version of the Views API you are using. For Views 7.x-3.x, use 3.
    'api' => 3,
    // Where your additional Views directory is, if you have one.
    'path' => drupal_get_path('module', 'mymodule') . '/views',
    // Where Views-related theme templates are located.
    'template path' => drupal_get_path('module', 'mymodule') .
      '/views/templates',
  );
}
```

Any files that contain Views classes (see the following sections) will also need to be added to your *mymodule.info* file, so that they are recognized by the Drupal 7 class loader:

```
files[] = views/name_of_my_include_file.inc
```

In addition, if Views integration is fundamental to the functioning of your module, you can make Views a module requirement by adding the following line to your *mymodule.info* file:

```
dependencies[] = views
```

Further reading and reference:

- "The Basics of Module and Theme Hook Programming" on page 23

Providing a New Views Data Source

A common need in a custom module is to *integrate it with Views*—that is, to make the data managed by the module available to Views. If you are storing data in existing entities or using standard Drupal fields to store the data, your data will already be integrated with Views. But if you are defining your own entity type in Drupal 7, or for some reason not using entities, you will need to provide Views integration yourself, by defining a new Views *data source* (also known as a *base table*). Once you've defined the data source, you can select it when setting up a new view: instead of selecting a Node-module Content view (the default), you can select your data source instead, or if appropriate, you can create a view using a different data type, and use a relationship to join it with your data type. Adding data sources is described in this section; the next section describes how to add fields and relationships to existing data sources.

Drupal 8

You can provide Views integration for non-entity data in Drupal 8 by using `hook_views_data()`, which is very similar to the Drupal 7 hook described here. This is not common, as most data in Drupal 8 should be stored in entities. Views integration for content entities in Drupal 8 is described in "Defining a Content Entity Type in Drupal 8" on page 139.

To define a Views data source in Drupal 7, assuming you have already followed the steps in "Setting Up Your Module for Views in Drupal 7" on page 174, start by creating a file called *mymodule.views.inc*, which must be located in the Views directory specified in your `hook_views_api()` implementation. In Drupal 8, the *mymodule.views.inc* file is located in the top-level module directory.

In this file, implement `hook_views_data()`. The return value of this hook, in both versions of Drupal, is an associative array of arrays, where the outermost array key is the database table name, and the array value gives information about that database table, the way it relates to other data tables known to Views, and the database table fields that can be used for filtering, sorting, and field display.

Here is an example, showing a subset of the return value of this hook in Drupal 7 for the User module (function `user_views_data()`, located in the *modules/user.views.inc* file under the main Views directory). The code has been slightly modified for clarity, and comments have been added (including notes about how you would do something similar in Drupal 8, which is mostly the same except where noted):

```
// The main data table is 'users'.
$data['users'] = array();

// The 'table' section gives information about the table as a whole.
$data['users']['table'] = array();
```

```
// Grouping name for fields in this table in the Views UI.
$data['users']['table']['group']  = t('User');

// Define this as a base table, meaning it can be used as the starting
// point for a view.
$data['users']['table']['base'] = array(
  // Primary key field.
  'field' => 'uid',
  'title' => t('User'),
  'help' => t('Users who have created accounts on your site.'),
  'access query tag' => 'user_access',
);

// Tell Views this is an entity.
$data['users']['table']['entity type'] = 'user';

// Define individual database table fields for use as Views fields,
// filters, sorts, and arguments (also known as contextual filters).

// The 'uid' database field.
$data['users']['uid'] = array(
  // Overall title and help, for all uses, except where overridden.
  'title' => t('Uid'),
  'help' => t('The user ID'),

  // Expose it as a views Field.
  'field' => array(
    // Name of the field handler class to use, for Drupal 7.
    'handler' => 'views_handler_field_user',
    // In Drupal 8, replace this with the ID of the field plugin:
    // 'id' => 'field',
    // Override a setting on the field handler.
    'click sortable' => TRUE,
  ),

  // Expose it as a views Contextual Filter (argument).
  'argument' => array(
    // Name of argument handler class to use, for Drupal 7.
    'handler' => 'views_handler_argument_user_uid',
    // In Drupal 8, replace this with the ID of the argument plugin:
    // 'id' => 'user_uid',
    // Override a setting.
    'name field' => 'name',
  ),

  // Expose it as a views Filter.
  'filter' => array(
    // Call the filter 'Name' instead of 'Uid' in the UI.
    'title' => t('Name'),
    // Name of filter handler class to use, for Drupal 7.
    'handler' => 'views_handler_filter_user_name',
```

```
      // In Drupal 8, replace this with the ID of the filter plugin:
      // 'id' => 'user_name',
    ),

    // Expose it as a views Sort.
    'sort' => array(
      // Name of sort handler class to use, for Drupal 7.
      'handler' => 'views_handler_sort',
      // In Drupal 8, replace this with the ID of the sort plugin:
      // 'id' => 'standard',
    ),

    // Define a relationship (join) that can be added to a view of Users,
    // where this field can join to another base Views data table. Only
    // one join per base table field can be defined; to define more, you
    // will need to use dummy field entries in the base table.
    'relationship' => array(
      // Call the relationship 'Content authored' instead of 'Uid'.
      'title' => t('Content authored'),
      // Also override the 'uid' default help.
      'help' => t('Relate content to the user who created it.'),
      // Name of relationship handler class to use, for Drupal 7.
      'handler' => 'views_handler_relationship',
      // In Drupal 8, replace this with the ID of the relationship plugin:
      // 'id' => 'standard',
      // Name of Views base table to join to.
      'base' => 'node',
      // Database table field name in the joined table.
      'base field' => 'uid',
      // Database table field name in this table.
      'field' => 'uid',
      // When you add a relationship in the UI, you assign it a label, which
      // is used elsewhere in the UI. This provides the default value.
      'label' => t('nodes'),
    ),
  );
```

Further reading and reference:

- "Programming with Entities and Fields" on page 129
- "Setting Up Database Tables: Schema API and hook_update_N()" on page 55

Adding Handlers to Views

A `hook_views_data()` implementation in Drupal 7 refers to the names of handler classes in various spots (fields, filters, sorts, etc.). In Drupal 8, your `hook_views_data()` or entity views data class instead refers to the IDs of the handler classes. In either case, you have the choice to use handlers provided by the Views module, or a class you create.

To create your own handler class in Drupal 7, here are the steps:

1. Usually, create a *handlers* subdirectory inside the Views directory specified in your `hook_views_api()` implementation.

2. In that subdirectory, create an include file named for your handler class, such as *mymodule_views_handler_field_myfield.inc* if your class is called `mymodule_views_handler_field_myfield`. Note that in contrast with the usual Drupal coding standards, for historical reasons Views-related classes are generally defined using all-lowercase names with underscores, rather than CamelCase names.

3. In that file, extend an existing Views handler class of the same type (field, filter, etc.), and override the appropriate methods to define the actions of your class. You can find existing Views handlers in the *handlers* subdirectory of the Views download. For instance, if you are making a field handler, you'll need to extend the `views_handler_field` class and override the `render()` method; if your field handler has display options, you'll also need to override the `option_defini tion()` and `options_form()` methods.

4. Add the handler file to your *mymodule.info* file, so that the class will be automatically loaded by the Drupal class-loading system:

```
files[] = views/handlers/mymodule_views_handler_field_myfield.inc
```

In Drupal 8, handlers use the Plugin API; see "The Basics of Drupal 8 Plugin Programming" on page 28 for details on how to define them. The information you'll need:

Namespace
The different types of handlers each have their own namespace. For instance, field handlers go in the `Plugin\views\field` namespace, and contextual filter (argument, in code) plugins go in `Plugin\views\argument`, under your main module namespace; therefore, in the *src/Plugin/views/field* and *src/Plugin/views/argument* subdirectories under your main module directory.

Annotation
Each of these types of handlers has an annotation class, such as `\Drupal\views\Annotation\ViewsField` and `\Drupal\views\Annotation\ViewsArgument`.

Base classes
Each type of handler has a base class, such as `\Drupal\views\Plugin\views\field\FieldPluginBase`, or you might want to extend one of the existing handler plugins in the appropriate *core/modules/views/src/Plugin/views/* subdirectory.

Further reading and reference:

- "Providing a New Views Data Source" on page 175 or in Drupal 8 for entities, "Defining a Content Entity Type in Drupal 8" on page 139
- "Automatic Class Loading in Drupal" on page 12
- "The Basics of Drupal 8 Plugin Programming" on page 28

Examples—handlers:

- In Drupal 7, the Views module's *handlers* directory contains general-purpose handlers. Use these as starting points when defining your own handlers. The Drupal 7 API (*https://www.drupal.org/project/api*) module also has some good examples of handler classes.
- In Drupal 8, the Views module's handlers are in subdirectories of *core/modules/ views/src/Plugin/views* in Drupal core. Some entity modules also have their own plugins in their *src/Plugin/views* directories.

Adding Fields and Relationships to an Existing Views Data Source

In addition to providing completely new Views data sources, as described in "Providing a New Views Data Source" on page 175, some custom modules may need to provide additional fields or relationships to existing Views data sources. To do this, implement `hook_views_data_alter()` in the *mymodule.views.inc* file that you set up in the previous section; this hook takes as input, by reference, the array of all of the `hook_views_data()` information from all implementing modules and allows you to alter it. Note that in Drupal 8 you would use `hook_views_data_alter()` to alter entity views data as well as non-entity views data.

This example from the Drupal 7 API module illustrates the two most common things you can do with this hook:

- Adding a relationship from an existing table to your table: in this example, the reason is that the API module allows users to comment on API documentation pages, so if someone were creating a view whose base data source is comments, they might want to add a relationship to the API documentation page that is being commented upon. Relationships are defined on the base table side, so this relationship needs to be added to the comment table's Views data.
- Adding an automatic join to your table (automatic joins provide additional database fields to a data source without having to add a relationship to the view): again, this example is comment-related: the `node_comment_statistics` table is normally automatically joined to the `node` base table, so that the number-of-comments field is available on node content items. Automatic joins are defined

on the table that is automatically joined to a Views base table, so this join needs to be added to the `node_comment_statistics` table Views data, to automatically join it when the `api_documentation` table is in a view.

Here is the code for Drupal 7 to make these two modifications, with notes added where Drupal 8 would be different:

```
function api_views_data_alter(&$data) {
  // Add a relationship to the Comment table. The array key must be
  // unique within the comment table -- do not overwrite any existing
  // comment fields.
  $data['comment']['did'] = array(
    'title' => t('Documentation ID'),
    'help' => t('The ID of the documentation object the comment is a reply to.'),
    'relationship' => array(
      // Table to join to.
      'base' => 'api_documentation',
      // Field in that table to join with.
      'base field' => 'did',
      // Field in the comment table to join with.
      'field' => 'nid',
      // Name of relationship handler class to use for Drupal 7.
      'handler' => 'views_handler_relationship',
      // For Drupal 8, this would be the ID of the relationship plugin, like:
      // 'id' => 'standard',
      // When you add a relationship in the UI, you assign it a label, which
      // is used elsewhere in the UI. This provides the default value.
      'label' => t('API documentation object'),
      'title' => t('API documentation object'),
      'help' => t('The ID of the documentation object the comment is a reply to.'),
    ),
  );

  // Add an automatic join between the comment statistics table and
  // the API documentation table.
  $data['node_comment_statistics']['table']['join']['api_documentation'] =
    array(
      // Use an inner join.
      'type' => 'INNER',
      // Field to join on in the API documentation table.
      'left_field' => 'did',
      // Field to join on in the comment statistics table.
      'field' => 'nid',
    );
}
```

Providing a Style or Row Plugin to Views

Another common custom Views programming need is to create new style or row plugins.

In Drupal 8, style plugins and row plugins use the Plugin API; see "The Basics of Drupal 8 Plugin Programming" on page 28 for details on how to define them. The information you'll need:

Namespace

Style plugins go in the `Plugin\views\style` namespace, and row plugins in `Plugin\views\row`, under your main module namespace; therefore, in the *src/ Plugin/views/style* and *src/Plugin/views/row* subdirectories under your main module directory.

Annotation

Style plugins have `\Drupal\views\Annotation\ViewsStyle` annotation, and row plugins have `\Drupal\views\Annotation\ViewsRow` annotation.

Base classes

The base class for style plugins is `\Drupal\views\Plugin\views\style\Style PluginBase`, or you might want to extend one of the existing style plugins in *core/ modules/views/src/Plugin/views/style*. The base class for row plugins is `\Drupal \views\Plugin\views\row\RowPluginBase`, or you might want to extend one of the existing row plugins in *core/modules/views/src/Plugin/views/row*.

Theming

Style plugin annotation refers to a theme hook, and row plugins can also set up render arrays with new theme hooks. You'll need to define your theme hooks using `hook_theme()`.

In Drupal 7, row and style plugins are detected by Views using a hook, so the process is a bit more complicated. Here are the steps to follow, assuming you have already followed the steps in "Setting Up Your Module for Views in Drupal 7" on page 174:

1. Implement `hook_views_plugins()` in your *mymodule.views.inc* file, which must be located in the Views directory specified in your `hook_views_api()` implementation. The return value tells Views about your style and row style plugin classes. For instance, you might have:

```
function mymodule_views_plugins() {
  return array(
    // Overall style plugins
    'style' => array(

      // First style plugin--machine name is the array key.
      'mymodule_mystyle' => array(
        // Information about this plugin.
        'title' => t('My module my style'),
        'help' => t('Longer description goes here'),
        // The class for this plugin and where to find it.
        'handler' => 'mymodule_views_plugin_style_mystyle',
```

```
        'path' => drupal_get_path('module', 'mymodule') . '/views/plugins',
        // Some settings.
        'uses row plugin' => TRUE,
        'uses fields' => TRUE,
      ),

      // Additional style plugins go here.
    ),

    // Row style plugins.
    'row' => array(
      // First row style plugin -- machine name is the array key.
      'mymodule_myrowstyle' => array(
        // Information about this plugin.
        'title' => t('My module my row style'),
        'help' => t('Longer description goes here'),
        // The class for this plugin and where to find it.
        'handler' => 'mymodule_views_plugin_row_myrowstyle',
        'path' => drupal_get_path('module', 'mymodule') . '/views/plugins',
        // Some settings.
        'uses fields' => TRUE,
      ),

      // Additional row style plugins go here.
    ),
  );
}
```

2. Create a file for each style or row style plugin class. For example, if you declared that your class is called `mymodule_views_plugin_style_mystyle`, create a file with the name *mymodule_views_plugin_style_mystyle.inc*. Put this file in the directory you specified in your `hook_views_plugins()` implementation (typically, plugins are either put into your Views directory or a subdirectory called *plugins*).

3. List each class-containing include file in your *mymodule.info* file, so that the class will be automatically loaded by the Drupal class-loading system, with a line like:

   ```
   files[] = views/plugins/mymodule_views_plugin_style_mystyle.inc
   ```

4. In each class-containing include file, declare your plugin class, which should extend either the `views_plugin_style`, `views_plugin_row`, or another subclass of these classes. You will need to override the `option_definition()` and `options_form()` methods if your plugin has options, and (oddly enough) that is usually all you'll need to override, because the work of formatting the output is done in the theme layer.

5. Set up `hook_theme()` to define a theme template and preprocessing function for your plugin. The theme template goes into the template directory specified in

---

your `hook_views_info()` implementation, and the name corresponds to the machine name you gave your plugin (in this example, *mymodule-mystyle.tpl.php* or *mymodule-myrowstyle.tpl.php*).

Further reading and reference:

- "Making Your Module Output Themeable" on page 25
- "Automatic Class Loading in Drupal" on page 12

Examples—plugin classes:

- The Views module has several general-purpose plugins, which are good starting points and examples. In Drupal 7, the `hook_views_plugins()` implementation is in the *includes/plugins.inc* file, plugin class files are in the *plugins* directory, and template files are in the *theme* directory, with theme-preprocessing functions in the *theme/theme.inc* file. In Drupal 8, plugins are in subdirectories of *core/modules/views/src/Plugin/views* in Drupal core.
- There are several contributed module projects that provide Views plugin add-ons (they may not yet be ported to Drupal 8). Commonly used examples are Views Data Export (*https://www.drupal.org/project/views_data_export*), Calendar (*https://www.drupal.org/project/calendar*), and Views Slideshow (*https://www.drupal.org/project/views_slideshow*). You can find others by browsing the "Views" category at *https://www.drupal.org/project/modules* (but note that only some of the Views-related modules in that list provide style or row plugins).

Providing Default Views

Once you have your module's data integrated with Views—either because it is stored in entities using the Entity API module in Drupal 7, core entities, or fields or because you have provided a custom data source as described in the preceding sections—you may want to supply users of your module with one or more default views. These views can be used to provide administration pages for your module or sample output pages, and they can either be enabled by default or disabled by default (administrators can enable and modify them as needed).

Here are the steps to follow to provide one or more default views in your Drupal 7 module, assuming you have already followed the steps in "Setting Up Your Module for Views in Drupal 7" on page 174:

1. Create a view using the Views user interface.
2. From the Views user interface, export the view. This will give you some PHP code starting with `$view = new view;`.

3. If you want to have the view disabled by default, find the line near the top that says `$view->disabled = FALSE;` and change `FALSE` to `TRUE`.

4. Implement `hook_views_default_views()` in a file called *mymodule.views_default.inc*, which must be located in the Views directory specified in your `hook_views_api()` implementation.

5. Put the exported view's PHP code into this hook implementation:

```
function mymodule_views_default_views() {
  // Return this array at the end.
  $views = array();

  // Exported view code starts here.
  $view = new view;
  // ... rest of exported code ...
  // Exported code ends here.

  // Add this view to the return array.
  $views[$view->name] = $view;

  // You can add additional exported views here.

  return $views;
}
```

In Drupal 8, views are configuration. So, to provide a default view in a module, here are the steps:

1. Create the view in the Views user interface.

2. Export the configuration to a file. You can do this on the configuration export page in the administrative UI (*example.com/admin/config/development/configuration/single/export*), which tells you the filename to save it as.

3. Remove the UUID line near the top from the exported file. This is part of your site configuration, but it should not be set in configuration for other sites to import.

4. Put this file in your module's *config/install* or *config/optional* directory.

Further reading and reference:

- "Programming with Entities and Fields" on page 129
- "Configuration file format and schema in Drupal 8" on page 42

Creating Rules Module Add-Ons in Drupal 7

The contributed Rules module lets you set up *reaction rules*, which are a set of *actions* that are executed in response to *events* under certain *conditions* on your website. For example, you could respond to a new comment submission event under the condition that the submitter is an anonymous user, by sending the comment moderator an email message. The configuration offered by the Rules user interface is quite flexible and powerful:

- You can define the events, conditions, and actions for a reaction rule in the Views user interface, without any programming.
- Conditions can be combined using Boolean AND/OR logic.
- Actions can have parameter inputs and can provide data outputs, so you can chain actions together, with the output data provided by one action feeding in as a parameter for the next action.
- Some actions provide arrays as output, and Rules has a special action that lets you loop over an array, doing one or more actions on each array element.
- You can also set up *components*, which are basically reusable subsets of reaction rules. Components can have inputs and outputs, as well as their own events, conditions, and/or actions.
- Once you have created a component, you can use it like an action in building a reaction rule.
- Components can also be used as bulk operations in the Views Bulk Operations module, if they take an entity or a list of entities as their first input value.

The Rules module comes with a set of standard events, conditions, and actions, including many related to entities and fields (in Drupal 7, these require the contributed Entity API module). This means that if your module stores its custom data in entities and fields, you will be able to use the Rules module with your module's data without any further programming. But you may occasionally find that you need to do some programming to add additional functionality to the Rules module; in my experience, this has always been to add custom actions to Rules; this is described in "Providing Custom Actions to Rules" on page 186.

In Drupal 7, reaction rules and components that you compose using the Rules user interface can be exported into PHP code and shared with others. One way to do this is by using the Features contributed module. But sometimes Features is cumbersome, and there is a direct method for exporting and sharing reaction rules and components described in "Providing Default Reaction Rules and Components" on page 188.

Drupal 8

As of September 2015, the API for Rules in Drupal 8 has not been finalized, but it will definitely be quite different from the Drupal 7 API. The following sections only apply to Drupal 7.

Further reading and reference:

- Rules module: *https://www.drupal.org/project/rules*.
- Features module: *https://www.drupal.org/project/features*.
- Views Bulk Operations module: *https://www.drupal.org/project/views_bulk_opera tions*.
- "Programming with Entities and Fields" on page 129.
- For programming with Rules not covered in this book, see the *rules.api.php* file distributed with the Rules module for documentation. For instance, it is possible to set up custom conditions and events, although it is unlikely you will ever need to, given the flexibility of the base Rules module and its entity integration.

Providing Custom Actions to Rules

Rules actions are responses to events and conditions detected by the Rules module, and they can take many forms. Built-in actions that come with the Rules module include sending an email message, displaying a message or warning, and altering content (publishing, unpublishing, etc.). As mentioned in the introduction to this section, you can chain together the input and output of several actions and you can also use action output for looping, so some so-called actions are really more like processing steps that exist solely to provide input for other actions that are actually doing the work (modifying content, sending email, etc.).

Whether you are defining a processing step type of action or one that actually does work itself, here are the steps you will need to follow to provide a custom action to the Rules module in Drupal 7:

1. Create a file called *mymodule.rules.inc* in your main module directory, and implement hook_rules_action_info() in that file. The return value tells Rules about your custom action: its machine name, a human-readable label for the Rules user interface, the data that it requires as parameters (if any), and the data that it provides as output (if any).

2. Create a callback function that executes your action. You can either put this function in your *mymodule.rules.inc* file, or you can implement

`hook_rules_file_info()` and specify a separate include file for callbacks. The name of the function is the same as the machine name you gave the action.

As an example, here is the code to provide a processing-step-type action that takes a content item as input and outputs a list of users (you could then loop over the output list and send each user an email message, for instance):

```
// Optional hook_rules_file_info() implementation.
// This specifies a separate file for callback functions.
// It goes into mymodule.rules.inc.
function mymodule_rules_file_info() {
  // Leave off the .inc filename suffix.
  return array('mymodule.rules-callbacks');
}


// Required hook_rules_action_info() implementation.
// This gives information about your action.
// It goes into mymodule.rules.inc.
function mymodule_rules_action_info() {
  $actions = array();

  // Define one action.

  // The array key is the machine name of the action, and also the
  // name of the function that does the action.
  $actions['mymodule_rules_action_user_list'] = array(

    // Label and group in the user interface.
    'label' => t('Load a list of users related to content'),
    'group' => t('My Module custom'),

    // Describe the parameters.
    'parameter' => array(
      'item' => array(
        'label' => t('Content item to use'),
        'type' => 'node',
      ),

      // You can add additional parameters here.
    ),

    // Describe the output.
    'provides' => array(
      'user_list' => array(
        'type' => 'list<user>',
        'label' => t('List of users related to content'),
      ),

      // You could describe additional output here.
    ),
  );
```

```
      // Define other actions here.

      return $actions;
    }

    // Required callback function that performs the action.
    // This goes in mymodule.rules.inc, or the file defined in
    // the optional hook_rules_file_info() implementation.
    function mymodule_rules_action_user_list($item) {
      // Because the parameter defined for this action is a node,
      // $item is a node. Do a query here to find a list of
      // users related to this node.

      // As a proxy for your real code, return a list of one
      // user -- the author of the content.
      $ids = array($item->uid);

      // Load the users and return them to Rules.
      return array('user_list' => user_load_multiple($ids));
    }
```

Further reading and reference:

- "The Basics of Module and Theme Hook Programming" on page 23

Providing Default Reaction Rules and Components

In some cases, you may find that you want to put reaction rules or components that you have created into PHP code, so that you can use them on another site. You have three choices for how to do this in Drupal 7:

- Define the reaction rule or component's events, conditions, and reactions using pure PHP code. This is somewhat documented in the *rules.api.php* file distributed with the Rules module, but it is not particularly recommended, as you'll need to read a lot of Rules module code to figure out the machine names of all the pieces, and there isn't really any documentation on how to put it all together.

- Create the reaction rule or component using the Rules user interface, and use the contributed Features module to manage the export.

- Create the reaction rule or component using the Rules user interface, export the definition to a text file, and implement a Rules hook to provide it as an in-code rule or component. This process is recommended if you do not want to use the Features module, and is described here.

Assuming you want to use the export-to-text option, here are the steps to follow:

1. In the Rules user interface, create your reaction rule or component. If you do not want a reaction rule to be active by default, be sure to deactivate it.

2. From the Rules user interface, export your reaction rule or component, and save the exported text in a file. Put this file in a *rules* subdirectory of your main module directory, and name it *sample_rule.txt* (for example).

3. Implement `hook_default_rules_configuration()` in a file named *mymodule.rules_defaults.inc*, with the following code:

```
function mymodule_default_rules_configuration() {
  $configs = array();

  // Read in one exported reaction rule.
  $file = drupal_get_path('module', 'mymodule') . '/rules/sample_rule.txt';
  $contents = file_get_contents($file);
  $configs['mymodule_sample_rule'] = rules_import($contents);

  // Add other reaction rules and components here if desired.

  return $configs;
}
```

Further reading and reference:

- Features module: *https://www.drupal.org/project/features*
- "The Basics of Module and Theme Hook Programming" on page 23

Programming with CTools in Drupal 7

The contributed Chaos Tools (CTools) module is a suite of APIs and tools designed to be used by other modules, including a generic *plugin* system, a system for packaging configuration data for export into code, a *context* system for detecting conditions involving the site and its data, and other components. If you are writing a module for Drupal, look through the contents of CTools, and you may find that you can use its tools rather than writing your own code for some of the basic tasks your module needs to do.

Implementing CTools Plugins for Panels

The contributed Panels module, which is based heavily on CTools, allows you to set up custom page layouts, which are managed using the CTools page manager tool. Panels also uses the CTools context system, which allows the content displayed in the panel layout's regions to respond to the URL path, properties of content being displayed, the logged-in user's role, and other conditions. Because Panels uses the CTools plugin system for almost all of its functionality, you can extend and alter the functionality of Panels by creating your own plugins (this process is known as *implementing* plugins, to distinguish it from the process of *defining* plugin types).

Drupal 8

The plugin system defined by the CTools module for Drupal 7 was not adopted for Drupal 8, which has its own plugin system in Drupal core. Thus, the information about CTools plugins provided here is only applicable to Drupal 7. As of September 2015, the Panels module has not been finalized for Drupal 8, but it will likely be using the Drupal core plugin system rather than the CTools plugin system described here.

This section describes the steps in implementing a CTools plugin for Drupal 7. The example used is a plugin implementation that adds a custom *relationship* to the CTools context system, for use in Panels. Specifically, the example plugin implementation provides a relationship from a user to the most recent node content item the user has authored. The steps to implement this plugin are described in the following sections.

Panels relationships are not the same as Views relationships. Also, although in Drupal 7 the Views module depends on the CTools module, Views does not use the CTools plugin system for defining and detecting its plugin and handler types. See "Creating Views Module Add-Ons" on page 171 instead if you are interested in Views.

Further reading and reference:

- Panels module: *https://www.drupal.org/project/panels*
- Chaos Tools (CTools) module: *https://www.drupal.org/project/ctools*
- Both Panels and CTools have help available on their API, if you install the Advanced Help module (*https://www.drupal.org/project/advanced_help*), and CTools has a *ctools.api.php* file with hook documentation. The Advanced Help topics in Panels and CTools also describe how to use the Panels user interface to create panel pages and use contexts and relationships.

Determining plugin background information

A CTools plugin implementation consists of an array of definition data and usually one or more callback functions mentioned in the definition array. Plugins come in many varieties, known as *types*, and each plugin type has a specific format for its definition array. So, before implementing a plugin in your module, you need to locate several pieces of background information about the plugin type:

- Whether the functionality you want to define can even be provided by implementing a CTools plugin
- If so, which module defines the plugin type that provides this functionality
- The machine name of the plugin type
- The elements of the definition array that plugins of this type need to define
- The callback functions that plugins of this type need to define, and their signatures
- Whether there are any restrictions on the machine name you will choose for your plugin

Unfortunately, modules that define plugin types do not have a uniform way of providing this information to Drupal programmers, so the rest of this section describes some steps you can go through to locate the information you'll need. If you already have this information in hand for the plugin you're implementing, you can skip the rest of this section.

A good starting point for determining if the functionality is covered by a plugin would be to look for a *README.txt* file, a **.api.php* file, or Advanced Help in the module whose functionality you are trying to add to. In the present example of adding a custom relationship to Panels, the Panels Advanced Help "Working with the Panels API" topic tells you that relationship plugins are part of the context system provided by the CTools module.

The next step is to find the plugin machine name. To do this, you'll need to locate the implementation of `hook_ctools_plugin_type()` in the module that defines the plugin type (this function should be in the main module file). In this case, because it is a plugin type defined by the CTools module itself, you are looking for a function called `ctools_ctools_plugin_type()` in the *ctools.module* file; if you had determined that your plugin type was defined by the Panels module, you'd be looking for `panels_ctools_plugin_type()` in *panels.module*. In either case, the return value of the function is an array of plugin type definitions, where the keys are the machine names of the plugin types, and the corresponding values are defaults for the plugin definition arrays.

Unfortunately, the CTools implementation of this hook does not include the definitions directly. Instead, it does this:

```
ctools_passthrough('ctools', 'plugin-type', $items);
```

The `ctools_passthrough()` utility (in the CTools *includes/utility.inc* file) delegates the work to functions called `ctools*plugin_type()` in include files called *includes/*

plugin-type.inc. Scanning the list of files matching this pattern in the CTools module download, you can eventually find the plugin type definition in the `ctools_con` `text_plugin_type()` function in CTools the *includes/context.plugin-type.inc* file:

```
$items['relationships'] = array(
  'child plugins' => TRUE,
);
```

This plugin type definition tells you two things. First, the machine name of the plugin type is `relationships` (note the final `s`!). Second, because the plugin definition array is very simple, this plugin type uses the standard CTools implementation methods described in this section. Most plugins have a simple array like this in their `hook_ctools_plugin_type()` implementation; there are two elements to watch out for that could be present in a plugin definition array that make slight changes to the implementation method described here:

extension

> The plugin definition should be placed in a file with a different extension than the default **.inc*.

info file

> The plugin definition should be provided in *.info* file format (like a module or theme *.info* file) instead of in a PHP array. The specifics of plugins using this format are not covered in this book, so you'll have to look for existing examples instead.

The next step is to figure out what data and callbacks this plugin type expects. Look for this information in a *README.txt* file, an Advanced Help topic, or in existing plugin implementations from the module that defines the plugin type. For the present example, there is a CTools Advanced Help topic that includes a description of the definition array elements, and there are several relationship plugins in the CTools *plugins/relationships* directory that you can use as examples.

Finally, you'll need to choose a machine name for your plugin; this example uses the machine name `mymodule_relationship_most_recent_content`. As with other Drupal programming, machine names must be unique, so it is customary to use the module name as a prefix, followed by a descriptive name. Be careful though: some types of CTools plugins have implicit (and likely undocumented) machine name restrictions, because they get stored in a database table field of that length. So to avoid trouble, it is probably best to pick as short of a name as possible that is still unique and descriptive. For instance, CTools content type plugins (which provide content panes you can insert into Panels layouts) have an implicit machine name length maximum of 32 characters.

Notifying CTools about plugin implementations

With the necessary background information in hand, the next step in creating a CTools plugin is to tell CTools that your module includes plugin implementations, and where to find them. Each plugin goes in its own file, and plugin files that you create must be placed in directories that are specific to the plugin type. The usual convention is to put CTools plugins into the *plugins* subdirectory under your main module directory, and organize them into subdirectories under that.

To tell CTools where your plugin directory is, implement `hook_ctools_plu gin_directory()` in your main *mymodule.module* file:

```
function mymodule_ctools_plugin_directory($module, $plugin) {
  return 'plugins/' . $module . '-' . $plugin;
}
```

The function parameters are the machine names of the module and plugin type; the return value is the directory name that you want to use for plugins of that type. You can make your directory structure from these inputs however you wish, as long as each plugin type you implement has its own directory. The example here means that an implementation of a relationship plugin defined by the CTools module goes into the *plugins/ctools-relationships* subdirectory under the main module directory.

Further reading and reference:

- "The Basics of Module and Theme Hook Programming" on page 23

Writing the plugin implementation code

The next step in implementing a CTools plugin is to create a PHP file for your plugin implementation in your plugin directory. The filename is the machine name you chose for your plugin, with a *.inc* extension (*plugins/ctools-relationships/mymodule_relationship_most_recent_content.inc* in this example).

The file starts with the definition of the `$plugin` array in the global scope, which contains the definition for your plugin implementation:

```
$plugin = array(
  'title' => t('My Module context relationship plugin'),
  'description' => t('Locates the most recent content item authored by a user'),
  'required context' => new ctools_context_required(t('User'), 'user'),
  'context' => 'mymodule_relationship_most_recent_content',
  'keyword' => 'node',
);
```

Notes:

- The specific elements of the definition array depend on the type of plugin you are implementing.

- Many plugin types use `title` and `description` elements, and these values should be passed through the `t()` function so that they are translated for display in the Drupal user interface.

- The `required context` element is specific to CTools context plugins; it tells CTools what the context input is for your plugin implementation. In this example, the one input is the user whose most recent content is to be found. If your plugin takes multiple inputs, you can make this an array.

- The `context` element is the name of the callback function that CTools will call when this relationship is selected as part of a Panels page.

- The `keyword` element is a suggestion for the user interface, which provides the default name for the relationship result.

The final step is to define any callback functions referenced in your definition array. These also go into your include file, and their signatures are specific to the plugin type. This example requires one function:

```
function mymodule_relationship_most_recent_content($context = NULL, $config) {
  // Read the user ID from the context. If you have multiple context inputs,
  // $context will be an array of contexts. But there is only one here.
  if (empty($context) || empty($context->data) || empty($context->data->uid)) {
    // If there is a problem, return an empty CTools context. This is also
    // used by CTools to determine the output data type of this plugin.
    return ctools_context_create_empty('node', NULL);
  }
  $uid = $context->data->uid;

  // Locate the most recent content node created by this user.
  $nid = db_select('node', 'n')
    ->fields('n', array('nid'))
    ->condition('uid', $uid)
    ->orderBy('created', 'DESC')
    ->range(0,1)
    ->execute()
    ->fetchField();

  // Load the node item if possible.
  if (!$nid) {
    return ctools_context_create_empty('node', NULL);
  }
  $node = node_load($nid);
  if (!$node) {
    return ctools_context_create_empty('node', NULL);
  }

  // Return the found node in a CTools context.
  return ctools_context_create('node', $node);
}
```

As usual, clear the cache: "The Drupal Cache" on page 10.

Providing Default CTools Exportables

CTools defines a concept of *exportables*, in which a set of configuration, such as a view from the Views module or a panel from the Panels module, can be exported into code. The user can modify the configuration in the administrative user interface, and this overrides the configuration in code.

If you want to create a panel, view, or other CTools exportable and save it to code in order to preserve it or share it, you can do so either using the contributed Features module, or directly. "Providing Default Views" on page 183 shows how to do a direct export of a view; this section describes how to do it for other exportables.

As an example, assume that you have a mini panel that you've created in the Panels UI and want to export into code. Here are the steps you would follow to get it exported:

1. Each exportable has a hook that allows you to provide it in code, and you'll need to locate the name of this hook.

2. The hook name is defined in some code that is in the defining module's hook_schema() implementation in the module's *modulename.install* file. In this example, mini panels come from the Mini Panels sub-module of Panels, so the function we're looking for is panels_mini_schema(), and this is located in the *panels/panels_mini/panels_mini.install* file.

3. In the hook_install() implementation, locate the data table related to the item you're trying to export, and within that, find the 'export' array. In this example:

```
$schema['panels_mini'] = array(
  'export' => array(
    'identifier' => 'mini',
    'load callback' => 'panels_mini_load',
    'load all callback' => 'panels_mini_load_all',
    'save callback' => 'panels_mini_save',
    'delete callback' => 'panels_mini_delete',
    'export callback' => 'panels_mini_export',
    'api' => array(
      'owner' => 'panels_mini',
      'api' => 'panels_default',
      'minimum_version' => 1,
      'current_version' => 1,
    ),
```

4. If the 'export' array contains an 'api' section, that means that in order for CTools to recognize your module as a valid provider of these items, you will need to implement (usually) hook_ctools_plugin_api(). Some exportables may use a

different API hook; if so, hopefully they have documented this fact. Here's the implementation:

```
function mymodule_ctools_plugin_api() {
  return array(
    // The API version.
    'api' => 1,
  );
}
```

5. The 'export' array may contain a 'default hook' element, which gives the name of the exportables hook we're looking for. If this is not provided, as in this case, the default name is 'default_' followed by the table name ('panels_mini' here). This value does not include the 'hook' prefix. So, in our example, the hook is hook_default_panels_mini().

6. To provide one or more exported items, implement this hook in your *mymodule.module* file. The return value is an array of exported items, keyed by the machine names of the items. Hopefully, the exportable will have a page that allows you to export the item into code, probably into a large text field on the page. Copy the exported code, and paste the value into your hook implementation function. For example:

```
function mymodule_default_panels_mini() {
  $minis = array();

  // Paste exported code here. It starts out:
  $mini = new stdClass();
  // ...
  // Find this line with the machine name in it:
  $mini->name = 'mymodule_test';
  // ...

  // After the export is pasted, you'll have $mini holding one exported
  // mini panel. Put it into the return array.
  $minis['mymodule_test'] = $mini;

  // Add additional mini panels here.

  // Return them all.
  return $minis;
}
```

7. As usual, clear the cache.

Further reading and reference:

- "The Basics of Module and Theme Hook Programming" on page 23
- "Setting Up Database Tables: Schema API and hook_update_N()" on page 55
- "The Drupal Cache" on page 10

## CHAPTER 5

Programming Tools and Tips

As you launch yourself into (or continue) what will hopefully be many productive years as a Drupal programmer, I hope that you will continue to keep the principles of Chapter 2 in mind and avoid the mistakes listed in Chapter 3. You should be able to keep returning to Chapter 4 and outside references such as Examples for Developers (*https://www.drupal.org/project/examples*) for examples and ideas. And for further study, there are suggestions sprinkled throughout this book.

In closing, I'd like to offer a few final tips, tools, and suggestions that you should find useful in your endeavors.

Where to Find More Information

Drupal Site Building and General Drupal Information

When I started using and programming with Drupal, there weren't really any books available on using Drupal to build websites, so I don't have any specific general Drupal book recommendations; the Drupal project maintains a list of current books about Drupal at *https://www.drupal.org/books*.

Here is a list of online resources on site building and the Drupal project in general:

https://www.drupal.org/project/user_guide
> The official User Guide for Drupal, which as of June 2015 is a brand-new work in progress, covers the basics of site building with Drupal.

https://www.drupal.org/documentation
> The Drupal Community Documentation, a wiki-like compendium of pages about nearly everything in Drupal (installation, site building, programming, etc.). It has a lot of coverage, but because it is open to editing by all members of

the Drupal community, it is of varying quality and only somewhat organized. Within this documentation, the "Developing for Drupal" section and the "Theming" section are of most use to programmers; other sections are aimed at setting up sites with Drupal, configuring modules, and the like.

https://www.drupal.org/planet
Drupal Planet, which is an aggregated feed composed of many Drupal-related blogs. Subscribe to keep up to date on new developments in Drupal and to read blog posts on programming topics.

https://groups.drupal.org
Central place to find topical and geographical Drupal groups, each of which has a forum. Many of them also have meetings and events (online or in-person) that you can attend.

https://www.drupal.org/irc
The Drupal community uses IRC for online chatting, and this section of the Drupal website contains a channel list and background information.

http://drupal.stackexchange.com
Questions and answers about Drupal.

https://association.drupal.org
Website of the Drupal Association, the nonprofit organization behind the Drupal project.

https://www.drupal.org/project/modules and https://www.drupal.org/project/themes
Search for downloads of contributed Drupal modules and themes. Some people prefer the search interface of *http://drupalmodules.com* for finding modules.

Drupal Programming Reference and Background

The Drupal API changes often enough that if someone tried to write an API reference book, it would probably be outdated before it was published. So, the following online resources are recommended (in addition, some of the general Drupal resources of the previous section have programming information):

https://api.drupal.org
The API reference site for Drupal. As of this writing, this site only includes Drupal core and a few contributed modules; *http://drupalcontrib.org* is a similar reference site that includes popular Drupal contributed modules. Use one of these sites to find documentation about a specific Drupal function, class, or constant whose name you know. See "Using api.drupal.org" on page 201 for more information.

https://www.drupal.org/developing/api
> Tutorials and conceptual explanations for core Drupal APIs. Use this reference if you do not know what function you need to use, or if you need more background information.

https://www.drupal.org/project/examples
> The Examples for Developers project, which is a set of tutorial-like example modules that aim to illustrate all of the core Drupal APIs.

https://www.drupal.org/writing-secure-code
> Documentation about writing secure code in Drupal. Also, Greg James Knaddison, one of the prominent members of the Drupal Security Team, has written *Cracking Drupal: A Drop in the Bucket* (Wiley), which is widely considered to be the definitive reference for Drupal security.

https://www.drupal.org/coding-standards
> The coding standards for the Drupal project.

https://www.drupal.org/new-contributors
> A list of tasks for people with a variety of skill sets, with step-by-step instructions, suitable for people who are new to contributing to the Drupal project.

https://www.drupal.org/novice
> Detailed instructions on how to contribute *patches* (code fixes) to Drupal.

Using api.drupal.org

The *https://api.drupal.org* website is an invaluable reference for Drupal programmers (note: I may be biased in thinking this, as I currently maintain the software that the site runs on and am also the Drupal core committer/maintainer for API documentation). Several contributed Drupal modules also run API reference sites that use the same software.

Here are some features that you can take advantage of; not all of them may be available on all API reference sites, depending on what version of the API software they are running:

- Every Drupal core file, class, interface, constant, function, method, service, etc. (item) has its own documentation page on the site. As of this writing, there are plans to include all of the contributed modules on this site as well, but until that happens, the *http://drupalcontrib.org* site (which runs the same software and includes many popular contributed modules) can be used.

- Most items are well documented and most of the documentation is accurate. The documentation is built from comments in the source code, so it tends to be updated when code is updated. (If you find a problem, you can click a link on the page to report an issue.)

- The source code of each item is shown, so if the documentation is unclear, you can read the code to see what's really going on.

- Hooks (places where modules can alter the Drupal core behavior) are also documented. The function body of hook documentation gives a sample hook implementation.

- You can search directly for any item by name, if you know the name of what you are looking for, using the search block in the sidebar. Note that when searching for function names, you do not include ( ) after the name.

- Topic pages provide additional documentation about the Drupal API: explanations and a list of related functions and classes. If you do not know the name of the specific Drupal function or class you want to use, try browsing the Topics list.

- The landing pages for Drupal 8 and (to some extent) Drupal 7 provide links to important topics and overviews.

- There is a lot of cross-linking:

  — File pages show all items defined in the file, and items link to their file. So if you are on a function page and want to find related functions, click on the file link to see what else is defined in the same file.

  — Topic pages show related items, and items link to topics. So if you are on a function page and it has a related topics link, try that link to find related functions.

  — Items in code listings link to their pages, as much as possible (e.g., names of called functions link to the function pages).

  — Each function page has a link to a page showing all the places in Drupal core that call the function. There are also pages showing string references to functions, where hooks are invoked, which classes use a particular class, etc. on their respective pages.

  — Classes and interfaces have extended hierarchy listings, showing which classes extend or implement them.

PHP Resources

There are hundreds of books about PHP, and you should be able to find one that suits your needs, background, and style preferences. My recommendations:

- I learned PHP, MySQL, and the basics of web programming from *PHP in a Nutshell* (*http://oreil.ly/PHP_nutshell*) by Paul Hudson (O'Reilly) and *Web Database Applications with PHP and MySQL* (*http://oreil.ly/web_db_apps_PHP_MySQL*) by Hugh E. Williams and David Lane (O'Reilly). These books are fairly old by now, so you can probably find a more updated reference—*Modern PHP* by Josh Lockhart (O'Reilly) looks promising.

- The newest PHP language features like traits and namespaces, which are used extensively in Drupal 8, may not be familiar to all PHP programmers. You can learn about traits at *http://bit.ly/php_traits* and namespaces at *http://bit.ly/php_namespaces*.

- For reference information about specific PHP functions, see *http://php.net* (that is always the most up-to-date reference; you can also download the entire reference for local or offline access).

- Coding practices for PHP: *http://www.phptherightway.com* (also created by Josh Lockhart).

Database Resources

Drupal can run on a variety of databases; most commonly, people use either MySQL, a MySQL clone such as MariaDB or Percona, or PostgreSQL. If you program with Drupal, you will need to use the Drupal Database API for maximum portability rather than writing MySQL or other database queries directly. Because of this, websites and references aimed at specific databases are of limited use to Drupal programmers. But I do recommend the following:

- *Web Database Applications with PHP and MySQL* (previously mentioned) as a good starting point for learning the basics of queries useful for web programming. Again, it is a bit old; you may be able to find a more recent book.

- *SQL Pocket Guide* (*http://oreil.ly/SQL_Pocket_Guide*) by Jonathan Gennick (O'Reilly), which highlights the similarities and differences between the various databases' query syntax and capabilities.

Other Web Technology Resources

Again, *Web Database Applications with PHP and MySQL* is a good starting point for learning about how the web server, PHP scripting language, database, and browser interact in web applications in general. For reference on HTML, CSS, and JavaScript, I recommend:

- *http://www.webplatform.org*—reference guide to HTML and CSS.

- If you prefer a book format, the O'Reilly pocket references are handy: *CSS Pocket Reference* (*http://oreil.ly/CSS_Pocket_Ref_4*) by Eric A. Meyer and *HTML & XHTML Pocket Reference* (*http://oreil.ly/HTML_XHTML_Pocket_Ref_4*) by Jennifer Niederst Robbins.

- For JavaScript, I am continually pulling out my well-worn copy of *JavaScript: The Definitive Guide* (*http://oreil.ly/JS_Definitive*) (O'Reilly), which contains both the basics of JavaScript programming and an API reference.

- Drupal makes extensive use of the jQuery JavaScript library, which has a comprehensive online API reference at *http://docs.jquery.com*.

Drupal Development Tools

The Drupal community has developed several very useful development tools that can help you avoid making programming mistakes, adhere to the Drupal coding standards, and debug your Drupal sites and Drupal code. Here is a list of the most useful development tools:

Coder
  A set of modules that points out coding errors and violations of the Drupal coding standards, and also helps you upgrade your code from one Drupal version to another. Some developers have, in the past, preferred to use the Drupal Code Sniffer project, which has now been merged into the Coder project. (*https://www.drupal.org/project/coder*)

Devel
  A set of modules containing a number of helpful functions for debugging and developing modules and themes, as well as a fake *lorem ipsum* content generator for testing. (*https://www.drupal.org/project/devel*)

Drupal for Firebug
  A Firefox/Firebug or Chrome web browser plugin that works with the Devel module to display information about how each Drupal-generated page was built. (*https://www.drupal.org/project/drupalforfirebug*)

Drush
  A project that provides a command-line shell that greatly speeds up the process of developing a site, with commands for downloading and installing modules, clearing the Drupal cache, and more. It also has an API for module developers that lets a module expose its administrative functions as Drush commands. Learning a few key Drush commands will save you a lot of time, because in one command and a few seconds of waiting, you can do things that would otherwise take you several clicks and page loads on a site's administrative interface. (*https://www.drupal.org/project/drush*)

Coding standards

It is a very good idea to follow the Drupal coding standards in your Drupal programming. This practice has several benefits:

- It makes your code more uniform, matching the style of existing Drupal core and contributed module code.
- It makes your code easier to read and maintain going forward.
- If you plan to contribute your code to the Drupal project, it will eventually need to comply with these standards, so it's best to start now.

Further reading and reference:

- Drupal project coding standards: *https://www.drupal.org/coding-standards*

Discovering Drupal API Functions and Classes

Programmers who are new to Drupal sometimes don't know about all of the useful functions and classes available to them in the Drupal API. Most PHP programmers know that they can go to *http://php.net* to find documentation on built-in PHP functions; the Drupal project has a similar API site at *https://api.drupal.org*, which lists all of the functions, constants, classes, and files in Drupal core. See "Using api.drupal.org" on page 201 for more information.

I'll also just mention that a lot of useful functions are defined in the *common.inc* and *bootstrap.inc* files in the *includes* directory of Drupal core (*core/includes* in Drupal 8). You can search for either file on the API site; browsing their function lists is a great way to familiarize yourself with what's available in the Drupal API. You might also want to browse the Topics list on the API site, and in particular the topics linked on the API site landing pages for Drupal 7 and 8, to get an idea of what general areas of functionality the API covers.

To help you figure out which functions are the most useful, here is a list, in order, of the 20 most-often-called functions within Drupal core version 7 (with Drupal 8 equivalents and notes where there are differences):

- t()
- variable_get() [see \Drupal::config() and \Drupal::state() in Drupal 8]
- db_query()
- variable_set() [see \Drupal::config() and \Drupal::state() in Drupal 8]

- url()
- drupal_set_message()
- db_select()
- theme() [eliminated in Drupal 8; use render arrays instead]
- db_update()
- drupal_static()
- check_plain() [eliminated in Drupal 8; theme system escapes unsafe text]
- drupal_get_path()
- db_delete()
- user_access()
- db_insert()
- module_invoke_all() [see \Drupal::moduleHandler() in Drupal 8]
- l()
- watchdog()
- drupal_static_reset()
- drupal_alter() [see \Drupal::moduleHandler() in Drupal 8]

Drupal 8 is a lot more object-oriented than Drupal 7. So, here is a list of the most-often-used classes and interfaces in Drupal 8 (the ones with the most use declarations):

- \Drupal\Core\Form\FormStateInterface
- \Symfony\Component\DependencyInjection\ContainerInterface
- \Drupal\Component\Utility\SafeMarkup
- \Drupal\simpletest\WebTestBase
- \Symfony\Component\HttpFoundation\Request
- \Drupal\Tests\UnitTestCase
- \Drupal\Core\Url
- \Drupal\Core\Session\AccountInterface
- \Drupal\Core\Language\LanguageInterface
- \Drupal\Core\Entity\EntityInterface
- \Drupal\views\Views
- \Drupal\simpletest\KernelTestBase

- \Drupal\Core\Render\Element
- \Drupal\Core\Routing\RouteMatchInterface
- \Drupal\Core\Entity\EntityManagerInterface
- \Drupal\Component\Utility\Unicode
- \Drupal\Core\Extension\ModuleHandlerInterface
- \Symfony\Component\Routing\Route
- \Symfony\Component\Validator\Constraint
- \Drupal\Core\Cache\Cache
- \Drupal\views\ViewExecutable
- \Drupal\Core\Form\FormBase
- \Drupal\Core\Entity\EntityStorageInterface
- \Drupal\Core\Database\Connection
- \Drupal\Core\Entity\EntityTypeInterface
- \Drupal\Core\Field\FieldStorageDefinitionInterface
- \Drupal\Core\Access\AccessResult
- \Drupal\Core\Field\FieldItemListInterface
- \Symfony\Component\HttpFoundation\Response

Other Programming Tips and Suggestions

Here are a few final suggestions that will help you improve your Drupal code and programming experience:

- Set up your own local development server with a LAMP stack (or WAMP, MAMP, etc.), rather than trying to develop using a remote server.
- On your development server, edit your *php.ini* file (or equivalent) so that you are displaying all PHP notices, warnings, and errors. Do not consider your code to be working unless there are no notices at all, as they generally indicate bugs. Also use the Database Logging module during development, and check the "Recent log messages" report to see any errors you might have missed.
- Get a good code editor that does syntax highlighting, automatic indenting, and parentheses matching. The classic editor choices are Emacs and Vim/Vi.
- A more powerful alternative to a good code editor is an integrated development environment (IDE), which offers many advantages (debugging, type hinting,

etc.). The most popular choice for Drupal development is PhpStorm, and most Drupal 8 developers would consider this to be an essential tool.

- Follow the Drupal coding standards. You should be able to set up your code editor to use the standard Drupal indentation practice (two spaces, never use tabs), and to display or remove extra end-of-line spaces.

- Write thorough documentation for every function, constant, and class that you define, preferably before you write the code. This will help you or others maintain your code going forward, and writing the documentation first will help ensure that you know what the function or class is really supposed to do before you start writing it.

- Test your code, preferably by writing automated tests.

- Use a revision control system, such as Git or Subversion, to keep track of the changes you make to modules and themes you develop.

Further reading and reference:

- Drupal coding standards: *https://www.drupal.org/coding-standards*
- "Principle: Drupal Code Is Tested and Documented" on page 68

Index

arguments, in Views, 173
Asynchronous JavaScript and XML (AJAX), 124
authenticated users, 8, 9
autocomplete, 119-121
autoloading
    classes, 12-15
    in hook_menu(), 90

B

Bartik (core theme), 22
base fields, entities, 130
base tables, Views module, 175
base theme, 22
base_table annotation (entities), 142
Block annotation class, 101
block system, 3
BlockBase class, 101
BlockPlugInterface interface, 101
blocks
    defining theme regions for placement, 71-79
    in HTTP requests, 9
    plugin manager, 31
    providing output in, 88
    registering in Drupal 7, 100-101
    registering in Drupal 8, 101
bug databases (issue queues), 83
build() method, block classes, 102
buildForm() method, form classes, 115
bundles, 130
Buytaert, Dries, 5, 82

C

cache
    clearing, 10
    page, 8
Cache API
    context, 12
    Drupal 7, 11
    Drupal 8, 11
    get() method, 11
    invalidate() method, 11
    set() method, 11
    storage bins, 11
cache service, 11
cache system, 10-12
Cache::invalidateTags() method, 12
CacheBackendInterface, 11
cache_clear_all() function, 11

cache_get() function, 11
cache_set() function, 11
callback functions, Ajax
    command-based, 127
    overview, 124
    wrapper-based, 127
CCK (Content Construction Kit), 5
check_markup() function, 63
check_plain() function, 63
check_url() function, 63
class autoloading, 12-15
Classy (base theme), 22
clearing the cache, 10
CMF (content management framework), 1
CMS (content management system), 1
code
    committing, 85
    contributing to Drupal community, 83-85
    overexecuting, 79
Coder module, 204
CommandInterface Ajax interface, 129
comment entities, 130
comment system, 3
Composer, 13
condition() method
    database queries, 62
    entity queries, 161
Config class, 45
config.factory service, 45
config/install directory, 42
config/optional directory, 43
ConfigEntityBase class, 151
ConfigEntityBundleBase class, 151
ConfigEntityInterface interface, 151
ConfigEntityListBuilder base class, 156
ConfigFormBase class, 115
Configuration API
    configuration entities, 46
    file format, 42
    get() method, 46
    getEditable() method, 46
    in Drupal 8, 42-47
    overrides, 46
    schema, 42, 150
    simple configuration, 45
configuration data, 40
configuration entity type
    configuration schema for, 150
    defining in Drupal 8, 149-160

tags, 36
services.yml files, 36, 39, 99
set() method, cache classes, 11
setErrorByName() method, form state object, 115
settings.php file, 8, 9, 40, 42, 46
settings.yml files, 42
Seven (core theme), 22
short names, 20
SimpleTest tests, 68
site building, information sources for, 199
software license, 1
SQL Pocket Guide (Gennick), 203
staging directory (for configuration), 42
Stark (base theme), 23
State API, 47
state information, 40
state service, 47
StateInterface interface, 47
StringTranslationTrait trait, 49
string_translation service, 49
structured form arrays, 109
style plugins in Views, 173, 180-183
StylePluginBase views class, 181
sub-themes, 4, 22
Symfony
    and event system in Drupal 8, 38
    and HTTP request handling in Drupal 8, 9
    and routing system in Drupal 8, 19
Symfony class-loading system, 14

T

t() function, 49-50, 63, 106
t() method, 106
taxonomy system, 3
taxonomy_term entities, 130
taxonomy_vocabulary entities, 130
template system, 2
template.php file, 21
testing, 68-70
theme .info file, 20, 77
theme .info.yml file, 20, 77
theme .theme file, 21
theme hooks, 18, 23, 26
theme preprocessing hooks, 18
theme processing hooks, 18
theme regions, defining for block placement, 77-79
theme system, 2, 3

theme template, 18, 26
theme template file, overriding, 23
theme template.php file, 21
theme() function, 18
    and render arrays, 26
    in Drupal 7, 25
theme(s)
    base themes, 22
    creating, 20-23
    creating sub-themes, 22, 77
    defining regions for block placement, 77-79
    directories for, 22
    functions/templates vs. render arrays, 26
    hook programming, 23
    inheritance, 22
    making module output themeable, 25-28
ticket systems (issue queues), 83
tips, programming, 207
top-level directories, 22
translations, 132
trusted users, 61

U

Unicode, 48
unit tests, 69
update function, 56
update.php script, 56
Url class, 63
URL registration, 88-102
    administrative links, 95-98
    altering in Drupal 7, 89-91
    altering in Drupal 8, 98-100
    in Drupal 7, 89-91
    in Drupal 8, 92-94
    providing dynamic routes in Drupal 8, 98-100
usability, 52
use declarations, 13, 14
user entities, 130
User Guide for Drupal, 199
user interface, internationalizing, 49
user-entered text
    cleansing/checking, 62
    insecurity of, 61-67
    internationalizing in Drupal 7, 50
    internationalizing in Drupal 8, 51
user_access() function, 65, 110
UUID (Universally Unique Identifier), 42, 130

V

validateForm() method, form classes, 115
value form element type, 111
variable_get() function, 40
variable_set() function, 40
view modes, 131
Views data source
    adding fields and relationships to, 179
    and Views integration, 175
Views integration, 147-148
Views module
    adding fields and relationships to existing
        Views data source, 179
    adding handlers to, 177-179
    creating add-ons for, 171-184
    default views for, 183
    defining base tables, 175
    module setup in Drupal 7, 172
    output construction, 173
    programming terminology, 172
    style/row plugins, 180-183
Views relationships, Panels relationships vs.,
    190

views.inc files, 175
views_default.inc files, 184
vocabularies, 130

W

Web Accessibility Initiative (WAI), 52
Web Database Applications with PHP and
    MySQL (Williams), 202, 203
WidgetBase base class, 165
WidgetInterface interface, 165
widgets, 131
Williams, Hugh E., 202
WizardPluginBase class, 148
World Wide Web Consortium (W3C), 52
wrapper-based callback functions, for Ajax, 127

X

XML, Ajax and, 124

Y

YAML format, 42

About the Author

Jennifer Hodgdon wrote her first computer program in 1982 and has been a professional software developer since 1994, using a wide variety of programming languages (FORTRAN, C, Java, PHP, JavaScript, and others). She started doing PHP/MySQL web programming professionally around 2002 and set up her first Drupal website in 2007. Soon after that, she started contributing volunteer time to the Drupal open source project and the Seattle Drupal User Group: organizing meet-ups and conferences, serving as the coleader and then the leader of the Drupal Documentation Team in 2011–2012, leading workshops, and making conference presentations. She is currently a freelance Drupal site builder and module programmer, the volunteer maintainer of several Drupal modules, the coorganizer of the Spokane Washington Drupal User Group, and the Drupal core maintainer/committer for API documentation and coding standards. She can be contacted through her business website, *poplarware.com*, or through her drupal.org user account (*jhodgdon*).

Colophon

The animal on the cover of *Programmer's Guide to Drupal* is a French angelfish (*Pomacanthus paru*). The French angelfish is native to shallow reefs in the Atlantic Ocean, from New York in the north to Brazil and Ascension Island in the south.

French angelfish typically pair up for life, beginning with an early morning rendezvous between April and September. Playfully chasing each other leads to spawning and then tending stable abodes hidden among the coral during the night. Pairs of French angelfish fiercely defend the territory of their chosen hiding places against neighbors but can also demonstrate a charming curiosity in the presence of snorkelers.

Juvenile *banderitas*, as they are called in Spanish, appear with markedly different coloring from that of the adults, for whom the vertical yellow stripes of youth have dissolved into pervasive, yellow-tinged black scales. When still young, French angelfish glean food by wiping ectoparasites with their pelvic fins from other fish on the reef who venture into "cleaning stations." Adults of the species live less symbiotically, consuming algae, sponges, and other invertebrates living on the reef.

Many of the animals on O'Reilly covers are endangered; all of them are important to the world. To learn more about how you can help, go to *animals.oreilly.com*.

The cover image is from Cuvier's *Animals*. The cover fonts are URW Typewriter and Guardian Sans. The text font is Adobe Minion Pro; the heading font is Adobe Myriad Condensed; and the code font is Dalton Maag's Ubuntu Mono.

Have it your way.

O'Reilly eBooks

- Lifetime access to the book when you buy through oreilly.com
- Provided in up to four, DRM-free file formats, for use on the devices of your choice: PDF, .epub, Kindle-compatible .mobi, and Android .apk
- Fully searchable, with copy-and-paste, and print functionality
- We also alert you when we've updated the files with corrections and additions.

oreilly.com/ebooks/

Safari Books Online

- Access the contents and quickly search over 7000 books on technology, business, and certification guides
- Learn from expert video tutorials, and explore thousands of hours of video on technology and design topics
- Download whole books or chapters in PDF format, at no extra cost, to print or read on the go
- Early access to books as they're being written
- Interact directly with authors of upcoming books
- Save up to 35% on O'Reilly print books

See the complete Safari Library at safaribooksonline.com

©2014 O'Reilly Media, Inc. O'Reilly logo is a registered trademark of O'Reilly Media, Inc. 14373